HITCH

Lucy Alexander was
nurse on a camping
had a spat with her boyfriend and was trudging
along the highway alone when a dark late-model car
pulled up beside her. The driver, a dark-haired,
clean-shaven male in a blue suit, politely inquired if
she'd care for a lift.

Lucy said no at first, but the friendly stranger persisted. It was late at night to be walking, and she at
last said yes. "How old are you?" he asked her after
she got in the car.

"Nineteen," she answered.

He seemed surprised. "You look younger than nineteen," the man repeated several times. "Are you
sure you're not younger?"

A short time later he stopped the car, declared himself an FBI agent, and told Lucy she was under arrest for hitchhiking. Before she could protest, he'd
handcuffed her wrists behind her and was driving
again. He stopped in a deserted field. He pushed
Lucy over the seat and down onto the back floorboard. "If you listen to me, I won't hurt you."

Lucy tried to believe him—but then the horror began. . . .

LETHAL SHADOW

**"A stunning study of an unspeakably horrible
criminal by one of the best reporters in the
business. Read only by daylight."—Jack Olsen**

LETHAL SHADOW

The Chilling True-Crime
Story of a Sadistic Sex Slayer

Stephen G. Michaud

AN ONYX BOOK

ONYX
Published by the Penguin Group
Penguin Books USA Inc., 375 Hudson Street,
New York, New York 10014, U.S.A.
Penguin Books Ltd, 27 Wrights Lane,
London W8 5TZ, England
Penguin Books Australia Ltd, Ringwood,
Victoria, Australia
Penguin Books Canada Ltd, 10 Alcorn Avenue,
Toronto, Ontario, Canada M4V 3B2
Penguin Books (N.Z.) Ltd, 182–190 Wairau Road,
Auckland 10, New Zealand

Penguin Books Ltd, Registered Offices:
Harmondsworth, Middlesex, England

First published by Onyx
an imprint of Dutton Signet,
a division of Penguin Books USA Inc.

First Printing, May, 1994

10 9 8 7 6 5 4 3 2 1

For Charlotte Doud Macdonald, absent friend

Author's Note

Some characters in this book have asked that their identities not be disclosed. They have been provided pseudonyms, as indicated throughout the text. Additionally, in certain cases biographical and geographical details have been changed to ensure an individual's anonymity. No material fact has been altered in any way.

Prologue

It had been one of the largest, most baffling manhunts in the 118-year history of U.S. Secret Service. Suddenly, it was now over.

Agent Dennis Foos, 37, first heard of the arrest at shortly past five o'clock on the warm Washington Wednesday afternoon of May 25, 1983. As Foos was wheeling his silver, government-issue Chevrolet Monte Carlo out of the Secret Service's ground-floor parking garage at 1800 G Street NW, the news came crackling over his two-way radio. The infamous phantom counterfeiter known to the service as the Mall Passer—for the canny practice of passing his bogus bills in suburban malls—at last had been apprehended near Knoxville, Tennessee.

Foos, a solidly built six-footer with blue eyes, a bushy mustache, and full head of brown hair, had been Washington case agent for the lengthy Mall Passer investigation. He had taken a personal, almost proprietary interest in the four-year, forty-four-state chase, and for a moment Dennis Foos was galled. "Damn!" he thought. "Knoxville got him instead of us!" Foos's pique soon subsided, however. "I was happy that the guy finally was in custody," he remembers.

In Knoxville, the glowering, bespectacled suspect himself absolutely refused to assist the Secret Service with its two main objectives: to identify the Mall Passer and to locate his printing operation. He wasn't answering any questions of any sort.

Agents found in his wallet a North Carolina driver's license identifying the Mall Passer as Roger Collin Blanchard of Charlotte. The license proved to be a fake. His car, a battered '71 Chrysler, bore stolen Tennessee plates, and was registered to a James R. Jones of Alexandria, Virginia. This information was radioed to Washington, where a surveillance team was dispatched to Jones's address, No. L-517 at the Oakwood Apartments on South Reynolds Street.

At midnight that Wednesday, agent Greg Mertz arrived at the service's ten-story, tan office tower two blocks west of the White House for his usual twelve-to-eight night duty shift. An ex-cop, the thick-shouldered, heavily muscled Mertz shared a cramped, windowless office with Dennis Foos. Mertz also had taken part in the Mall Passer investigation. Like Foos, he felt a special stake in its outcome. When he heard news of the Knoxville arrest, Mertz hurried upstairs to the seventh-floor duty room.

There, using the service's mammoth, computerized Master Control Index, and the WALES (Washington Law Enforcement System) data base, Mertz learned that Mr. Jones had registered his Chrysler not only in Alexandria, but also in Albany, New York. Jones appeared to be living two lives. But what was his connection to the suspect, Blanchard?

Mertz found the answer via the Virginia Department of Motor Vehicles. The DMV computer reported that Jones was six feet tall and weighed 158 pounds. His hair was brown, as were his eyes, and he wore spectacles. Mertz then consulted Blanchard's description as provided by the Knoxville office that afternoon. It was a perfect match: Jones was Blanchard. He reached for the telephone.

"Hey, I think Blanchard and Jones are the same guy!" he nearly shouted over the wire to Knoxville. It was two in the morning. Then Mertz called his immediate superior, 34-year-old agent Jane Vezeris, awakening Vezeris at her suburban Maryland residence. "I'm gonna call Denny Foos," he told her after sharing his discovery. "We need to start writing the search warrant affidavit."

Midmorning of the 26th brought the next surprise. As Mertz and Foos were busily typing up their affidavit, word came from the FBI's fingerprint identification unit that the Mall Passer was neither Blanchard nor Jones. He was a third individual altogether, a career criminal named James Mitchell DeBardeleben II, known as Mike. Moreover, DeBardeleben's rap sheet showed that he already was known to the Secret Service as a counterfeiter. The treasury agency had busted him once before, in 1976, for passing phony hundreds. He'd done two years of federal time for the offense.

After a brief interval of embarrassed silence, Foos retrieved DeBardeleben's file and reviewed it. His worry turned to alarm as Foos leafed through the old records, especially the inventory of what was found in DeBardeleben's house, and a report by agent Mike Stephens of his 1976 interview with DeBardeleben's estranged wife. Foos found the six-feet, four-inch tall Stephens, called "Stretch," at his desk in the Special Investigations squad area. "Hey, Stretch," said Foos as he dropped DeBardeleben's arrest photo on Stephens's desk. "Recognize this guy?"

Stephens did, instantly, and in the same moment felt something twist in his stomach. He looked up and answered slowly. "Yeah, I do."

The pieces had begun to fall into place.

In Knoxville, a search of DeBardeleben's Chrysler had turned up guns, thousands of dollars in counterfeit bills, a substantial quantity of pornography, a portable pharmacy of legal and illegal drugs of nearly every sort, eighteen license plates (most stolen) from a variety of states, nine forged driver's licenses (all bearing DeBardeleben's photograph), and a mail order police badge inside a commission book. There were, as well, dozens of paper bags filled with inexpensive merchandise, what the Secret Service calls the "proceeds" of counterfeit passing. The agents found, for example, two JCPenney sacks; one contained two pairs of socks, the other an oven mitt; a Pet Center bag with a new dog collar in it, three new Flair pens in a plain brown sack, and a Gateway Bookstore bag that contained a greeting card and a squeeze toy. What they couldn't find was any clue as to where DeBardeleben kept his press and printing supplies, his "plant," in Secret Service parlance.

The post-arrest investigation's focus therefore shifted back to Washington, where Dennis Foos and Greg Mertz finished with their search warrant affidavits at about midday. At approximately 4:30 on the 26th, as thunderstorms threatened from the northwest, Foos and Mertz, their boss Jane Vezeris, several other agents, and two technicians arrived at the Oakwood Apartments to conduct their search.

They found a large and relatively new rental complex of well-maintained, brown brick buildings, parking lots, and a swimming pool in the southern part of the city. Apartment L-517, a furnished studio, had been rented the previous autumn for $485 a month by DeBardeleben posing as J. R. Jones. According to a card he'd given the Oakwood manager, Mr. Jones was a "district representative" for Optikon Electronics, Inc., in Glen Burnie, Maryland.

The apartment was located at the end of a hallway. Foos opened the door using the manager's key, quickly surveyed the single room, then turned to Mertz.

"We ain't done yet," said the agent.

Instead of DeBardeleben's plant, the Secret Service team found a wholly unremarkable-looking bachelor's apartment with dirty dishes in the sink, articles of clothing lying about in casual disarray, a bed, a table or two, and a television. It might have been a traveling man's room at the Holiday Inn—white walls, brown rug—for all DeBardeleben's personal imprint on the place. The only truly individual features of the studio were his sizable collection of paper bags of greeting cards and men's black socks—more "proceeds"—plus, on a telephone stand, several pages and scraps of paper with dozens of names, addresses, and telephone numbers written on them.

"Essentially, that was it," remembers Greg Mertz. "We were both disappointed and dumbfounded. Here was this major investigation. We were looking for a whole printing operation; press, plates and negatives, and sizable quantities of counterfeit cash, too. And after working all night and day we came up empty-handed. Unbelievable."

Disturbing, too.

No Secret Service counterfeiting investigation is considered complete until the forger's plant is found. With a totally uncooperative suspect, the Mall Passer team sensed their chances of finding Mike DeBardeleben's printing equipment were rapidly slipping past slim toward none.

"Everybody else had left the apartment," Mertz continues. "It was just Denny and Jane and I left. We thought, 'Well, *maybe* there's something the guys missed. Let's go over everything again.' So we just started tossing the whole place once more, looking for any evidence of where his stash was.

"I started going through the telephone book white pages—which for northern Virginia is huge—looking for any possible marks he'd made. This was page by page. I found nothing. Then I went to his Yellow pages and started through them.

"I got to the M's. Inside the section for Moving and Storage I found a little tiny piece of blank paper about the size of a business card slipped between two pages. That's when the light bulb lit. I yelled at Denny, 'Come here!' "

Acting on Mertz's strong suspicion that they'd find DeBardeleben's plant stashed somewhere in storage, Dennis Foos on Saturday, May 28, began a canvass of likely locations at Landmark Mini-Storage on Edsall Road in Alexandria, the facility nearest to DeBardeleben's apartment. "I've been expecting you guys," manager Linda E. Johnston told Foos after glancing at DeBardeleben's photo. "I've been waiting for the cops."

Johnston explained that she knew the man in the photo as J. R. Jones, resident at the nearby Oakwood Apartments, who'd rented mini-storage locker #230 at Landmark for $28 a month in November 1982. Some weeks before, Jones had left locker #230 lit and unlocked one evening. When she reached inside to turn off the unit's single electric bulb, Johnston had been shocked, and a bit scared, to see a red bubble light of the type police sometimes use, resting on the floor. Also out in plain view were a large flashlight, photographic equipment, some tools, a ski mask and what Johnston took to be a police radio. She'd called the local police with her discovery, but had been brushed off. Since then, Johnston said, she figured it would just be a matter of time before the police came to *her*.

At eight o'clock that Saturday night, Foos, Mertz, and Jane Vezeris, plus several other agents gathered at Landmark for the search. Foos snapped DeBardeleben's padlock with a heavy bolt cutter, pushed aside locker #230's beige door, switched on the dim electric light and saw, first of all, a set of red and blue police bubble lights and a siren, outfitted with a wire and plug so the devices could draw power from an automobile cigarette lighter. The second conscious impression registered both by Foos and Mertz was that there was nothing big enough in the locker bay to be a printing press.

"This was another disappointment," remembers Foos. "Our main goal still was the press and plant and all. But at the same time, as soon as we opened the door the things that had been in the backs of our minds—what Mike Stephens had told us, and the information we'd received from Knoxville—suddenly came flowing to the front. Right off the bat it was, 'Wait a minute here!' "

The locker's interior was a jumble of vinyl briefcases, plastic envelopes, bulging paper bags, portfolios and other containers, including two large footlockers. Foos opened one, and Mertz the other. The agents' notes indicate that the second item they inspected that evening was a bag containing an empty gun case, ammunition, handcuffs, and twine. Then a dark blue ski mask and an Icoflex large-format camera, ideal for counterfeit work.

Photographing everything as they handled it, the search team inspected a red plastic pouch containing counterfeit money and a police badge. Another bag from the footlockers were filled with handwritten notes, phone numbers, and women's names and addresses. There were drugs, too, plus a coke kit (mirror and razor blades) and a kit for testing drug purity, complete with a gram scale.

Over the next three hours, the agents identified and seized a single aluminum printing plate and $52,760 worth of counterfeit money in various stages of completion, much of it sorted into stacks and graded A, A-, B+ and so on according to color-coded wrappers around each stack. They found a camera tripod, eyebolts, a man's hat with a bloodstained visor, a device for punching out auto ignitions (a car thief's standard tool), various fake identifications, a pair of women's underpants with a severely distended elastic band, whips, a dildo, and another bag containing what Greg Mertz took to be, in his words, a "death kit": shoelaces, a choker chain, K-Y jelly, and handcuffs.

There were wads of clay for taking key imprints and several metal key blanks. The agents found an abundance of newspaper clips, most reporting on crimes of various sorts, an ample collection of self-help texts, works of pop psychology as well as scholarly and extensively underlined psychiatric texts, and a wide sampling of raunch books, magazines, tapes and photos—hundreds of photos.

Everyone recognized early on in the search that it would be impossible, at the site, to sort through the enormous volume of material; evidence connecting DeBardeleben with counterfeiting, as well as documents that might point the investigation toward its Grail, his press and plates, were hopelessly intermixed with the rest of his papers and gear, both innocuous items such as clothing and the seriously troubling police equipment and handcuffs and brutally explicit pictures of females, some hardly pubescent and many looking either drugged or battered or frightened for their lives.

At eleven o'clock that night, the Secret Service team transported the bulk of the locker's contents to a makeshift evidence room at the Washington Field Office (WFO), where Greg Mertz began sifting through it. For several hours that night it was more of the same. Then, at about four in the morning, Mertz shoved one of DeBardeleben's audiocassette tapes into his Dictaphone. What he heard has burned in his memory ever since. Stunned by the experience, Mertz drove home alone through the capital's empty streets that Sunday morning, lost in a fog of bewilderment.

The horror had only just begun.

In the months ahead, Mertz together with Denny Foos and Stretch Stephens would confront a species of evil totally beyond their experience, or their imaginations. DeBardeleben's sheer criminal catholicity was startling in itself. Car thief, con artist, bank robber, forger, kidnapper, rapist, and suspected serial murderer of monumentally perverse appetites, he appeared to have committed practically every known felony. Some authorities consulted by the agents believe DeBardeleben's criminal history is unmatched anywhere for its sadism, its scope and his success at eluding detection. Not only the Secret Service, but federal, state, and local law-enforcement officials all over the United States—together with judges, prosecutors, jurors, and jailors alike—would come to regard the name Mike DeBardeleben as synonymous with ineffably evil criminal intellect. Many investigators would tell agents Foos, Mertz, and Stephens that DeBardeleben was the most dangerous felon ever at large in America.

Inevitably, DeBardeleben's been compared to other degenerate offenders of his order: Ted Bundy, Jeffrey Dahmer, John Gacy, and the rest. Where these comparisons falter, however, is in the breadth of DeBardeleben's depredations, and in his painstakingly patient and methodical approach to murder, which allowed him to remain at large far longer than his putative peers. Ted Bundy, for example, bumbled as a thief and failed outright as a fugitive. What is more, he may have roved free, killing, for fewer than five years in all. Bundy ultimately admitted to thirty slayings. DeBardeleben, by contrast, is believed to have committed his first killing in 1965 or earlier, at least eighteen years before he finally was caught. The arithmetic is chilling.

Even in custody, DeBardeleben has remained an enigma. In the end, he'd be indicted eleven times in nine states (twice for murder), tried and convicted in six cases and sentenced to a total of 375 years. No one, however, thinks that these known offenses comprise any more than a tiny fraction of Mike DeBardeleben's full history of offenses.

As horrifying—and heartbreaking—as his story may be, it is still not fully revealed. And may never be. Once again unlike other aberrant offenders in his category, DeBardeleben did not acquiesce in his imprisonment, or acknowledge his guilt or seize the occasions of his several sensational trials to reach for the black celebrity that America accords its truly weird and outrageous criminals. Paradoxically, he would become the most infamous largely anonymous felon in American criminal history.

But not before agents Foos, Mertz, and Stephens completed an odyssey that all three would prefer never to have begun. Wretched as the unnerving experience would be, however, the story of their investigation and the mind-boggling breaks that allowed the three agents to make their major cases against DeBardeleben is also a tale of justice served—at least in part—with an improbable note of redemption at its surprise conclusion. What unfolded was one of the scariest, most incredible true crimes sagas—ever.

PART
ONE

1

The Friendly Stranger

This is a tape, regarding my goals.

Number one on my list of goals is to establish a new identity; complete with background, school records, employment records, driver's license, Social Security card, passport, checking accounts, savings accounts. Rent an apartment. Buy a car. Have a job—or a job front. All under a new identity. This new identity would not be able to be traced to me under *any* circumstances. It may have to be set up in a different location, a different city.

Second on my list of goals is to buy a house; preferably, buy some land and build my own house according to my own *custom* specifications, and needs. Number one would be a garage, one- or two-car garage, to completely enclose a car with no windows so that no one could tell if a car was there or not there. Also a basement area—or *work* area—which is hidden and unable to be detected by ordinary means.

Naturally, of course, I would need as a requirement a secret hidden compartments built into the house for stash areas, for various things, as well as along with the secret work area for a press and darkroom facilities, a *fun* area—secret *fun* area—which would include a *cage* so that I could have (a female victim) locked *up!*

Also of *prime* importance—top priority—would be an *incinerator* capable of incinerating at extremely high temperature—*total* incineration. This could be connected as the lower part of the fireplace in the living room above.

> *Third* on my list of goals would be Caryn*
> or another female victim first, then Caryn. How about
> eventually *both*?
> I would also want as goal number four enough money
> to last for a year without working.
>
> —from an audiocassette tape recorded
> by James Mitchell ("Mike") DeBardeleben

On May 5, 1978, Mike DeBardeleben was released to a District of Columbia halfway house after serving twenty-three months of his 1976 counterfeiting sentence in the Federal Penitentiary at Danbury, Connecticut. In June, the sallow, softly drawling 38-year-old ex-convict moved back into the shabby two-story house he owned at 1201 South Columbus Street in Arlington, and took a barbering job—a condition of his release—but soon stopped showing up for work.

In late July, at Brown's Tyson Corner Dodge in Fairfax, Virginia, he bought a dark blue '77 Thunderbird. This is the car with which the Secret Service believes DeBardeleben abducted student nurse Lucy Alexander.*

Labor Day weekend, 1978, the luminous dark-blond Alexander went camping with her boyfriend on the Indian River in southwestern Delaware, not far from the Maryland border. On a partly cloudy Sunday, September 3, the afternoon high temperature in the 70s, the couple drove a few miles south across the state line to Ocean City, where they went partying at a bar called Back of the Rack. Sometime shortly past midnight, after several hours of drinking, Lucy and her boyfriend fell into a quarrel. Provoked, she stalked out the door and headed north, alone, on foot, intent on walking the full distance back to their campsite.

By 1:30 A.M., Alexander had trudged approximately five miles, and had gained Fenwick Island, Delaware,

---

*denotes pseudonyms

on Route 1 when an automobile she'd later describe as a dark, late-model luxury vehicle slowed to a stop beside her. The driver, a dark-haired, clean-shaven white male clad in a blue leisure suit, and very thin—"wimpy" looking, according to Alexander's statement—politely inquired where the teenager was headed, and if she'd care for a lift. "The Indian River campground," Alexander replied to his first question. "No," she said to his second. She'd just as soon walk.

The friendly stranger persisted. He was headed directly past the campgrounds, he said, and it'd be no trouble for him to drop her off. Lucy Alexander, perhaps considering the hour and the miles she'd walked, relented and climbed into the dark car's passenger-side bucket seat.

"How old are you?" he asked easily as they drove on.

"Nineteen," she answered.

He seemed surprised. "You look younger than nineteen," the man repeated several times. "Are you *sure* you're not younger?"

The stranger was careful not to betray his intentions until they reached the campground, where he stopped the car, brandished an official-looking badge, declared himself an FBI agent and told Lucy she was under arrest for hitchhiking. Before she could protest or even consider escape he'd handcuffed her wrists behind her and was driving again.

At first he said he planned to deliver Alexander into the custody of local authorities at Rehobeth Beach, about ten miles to the north. Then he said he'd changed his mind and would drive her to the Sussex Correctional Institution in Georgetown, about twenty miles to the west. Only after they'd traveled well into the Delaware countryside did he drop the law-enforcement charade.

He stopped the car in a field. When Alexander started screaming, he gagged and blindfolded the terrified girl with adhesive tape. He then pushed Lucy over the seat and down onto the back floorboard, covered her with a blanket, and said, "If you listen to me, I won't hurt you."

She tried to believe him.

Alexander spent the next two hours bound, gagged, and blindfolded as they drove on, the kidnapper chain-smoking cigarettes and belching frequently from the root beer he kept handy in an ice chest. She would remember little else of the trip except that about halfway through it they slowed for a moment and she heard the distinctive tinkling of highway tollgate bells.

He finally pulled to a stop in what she sensed was a residential neighborhood. A dog barked in the near distance. The man guided her from his car to some low steps, then across a porch or landing and into the house where he shoved her upstairs and to the right into what seemed to Alexander to be an empty room. There was a mattress on the floor, covered with a blue blanket.

Drawing next to her, he removed Lucy's adhesive-tape gag, but left the blindfold in place, explaining that if she saw him in the light he'd be obliged to kill her. Then, as she listened to him rifle through her purse, he announced that he was going downstairs to negotiate a ransom with her parents.

That turned out to be a lie.

He did leave—probably to move his car away from the house—but moments later was back in the room, trailing his aura of root beer and stale cigarette smoke. Deprived of sight, Alexander's only sense was of his fingers as they removed her clothing. He commanded her down onto her back on the mattress. She obeyed and lay still, listening as he masturbated before dropping atop her and forcing himself inside her.

He raped her, steadily, for an hour without ejaculating. "Turn over!" he at last demanded, and then sodomized her. Alexander later remembered the rapist urgently insisting she call him "Daddy" again and again until he could climax. Afterward, he rolled off her and slept.

Her next recollection was of a second vaginal rape, followed by another anal rape, and intermittent periods in which he drank more root beer, smoked cigarettes and ate some cheese while forcing her to fellate him. Fellatio also alternated with the rapes. During the former he frequently warned Lucy that he'd kill her if she didn't keep his penis in her mouth. During the latter, he verbally as well as sexually abused her. He also had difficulty maintaining an erection. He repeatedly instructed Alexander to call him "Daddy" as he neared orgasm.

"Subject would also talk about his ex-wife," read the later FBI report in part, "saying such things as how they were hard up for money and all she did was spend money and he couldn't afford to pay the bills. Alexander said he would talk about his ex-wife after he raped her."

In all, Lucy Alexander reported that she was raped at least four times, vaginally and anally, and forced to fellate her attacker four or five times over a period of eighteen hours. When she pleaded with the man to stop and let her go, he said he would, "When I think the time is right."

That was late the following night.

She could not recall how she was reclothed, only that he took her back downstairs, gave her a drink of water, and then hurried her out to his car with a blanket over her head. Again he seemed to drive interminably. At one point, he told her that if anything went wrong and a cop stopped them, he'd shoot the officer first and then kill her.

By that time, death held far less terror for Lucy Alexander than it had the day before. Yet she did survive. At around 2:30 A.M. on Tuesday, September 5, 1978, he released her in an isolated area known as Hardscrabble, about five miles east of Georgetown,

Delaware. As her abductor sped away, she peeled off her blindfold in time to glimpse his brake lights, but nothing else. The next driver she saw was a Delaware State Trooper in his patrol car.

2

"Pass Out, Bitch!"

I feel that I have been unjustly tormented, degraded, and shit upon by society (specifically the Amerikan Criminal Justice System—which is rotten to the core.) In order to regain an adequate self-image, I feel compelled to somehow restore my self-respect. If I were to shit upon society for an adequate monetary gain, commensurate with the pain I have suffered, and not get caught, it would accomplish my objective . . .

I'M GOING AFTER THE WHOLE BALL OF WAX
THE BIG BANANA!
THE WHOLE ENCHILADA!
THE LAST BIG SCORE!!!!!!!!!!!!!!!
I've paid my dues, now I'm gonna COLLECT!!!!!!!!!

Several weeks following Lucy Alexander's Labor Day abduction, Mike DeBardeleben put his South Columbus Street house on the market and began, patiently, to travel up and down the mid-Atlantic states, answering want ads, visiting printing supply houses, and scouting hideouts where he could assemble the paraphernalia necessary to resume his craft—currency counterfeiting.

Progress was slow. The two-story Arlington residence, painted white with rust-colored trim, didn't sell until early 1979. Even then, after retiring the various trusts on the property, DeBardeleben cleared only $15,000.

It was at about this time, February of 1979, that the

Secret Service believes Mike DeBardeleben went on another hunting trip.

At approximately 3:30 on February 4, 1979, a bright Sunday afternoon in a nearly completed tract development outside Fayetteville, North Carolina, 31-year-old Elizabeth Mason* was seated alone at a kitchenette table, inside the subdivision's utility trailer sales office, doing her monthly bills, when a casually clad stranger wearing aviator sunglasses quietly walked into the office and appeared as if out of nowhere before her, startling the real estate agent. The man introduced himself as Al, possibly Al Wise, or Al Weiss; Mason is not sure of his name. He said he was a federal employee about to be transferred down from Arlington, Virginia, and he explained to Mason that he was doing some preliminary scouting for a house in the area. He and his wife, the man added, soon would come down together to make their final choice.

Mason, an amateur actress as well as a Realtor, was five-five, blue-eyed with naturally dark-blond hair she recently had grown long and bleached to portray the toothsome naif, Billie Dawn, in a local little-theater production of Garson Kanin's comedy, *Born Yesterday*. A photograph of Mason, in costume, had appeared in the local newspapers, as well as around town on posters advertising the play's run. That Sunday afternoon she was wearing taupe slacks, a matching plaid shirt, and her brown leather jacket, lightweight attire appropriate to a clement late winter's day in central North Carolina.

She recalls that her most vivid physical impressions of the stranger were of his severely close-cropped, salt-and-pepper hair, and his pale, pockmarked complexion. Neither his height nor his weight registered with her, although she does not think he was more than six feet tall. Mason does remember how uncomfortable she felt in Al's presence. She was accustomed to being relaxed with other people, and was used to putting them at ease, as well. But not on this occasion.

"He was real agitated," she says. "Fidgety. He *never relaxed*, and neither could I, which was real strange. I kept telling myself it was only because he'd surprised me."

Al, who indicated he was willing to spend $100,000 or more for a house—a moderately upscale price for Fayetteville in the late '70s—accompanied Mason on a short walking tour of the subdivision before mentioning that what he *really* was interested in was a country place, preferably on a lake. Could Mason show him some properties that afternoon?

"I took him back to the trailer and sat him down and started showing him pictures," she says. "It was late, and I knew he wasn't going to buy that day. Therefore, I wasn't going to drag ass out to the country. But he kept asking, so I told him I would show him a few neighborhoods in his price range, in town. Then when he and his wife came back we could go look at some country properties."

He acceded to the suggestions. "I think if he'd gotten any more obvious it would have been a problem," observes Mason, who drove Al in her blue 1977 Oldsmobile to a nearby community known as Warrenwood. "After looking at the house in Warrenwood," read the later Fayetteville Police Department report of the case,

suspect stated that he was running short on time, and had to go back to pick up his car . . . While en route back to the office, suspect stated that he wanted to look at some more houses in a higher price range. He further stated that he did not want to leave his car parked at the real estate office because he did not feel that the car would be safe there. Suspect picked up his car—maroon in color and could have been a Volvo or more likely an Audi Fox—and drove to the

Highland Presbyterian Church at 111 Highland Avenue. He parked the car there. . . ."

Try as she might, Elizabeth Mason could not shake the vague dread she'd felt from the moment that Al had suddenly loomed in front of her. Without thinking—and contrary to practice—she radioed her home office as they left, telling her boss where she was headed, as well as her prospective customer's name. "My boss," she says, "thought it was really strange that I did that. Several different real estate companies used the same radio frequencies. Ordinarily, we'd never used a buyer's name."

As the tour continued, Mason remembers, her customer spotted an empty and secluded-looking white-brick ranch house at 402 Foxhall Drive, a corner lot abundantly set about with trees and shrubs. Al asked Mason several questions about the place, which the Realtor could not find in her listings. Twice, Al requested that they circle back for a closer look.

Mason finally pulled into the driveway and accompanied him to the back of the house, where they found a lockbox securing the kitchen door. Inside, the man walked through the kitchen to the living room where he made an elaborate display of figuring out how and where his various pieces of furniture would fit. Mason recognized an act when she saw it. *"He's not buying this house,"* she thought to herself as she turned on some lights, and then walked outside to radio her office for information on price and availability. But why the intricate ruse?

When she returned, Al was still in the living room, still in character, carrying on his performance. She strode past him again, down a long hallway to the back of the house. Then she retraced her steps to the living room. This time, Al was standing still and silent, staring at her, a .380 automatic in his right hand.

His eyes, two voids, told Mason everything.

"Now, I had never really *thought* of being *prepared* for rape," she says. "But years before I had read a magazine article by Carol Burnett. She wrote that she had been walking down a street in New York or somewhere, and somebody walked up behind her. She decided to try to scare him and perhaps he would go away. So she turned around and just acted *totally crazy*, screaming and hollering and totally freaking out. And it worked. She scared the guy and he ran away.

"At the time I thought, 'If anything like that ever happens to me, that's what I'm going to do.' And that's what I did. I just went *bananas!* I started screaming and flailing my arms and jumping up and down. Just berserk! Attacking him and screaming real loud."

Mason's staged fit did catch Al off guard—she could see the surprise in his face—but he didn't panic. As she yelled and scratched at him, Al clubbed her with his handgun, hitting her face and head again and again.

"Then he tried to *shoot* me!" she continues. "But the gun didn't go off. We both heard it click, and it clicked again. So I attacked him again. I just *attacked,* trying to get by, clawing at him and hitting."

There are a couple possibilities why Al's automatic would not discharge. He may have left the safety on or, for some reason, neglected to chamber a shell. The gun also might simply have failed to work. Police later recovered a full .380 ammo clip inside the house, and surmised that Mason's attacker inadvertently had hit the clip release mechanism as he assaulted the Realtor.

"He took the gun and started hitting me again on the head," Mason says. "Well that hurt, so I backed up. And when I did he tried to shoot me again, but it wouldn't go off. And when it wouldn't go off I attacked again. This went on for a while. I had blood just pouring down my face."

Mason remembers it was at this moment that Al suspended his assault. "I just want your purse," he repeated several times in a low, steady voice. "I just want your purse. I just want your purse."

"Now, I *knew* that this is not true," she explains. "But you want to believe it. So I screamed, 'It's in the car! Just take the keys and go!' Then I thought that I only had eighteen cents in my purse. 'If you tell him that,' I thought, 'it's just going to piss him off.' So I said, 'My billfold's in it! My checkbook is in it! Just go! Leave!' "

Before he would, Al said that he wanted to tie her up to ensure his getaway. She resisted as he pushed her farther down the hall into a back bathroom. "He was talking real fast, trying to tell me that he was just going to take my stuff. 'I'm going to tie you up and then I'll leave,' he said."

Out of fear and desperation Mason chose to believe him, begging the stranger for a single mercy. "Look, I'm hurt and nobody knows where I am," she pleaded. "Will you call somebody and tell them where I am?" He promised that he would. "I gave him a number and he repeated it. Then he pulled a roll of adhesive tape out of his jacket and put my hands behind my back and tied them up. He also gagged me with it."

As the battered Mason stood there, bound and bleeding, Al then grabbed for her throat and violently slammed Mason to the bathroom floor. He pounced on her, throttling her and hissing *"Pass out, bitch! Pass out!"*

On her back on the floor with only her feet free, she tried to kick him and to use her shoulders to protect her neck from his frenzied assault. "He kept coming down on my throat," yelling *'Pass out! Pass out!'* Finally I did pass out."

While unconscious, Mason underwent an out-of-body

experience. "I was just kind of floating through time. I have a real vivid memory of a Being, a spirit-type Being, with me, whose face I could see. It was female. There also were two others that I couldn't see; one behind me and one above me. And we all were just floating through time. Very pleasant. It was just very, very pleasant. We were above everything and I said, 'Gee, can I go back?' One of the three seemed to be speaking for the others—'No, we don't think you can. It doesn't work that way.' This didn't upset me, but I said, 'Well, would you mind asking again? I'm really not ready,' At some point they said, 'Well, okay. You can go back.' "

The police reckon that Elizabeth Mason regained partial consciousness about forty-five minutes later. Her blurry recollection is of first trying to stand up in the blood-smeared bathroom, then a blank period, then of looking out the living room window to discover that her car was missing.

"I don't know how I got out of the house," she says. "My hands were still taped behind my back and my panty hose were around my ankles. I was carrying my slacks in my hands behind me."

Somehow she found her way through a thick hedge and across a neighbor's front lawn to their porch. "I don't remember doing that. My only memory is of waking up on that doorstep, and I was ringing their doorbell with my chin. And they were staying to me from behind the door, 'We told you to sit down! We called the police. We called for help. Just sit down.'

"They were too afraid to open the door. Isn't that sad?"

Sergeant Jimmy Cook, a wiry, veteran Fayetteville police detective who was placed in charge of the Elizabeth Mason case, remembers that it was two days before he could question the victim at Cape Fear Hospital. Doctors had taken thirty-one stitches in Mason's head. "She was beaten unmercifully," says Cook. "When I first saw the lady she was wrapped up like a mummy. It is just a miracle that she is alive today."

At the hospital, Mason recollects, she temporarily was lucid enough to visit the women's room on her own. "My Tampax came out," she says, "and I just started screaming: 'I HAVE NOT BEEN RAPED! I HAVE NOT!' And I don't think that I was."

Mason would not, however, allows swabs to be taken. "I wouldn't let them do *anything* after that. As far as I was concerned, I had not been raped. I think that the police felt that maybe I had been abused in other ways while I was out. But I don't have any memory of that."

As Mason recovered, the official investigation went nowhere. Her car was found, but a search of it revealed only that Al apparently had taken Mason's purse and her eighteen cents with him, no doubt as a souvenir. When a $10,000 reward for information was posted by the area Realtors association, a witness came forward to relate how he'd encountered a blood-covered individual struggling to open Mason's car in front of 402 Foxhall that afternoon. The red-soaked man said something about having hurt himself, so the neighbor helped him sort through Mason's key ring, which was slippery with blood, and into the driver's seat. "And that guy *did not* call the police until a reward was posted," observes the victim. "Isn't that amazing?"

Mason also relates how, a couple days after she went home from the hospital, she received a telephone call from her assailant. "I know it was he," she insists. "He couldn't believe I was alive. I know he couldn't.

"He said, 'Is this Elizabeth Mason?'

"And I said, 'Yes.'

" 'Elizabeth Mason the real estate agent?'

" 'Yes.'

"Then there was just *silence*—and he hung up. I *know* who it was. I recognized the voice."

Mason, according to Jimmy Cook, said she was certain from the start that she'd recognize Al anytime, anywhere. "There was no question in her mind that she could identify him," says Cook. She said she'd *never* forget him."

3

A Sweet Little Girl

Sadism. The wish to inflict pain on others is not the essence of sadism. The central impulse <u>to have complete mastery over another person, to make him/her a helpless object of our will, to become the absolute ruler over her, to become her god, to do with her as one pleases, to humiliate her, to enslave her are means to this end. And the most radical aim is to make her suffer. Since there is no greater power over another person than that of inflicting pain on her. To force her to undergo suffering without her being able to defend herself. The pleasure in the complete domination over another person is the very essence of the sadistic drive.</u>

In May 1979, after a four-month search, DeBardeleben found just the right dead-end street and suitable printer's lair—a grayish, wood-frame bungalow at 1913 Hileman Road in Falls Church, Virginia, which he leased for $320 a month. He now was ready to set up his press, a 1250 Multilith.

Posing as Frank A. Turner, he bought the offset press for $600 from BPS Printing Service in Wheaton, Maryland. Days later the residents along Hileman Road noticed their new neighbor, bespectacled, pale and aloof as usual, assiduously sealing his house's windows. Once DeBardeleben felt secure from inquiring gazes, he deftly reassembled the heavy, bulky Multilith in an upstairs bedroom, and then set to work shooting his negatives, burning them onto thin aluminum plates, and mixing his inks to take advantage of late spring and early summer's favorable nighttime temperature and humidity conditions for printing counterfeit. In a few weeks it would be too hot in eastern Virginia, and too damp, to manufacture quality funny money.

Memorial Day weekend, 1979, he returned to the Delaware—Maryland seashore.

Like Lucy Alexander, doe-eyed Laurie Jensen*, 20, of Howard County, Maryland, was warm, soft, and trusting. If possible, the dark strawberry blond with a slight overbite was even more naive than Lucy. "She was a sweet little girl who easily could be taken advantage of," says FBI agent Cathy Kiser, who'd later work both the Alexander and the Jensen cases. "Both she and Lucy were very much the same type."

Just before midnight on Friday, June 1, Laurie Jensen closed the Ocean City convenience store she'd been hired to manage that summer, then set out, as usual, for her brief walk home. The day had been warm, with a high in the 80s, but the nighttime temperature was dipping toward the 50s, chilly for the light clothing Jensen wore. A half block from the rental home she shared with a roommate, Laurie met a jogger, unknown to her, with whom she exchanged a casual "Hi."

Just then, a white male in a blue leisure suit pulled over his dark-blue two-door sedan beside her and stopped.

"Police," said the driver, who was slender and appeared to be in his thirties.

"What?" asked Jensen, alarmed.

He leaned across the passenger seat and flashed an oblong gold shield at her. "Get in the car," the stranger ordered.

Laurie Jensen obeyed.

"I want to ask you a few questions," he said after examining her Maryland driver's license, which he tucked into his shirt pocket. "There's been a store broken into by a man and a woman. I saw you talk to that guy who ran by you, and I think he might be your accomplice."

Jensen courteously advised the "officer" he was mistaken. She couldn't have committed any burglaries that night; she'd been at work since 2:30 in the afternoon.

"Is there anyone who can verify that you were at work?" he asked.

"Yes," she answered. "My boss can."

Cool and controlled as he'd been with Lucy Alexander, he asked Laurie to direct him to her employer's Ocean City residence. Once they found the house, however, he drove past it and stopped. "You're under arrest for robbery," he announced abruptly. Then he turned the unresisting Jensen around in her seat and handcuffed her.

From this point the abduction and assault proceeded as had the previous one—what the police sometimes call a "layover" because so many elements of both crimes exactly matched. Once again he drove north on Delaware Route 1 from Fenwick Island, and then west along secondary roads, assuring Jensen that they were headed for the Sussex Correctional Institution. When they were deep into the countryside, he stopped as before.

"At this time," wrote Howard County police detective Richard Witte in his subsequent report, "the victim claims that she realized that the

subject was probably not a police officer. She opened the door, got both feet on the ground, screamed, and tried to get away. Suspect grabbed her and said, 'I'll kill you.' He then put handcuffs on her ankles, bunched her hair up behind her head, took a rubber band and tied it in a ponytail, and then took white adhesive tape and began taping her face going down across her face behind her neck, around her face again numerous times. He then taped above her eyes, down under her chin. The victim was struggling at this time, very scared. The suspect said, 'Cool it. Didn't anybody ever tell you what to do in case something like this happened to you? You're defenseless. Don't even struggle. There's nothing you can do.' The suspect at this time pushed her on the floor with her head resting against the bucket seat facing the door. The suspect said, 'I have a gun and I'll use it. I have nothing to lose because I've already kidnapped you.' "

The drive again lasted approximately two hours. Jensen, as had Alexander, would distinctly remember passing through a toll plaza about halfway through the trip. Once arrived at their destination, he freed her ankles and then hustled Jensen indoors. He guided her through what seemed to be a back door, across his kitchen, up a low incline and to her left into a bedroom equipped with an alarm that buzzed angrily as he opened the door. From what little she could discern looking downward, the house was small and seedy and littered with everything from Pepsi bottles to random tools to the package of Stove Top Stuffing she noticed in a cardboard box resting on the tan linoleum kitchen floor.

Before disrobing Jensen—she refused to undress herself—he offered her a sip of his root beer. Then he removed the adhesive tape from her mouth and nose and neck, and took off his own clothes.

"Lay down beside me," he commanded.

"Don't hurt me!" Laurie pleaded. "I can get money for you!"

"Shut up!" he answered. "I'll tell you what to do. I want you to give me a blow job."

As before, he had trouble staying hard and inordinate difficulty achieving orgasm. Once he did, he immediately forced Jensen onto her knees, applied a lubricant, then sodomized her as he had Lucy Alexander. Again, he compelled his victim to call him "Daddy" through her screams, and to beg for further degradation between sobs.

Afterward, she was placed on a pad in the locked bedroom closet, naked and bound and chained to an eyebolt in the floor with handcuffs. Five or six hours later, Jensen guessed, he awakened her. Though still blindfolded, she could tell that daylight had arrived. Dogs were barking. A television played somewhere in the house; Laurie heard mention of the game show, *Family Feud.*

"Let's go," he said, and led her over to the bed.

"When can I go home?" she pleaded again.

"I told you, don't piss me off or I'm going to start punching you each time you ask," he warned stonily. "Now slide down and give me a good blow job. Go down on it." The fellatio—Jensen would recall his penis was quite small—was followed by vaginal rape, during which he called her "Becky" for no explicable reason. He seemed to Laurie to be manipulating one or more small mirrors to observe the sexual assault from different angles. Then he returned her to the locked closet.

That afternoon, he photographed and audiotaped her as he again forced her to fellate him, and then sodomized her. He also ordered her to insert an oversized dildo he called "the biggie" into her vagina. Back in the closet, she listened as he prepared a Salisbury steak TV dinner, and braced herself as he returned again to the bedroom.

"I'll tell you what's going down," he said. "I had an ex-old lady who really pissed me off and fucked me over. I just want to get back at women." He added that he would take her home soon—after one more fellation. "Give me a good one," he said. "Make me come quick so you can sleep some hours before we go."

When she couldn't satisfy him, he sodomized her

again before returning her a final time to her closet cell. Not until early Sunday, June 3, more than twenty-four hours after her abduction, did the rapist finally allow Laurie to reclothe herself. Then he removed the tape, bound her eyes with a bandanna and her hands with a length of heavy string and drove her home to Maryland. Before releasing her a few block from the Jensen family residence, he warned Laurie that if she went to the police he'd make sure everyone saw the naked pictures he'd taken.

4

The Mall Passer

The United States Secret Service, among the oldest of all federal law-enforcement agencies, is unique in the world for its curious mix of missions—protection and investigation. What is more, although the Secret Service traces its origin to the day Abraham Lincoln was assassinated, the two events were unrelated.

In 1865, four years after the U.S. had resumed printing paper dollars for the first time since the Revolution, counterfeiting of the new national currency was blossoming into something of a country-wide criminal pastime. According to estimates of the day, more than a third—and as much as half—of all Union paper dollars in circulation were fake. The Confederacy's problems were even more severe.

Alarmed at the flood of counterfeit, Treasury Secretary Hugh McCulloch on April 14, 1865, suggested a solution to President Lincoln during an afternoon Cabinet meeting at the White House. McCulloch told the President that, in his view, half measures such as the rewards then offered for turning in counterfeiters, would not suffice. "I believe there should be a continuous organized effort, aggressive rather than merely [a] defensive [one]," McCulloch told the President. "The work," he added, "should be undertaken by a permanent force managed by a directing head."

"Work it out your own way, Hugh," Lincoln answered. "I believe you have the right idea." Hours later, John Wilkes Booth assassinated Lincoln at Ford's Theater.

On July 5, 1865, William P. Wood, a sometime Federal spy and keeper of the Old Capitol Prison, was sworn in as the first chief of the Treasury Department's new Secret Service. Wood deployed a force of thirty so-called operatives in eleven eastern cities and soon began to show results. Within a year, fully two hundred counterfeiters had been put behind bars.

Two more U.S. presidents were assassinated by gunshot—James A. Garfield in 1881, and William McKinley in 1901—before Congress officially authorized the treasury's forgery investigators to also protect the Commander in Chief, a job they'd performed intermittently and informally for some time. Since then, the list of Secret Service protectees has lengthened to include all members of the First Family, the Vice-President and his family, designated presidential candidates (since Robert Kennedy's murder in 1968) plus foreign heads of state when they visit the U.S.

The Secret Service's investigative responsibilities expanded over the years, as well. Besides paper money, coins, and food stamps, the agency's 2,000 special agents police the authenticity of all government securities, such as treasury bills and savings bonds, and investigate financial crimes, as well as credit card and computer fraud. Suppressing bogus currency lately has been complicated by the emergence of sophisticated foreign operations—as much as a third of all counterfeit U.S. money is now printed abroad—and the appearance of new domestic players such as drug and bike gangs who find counterfeiting a convenient and complementary sideline in their strictly cash-only business transactions.

Still, the overwhelming majority of counterfeiting cases begin—and end—in much the same way. "Generally what happens," says David Butler, an ASAIC (Assistant Special Agent in Charge) at Headquarters

Counterfeit Division in Washington, "is that you and I get together. You're a printer and we both have larceny in our hearts. Obviously, you just don't go out and find somebody. There's a tie there, a connection, between me, the guy that wants it done, and you, the printer. We decide, 'Okay, we'll print a million dollars.'

"You ask, 'How're we gonna get rid of it?'

'Well, there's this guy who lives next to me. We can trust him. Let me talk to him.'

"So I talk to him. He says, 'Yeah, give me a hundred thousand dollars, and I'll pay you ten grand in genuine'—whatever they decide on. Then it just breaks down from there."

According to Butler, roughly $18 million in forged notes (sixty percent of which are twenties) reached the public in 1992. Secret Service agents seized another $50 to $70 million worth before it can be distributed.

Most of this counterfeit is interdicted in the same way. "It's a typical police investigation," says Butler. "In a classic example, a gas station attendant alerts police that he's taken in a counterfeit note. The cops call the Secret Service. Maybe the attendant has a car description and a tag number. We find the driver and talk to him. He confesses he's got, say, five more bills, and he tells us where he got 'em. We send him back for more and then bust his supplier. Then we just move right on up the line until we find the plant—the press, the plates, and paraphernalia of counterfeiting. There's really nothing spectacular about it in ninety-five percent of the cases. Just police work."

The perils of snitching and betrayal notwithstanding, it remains axiomatic among counterfeiters that to be an independent printer-passer is to take an imbecile for a partner. Much better, writes British master forger (and ex-con) Charles Black in his 1989 memoir, *Counterfeiter*, that a forger "dispose of his crisp and entrancing product through no more than one or two buyers in large quantities at tremendous discounts. And he must ensure that his customers are sound villains who won't drop him in it if their collars are felt by the law."

Given the scarcity of sound villains, it is no wonder that many of the Secret Service's toughest cases have involved solitary operators. "You run into a printer-passer," explains Butler, "and you *really* have problems. If you know something and tell nobody, then nobody knows. But if you tell me, things start unraveling at that point."

Over the years, among the more artful independents was a German immigrant and quiet family man, Emanuel Ninger, known to the 19th-century operatives who pursued him as Jim the Penman. Ninger, a sign painter by trade, owned a farm in New Jersey where he secretly handcrafted brilliantly deceptive $50s and $100s that he spent monthly in New York City for farm supplies. Beginning in 1882, Jim the Penman anonymously created and passed an estimated $40,000 in counterfeit paper money. According to one story, he might have continued to do so indefinitely save for an accident in 1896 when Ninger absently dropped one of his small masterpieces on a bar top. To his horror, the bill blotted up some water and began to bleed its color across the bar. Before he could flee, the constables took Jim the Penman into custody.

Another solo practitioner, machinist Marion John Williams, began his counterfeiting career manufacturing fake coins in the 1920s, and stayed with it for more than fifty years. According to David Butler, Williams printed some of the finest counterfeit paper money the Secret Service ever has encountered, and continued to do so into his 70s. "He would pass one note at a time, by himself," says Butler. "The only reason he got caught was that he got sick and needed some help moving his personal belongings. A kid was helping him, and he noticed some counterfeit that Williams later told us he never would have tried to pass. It wasn't ready yet. But the kid hit him over the head, took some of the money, tried to pass it and was arrested. Then he took us back to Marion John Williams."

Printer-passers also enjoy an advantage of scale. In large cities where counterfeiting is relatively common, a typical operation might inundate a town's merchants with tens of thousands of dollars' worth of funny money in a day or two. Capers of this scope inevitably yield tips and leads.

By contrast, there was the case of elderly New York City junk dealer, Emerich Juettner. In 1938, Juettner set up a press in his Manhattan apartment and began printing *one* dollar bills, which he passed throughout the city as his finances required. So varied were Juettner's targets and so modest his take—he later explained that in an effort to be equitable he never passed twice in the same store—the Secret Service pursued "Mr. 880" (his federal case number) without success for a full decade. Only after Juettner's Manhattan apartment caught fire was his operation exposed. After pleading guilty, at age 72, Juettner was sentenced to nine months behind bars and was fined, appropriately enough, one dollar.

Mike DeBardeleben, the Mall Passer, would become the most notorious of them all, the slickest printer-passer in Secret Service history. DeBardeleben devised six steps to his printing process. First, came a yellowish-black halftone screen applied to his blank 8½ x 11 sheets of twenty-pound Cranes Crest White—widely regarded as the best paper stock available for currency counterfeiting—with which he approximated the familiar ivory hue of genuine currency paper. Then the actual printing began with the back plate's green-ink portrait of the White House and south lawn, its trees and shrubbery. Third, he affixed the green treasury seal on front, as well as the bill's serial numbers. Fourth, he printed the black-ink portions of the note, including the three-quarter view of President Jackson, and the tall

"TWENTY" superimposed over the treasury seal. On press runs five and six he added the wispy red and blue traces with which he sought to mimic the colored synthetic threads imbedded in genuine linen-and-cotton "rag" currency stock.

Once the printed sheets were dry, DeBardeleben cut his individual bills to a uniform 6.14 x 2.61 inches, steeped each one in a tea solution to chemically age them ("selking" as he called it in his handwritten diaries) and donned gloves to meticulously hand crumple, or "wraggle" the notes to further disguise them. Finally, in late July 1979, he selected a batch of his best notes, climbed in the blue T-bird and hit the road.

On Tuesday, July 31, his new twenty-dollar bills debuted at a Super Sam's franchise fast-food outlet in the Florence Mall in Florence, Kentucky, just south across the Ohio River from Cincinnati. The next day, a bank teller discovered the counterfeit in Super Sam's deposit bag. According to standard procedure, the bank sent the bill to the Secret Service field office in Cincinnati, which then forwarded it to headquarters on "G" Street in Washington.

There, document analysts in the Forensic Services Division labs could tell at a practiced glance that the bill was a fake. As is true of almost all counterfeit paper money, it obviously had been printed on an offset machine—the Multilith 1250—which yields a bill lacking the crisp detail and familiar raised-ink feel of genuine notes printed by the intaglio process from hand-engraved plates. This new counterfeiter hadn't even tried to match the magnetic inks used by the U.S. Bureau of Printing and Engraving. On the other hand, he had done a pretty fair job of reproducing the treasury seal which, with its interior detail including thirteen stars inside bars and exterior circular pattern of tiny coglike teeth, is one of the most difficult parts of a U.S. bill for a counterfeiter to get right. Also, the green of his greenbacks was close to exactly the shade of the real thing.

All offset counterfeit bears telltale flaws. This note's major identifying defects included a small black diagonal in the field to the left of the "J" (for Kansas City) in the black Federal Reserve Board (FRB) seal on Andrew Jackson's right, plus a defect in the interior outline of the zero in "20" in the upper-left corner of the face of the bill. On its reverse side, the document analysts isolated another artifact, a green curl in the sky above the White House and below the letter "T" in "UNITED."

In all, the experts described the new bill as technically competent but hardly a masterwork—"not a deceptive note," in Secret Service parlance, meaning that an agent would not be fooled by it. A busy clerk, on the other hand, might well be. James E. Brown, a twenty-two-year veteran of the Forensic Services Division, explains. "This may have been an average counterfeit, maybe a four or a six on a scale of ten. If I were to compare it to some of the best notes we've seen, maybe I'd move it down to a two. But in counterfeiting, quality is not everything. Remember, you only have to fool someone with it *one* time. Obviously, this note was *good enough.*"

The note's identifying characteristics were typed up and telexed to all sixty-three Secret Service field offices in the U.S., together with its code, or Circular, number, which was 7215—meaning that the new bill was the 7215th separate example of counterfeit currency detected by the Secret Service since its classification criteria were systematized in the late nineteenth century.

No one at Super Sam's remembered who'd passed 7215. However, a clerk at another Florence Mall shop, the Donut Palace, also had been approached that Tuesday. She refused to accept the bill, and had a clear recollection of the man who tried to pass it. According to her and other Donut Palace employees, the suspect was a white male in his middle thirties, about six feet tall, and around 160 to 170 pounds. His hair was black, she said. He was dressed in a white shirt with a polka-dot pattern, navy blue trousers, and wore a gold wrist-watch, as well as wire-rimmed glasses. Also, there was something unusual about the bridge of his nose, a pro-trusion or irregularity that the witnesses could not quite describe.

On August 1, another of DeBardeleben's notes turned up in the till of a United Dairy Farmers store across the river in Cincinnati. Then nothing until the 21st, when a 7215 was passed at a Cincinnati Burger Chef. This note may have been what the Secret Service calls a floater, a counterfeit bill that is passed and then unwittingly repassed, perhaps several times, across days or weeks and sometimes great distances until it is finally detected.

There were no further passes until November 13, when the manager of the Empress Shop franchise in Elizabeth, New Jersey, took in a new example of DeBardeleben's Hileman Road handiwork. In Wash-ington, the Secret Service currency experts compared the new bill to a 7215 and determined that the same plates had been used to print both, except that the FRB seal had been changed from Kansas City (J) to New York City (B). This twenty was designated Circular 7373, and described in another telex to the field.

DeBardeleben stayed busy. A third new note, Circu-lar 7404, was recovered from a cash drawer at the United Pennsylvania Bank in Scranton, Pennsylvania, on December 14. Circular 7404 was printed with most of the same aluminum plates used for 7215 and 7373. Hence, it featured most of the same flaws, including the free-floating curl in the sky above the White House. On the front of the note, however, he changed the FRB seal again; this time the letter was C, for Phil-adelphia. Otherwise (and except for another new serial number) 7404 and 7373 were exactly like their "parent" note, 7215.

As was true of 7215 and 7373's initial appearances, the Secret Service had no description of the person who passed 7404 nor, in this case, any way even to establish which Scranton-area business had accepted it. Except for the bills themselves and the single physical description provided by the staff of the Donut Palace, the treasury agents knew nothing about this clever new counterfeiter, except that he was deliberate and careful. He was going to be difficult to catch.

DeBardeleben started out cautiously, but by early 1980 he began to hit his stride. From March 1st through the 10th, examples of his work turned up in Durham, North Carolina, Charlottesville, Fredericksburg and Sterling, Virginia, and in Columbus, Ohio, too. On April 12th he hit the Blue Hen Mall in Dover, Delaware. Two days later, it was a Penney's store in St. Louis. Eight days after that he conducted a sixteen-note blitz of malls in the Charlotte and Greensboro, North Carolina, area.

An early-summer note-passing tour of the south started June 11 at the Western Hills and Century Plaza Malls in Birmingham, Alabama. Next stop: the Cumberland Mall in Atlanta on June 13. Less than a day later he toured the Valley View mall in Dallas, passing a total of nineteen fake twenties at stores ranging from Sears to Waldenbooks to Sound Town and Susie's Casuals. June 16 and 17 the Mall Passer visited New Orleans and Shreveport, Louisiana. June 18 and 19 he was back in Dallas at North Park Center. June 20: Kansas City. June 30: Charlotte, again.

He rested a month, then began a northern swing, on July 31, at the Twelve Oaks Mall in Novi, Michigan, and continued in early August through Minneapolis, Milwaukee, Niles, Illinois, Milwaukee again, and on to the Manor Mall in Louisville, Kentucky, before his trail of counterfeits abruptly halted over Labor Day in Tulsa, Oklahoma.

From then until late in the year, DeBardeleben's principal passing occurred nearer to home, at Giant Food stores in Greenbelt and Wheaton, Maryland, as well as the Giant Food outlet in Fairfax, Virginia. Total amount passed in 1980: Approximately 1,500 counterfeit notes, or $30,000 worth. Including floaters, one or more of DeBardeleben's counterfeits were recovered from cash registers in thirty-eight states that year.

5

Unsub

MY BELIEFS:

"I'M TOO OLD/UGLY/POOR ETC. TO ATTRACT/FUCK YOUNG
PRETTY GIRLS . . .

I NEED SPD., DAR. ETC. TO 'GET GOING' ACCOMPLISH THINGS

BECAUSE C. REJECTED ME: I AM LESS OF A PERSON (IRRATIONAL
BELIEF)/MUST GET EVEN/ALL PRETTY GIRLS (LIKE C.) WILL REJECT
ME/ I HATE WOMEN (MOTHER–CARYN* REINFORCES THIS)

DID BECKY ACCOMPLISH GOAL?

PRO: TEMPORARY A-H FUCK

   TOTAL CONTROL

CON: LOW SELF ESTEEM . . .

   COMPLAINING TROUBLESOME

   LONG DRIVING, NO SLEEP, ANXIETY, FEAR

   <u>TWO DAYS</u>

   VERY TEMPORARY

   A LOT OF TROUBLE—NO TIME FOR MUCH ELSE

As the Secret Service began stirring to what the
treasury agency still regarded as more the Mall
Passer's impertinence than any grave threat to the dollar's integrity, other law-enforcement agencies were
struggling with much more disturbing unsolved crimes.

In Fayetteville, according to Sergeant Jimmy Cook,
there were no likely suspects in the Elizabeth Mason
assault, and no leads, either. To the north in Delaware
and Maryland, FBI and state investigators felt certain
from the outset that the same deviant offender was responsible for both the 1978 Alexander and the 1979

Jensen oceanside kidnap-assaults. But that rational investigative premise didn't tell the law-enforcement agencies anything about who their Unsub (for Unknown Subject) might be, or where to look for him. The federal agents and local detectives also had no leads and only a general description of the assailant; neither victim had gotten a very good look at the man.

In view of what they did know of his apparent pattern, the FBI attempted a pro-active ploy. Over the Independence Day weekend, 1979, a Bureau Special Operations surveillance group was detailed to Ocean City where agent Cathy Kiser (blond and attractive, like the victims), and another female FBI agent had volunteered to stroll around late at night, hoping to attract the rapist's attention. "We were there for the entire weekend," Kiser remembers, "taking turns walking up and down, wearing shorts, hoping that if this person was in fact in the area we could snatch him up."

The FBI temptresses had no luck. "What can I say?" Kiser asks with a laugh. "We were a little older than the victims. We did get a few honks, but we didn't get picked up. We were out there, though. Going up and down the road, trying to be targets."

A month later, the frustrated investigators turned to their last resort, the Bureau's Behavioral Sciences Unit (BSU), a special team of experts on aberrant crime who work out of a converted bomb shelter beneath the FBI Academy in Quantico, Virginia. Unlike traditional detectives, the BSU's so-called Criminal Personality Profilers focused then, as now, on behavioral aspects of irrational crimes to develop conjectural portraits of deviant Unsubs.

The body of fact and lore from which these profiles are fashioned is rich and varied. Some of this knowledge, such as the fact that murder is largely an intra-racial crime committed for the most part among family, friends, and acquaintances, is evident from a quick look at any police arrest statistics. Other indicators are more subtle, and have been gleaned, in part, from law officers' cumulative empirical experience with homicide. Example: If a victim's face is mutilated—especially the eyes—this fact in conjunction with other clues often suggests that she or he and the assailant knew each other. Still another critically important source of insight for the BSU has been the intimate recollections of aberrant offenders themselves. In order to know more about their appalling subject, the BSU agents have toured the country's prisons, interviewing serial killers, serial rapists, pedophiles, and other sex criminals to learn directly from them the specifics of what they did before, during and after their crimes, and how they did it.

BSU Special Agent John Douglas—later to become chief of the team—was a 33-year-old Air Force veteran with two years' experience as a profiler in August of 1979 when he was assigned the Alexander and Jensen cases. "Generally," Douglas noted at the start of his report, "subjects involved in criminal offenses such as this . . . were raised by a domineering overbearing mother, and a father who was passive, weak, and indifferent when expressing his feelings to his son and other members of his family. By . . . puberty he has already been involved in criminal offenses and in all probability has been confronted by local police agencies."

In short, the Unsub surely had a rap sheet.

"His arrest record," Douglas continued, "will reflect offenses [including] voyeuristic activities, burglary, and assault. While he was attending elementary and secondary schools he was a problem in the classroom and in all probability was expelled on numerous occasions."

Douglas surmised that the Unsub joined the military after high school. Although his subsequent discharge might have been honorable, there would have been "major problems on his part in adjusting to the military way of life."

The profile also addressed the offender's probable sexual orientation.

> Your subject has had a problem throughout his life in adjusting to females and heterosexual relations in general. Your subject can be classified as a sexual experimenter who by his own inadequacies believes his assaults upon his victims are desired by them. Much of his warped thinking comes from pornographic literature, which he is obsessed in reading and buying. The pornographic literature that is most appealing to his sexual fantasies are those magazines depicting sado-masochistic types of behavior; behavior that reflects total domination and degradation of the female by the male. Although your offender can be classified as being sexually inadequate, it is not surprising to find offenders such as yours either married or recently divorced. Interviews of former spouses generally will reflect a stressful marriage; a marriage that included sexual experimentation and degradation of his own wife.

Douglas noted that this Unsub might cruise for victims nightly, but that he was intelligent enough not to take undue chances. The dark-blue car was consistent; these offenders often troll in vehicles that are "subdued in color," as Douglas put it, "and appear to be somewhat police looking." In fact, the rapist was likely to be a police "buff," wrote the agent, and may have tried on one or more occasions to become a cop himself. "His obsession," Douglas continued, "will consequently find him reading various detective magazines. It is from these . . . that he may go one step further and send away for various police badges . . . which will satisfy his police fantasy."

The profile explained the Unsub as a type that may

threaten to kill his victims but would not do so, "as long as he can maintain some control over them. He is not the type of offender that desires his victims to fight back and struggle with him."

Finally, Douglas offered some thoughts on the Unsub's future actions. Noting the photography, Douglas opined that

> the subject in future weeks and months will use these photographs and perhaps articles of clothing from his victims to fantasize and relive his conquest. The clothing and photographs, however, will not always be sexually satisfying for him, so generally it is at this point that we find offenders returning to the victim's residence in a hope that he can personally observe her. . . . He will probably return and observe the victim from a distance, and while there, fantasize once again in his mind the sexual relationship that he had with her. He is smart enough, however, not to confront the victim inasmuch as this could result in an identification of him as her abductor.

6

"Somebody Help Me!"

*JUST BECAUSE I FELT FEAR (GUILT, IN REALITY)
WHEN I HAD LAURIE, LUCY, ETC. DOESN'T MEAN
THAT I WILL AUTOMATICALLY FEEL THE SAME WAY
(FEAR) IN A SIMILAR/SAME SITUATION IN THE FU-
TURE. SOLUTION: ANALYZE WHY I FELT FEAR
WITH THEM + WHY I FEEL EVEN STRONGER FEAR
WHEN I 'IMAGINE' THE SAME SITUATION WITH C.*

On the evening of November 1, 1980, 25-year-old Dianne Overton brushed her curly dark-blond hair, pulled on a burgundy terry cloth dress and high heels and headed southeast from her parents' house in tiny Knoxville, Maryland, near Frederick, for the California Inn in Laurel, an hour and a half away. "A bunch of us were supposed to go that night," recalls the lively and assertive Overton, who at the time was working as a data-entry clerk. "But they all called me at the last minute to say they'd decided not to go. I'd never driven to Laurel on my own, but I was determined to go anyway. A band called Summer was playing at the California Inn that night, and I had a crush on the drummer."

It was cool and clear and the roads were dry that Friday night. Some time soon after 9:30 Overton found the California Inn—"a big nightclub-type thing, very nice"—and went in. At the crowded bar, she ordered a tequila with orange juice, then sat poised for her ardor's object to notice her.

"He came over and spoke to me a couple of times," she says. "But we didn't confer with each other that much." The night dragged on. "I kinda got the feeling, 'Uh, I don't know if he really wants me to be here or not.' So I had another drink and then I decided, 'I'm going on home.' "

It was the shank of the evening, past one-thirty. "When I got out to the parking lot I thought, 'Now which way *is* home? It was dark. So I worked my way to a Seven-Eleven, walked in and asked, "Can you give me directions to Frederick?' The person told me the wrong way, so I stopped again at a Big Boy and finally got the right directions."

Overton was driving her new Olds Firenze, white with black stripes, an easy car to follow. According to directions, she first steered south from Laurel on I-95 for approximately seven miles until she reach I-495, the Washington Beltway, which she took a short distance west to I-270, the main route northwest to Frederick, about forty-five miles away. "I took my time getting home," Overton explains. "I was kinda heartbroken because basically this guy didn't want to talk to me. That's what it boiled down to."

At Frederick, she turned west on four-lane State Highway 340 and followed it across the dark countryside to two-lane Route 180, the road into Knoxville. About half a mile from town, Overton crossed the deserted, unlit intersection of routes 180 and 478.

"Right there," she says, "is where the whole thing started."

It was approximately 4:00 A.M.

"I proceeded across the intersection and looked in my mirror and saw like a light flash. I thought, 'Oh, that's just a car turning around in the intersection.' I paid it no mind."

A short distance farther, as Overton approached the top of the long hill that wends down into Knoxville, she saw a flashing red light in her mirror, and may have heard a short blast from a siren. "I said, 'That's a cop! I don't believe it!' Then it dawned on me that it must have been the same car I'd just seen in the intersection."

She pulled over onto Route 180's narrow shoulder and waited as the man she took for a police officer approached her. He produced a silver badge from his pocket. "My doors were locked. I cracked my window and he said, 'I'd like for you to pull off down here on the next road to your right.' " Suspicious of this suggestion, if not yet of the situation itself, Overton decided to do otherwise. "I thought to myself, 'I'm not going to pull off on the next road. I'll just go on into town underneath the lights.' And that is what I did."

She stopped at the bottom of the hill in front of Miller's General Store, opposite a darkened gas station and the Knoxville post office. There was just room enough for the "officer" to pull in behind her, the red light still flashing on his dashboard. Immediately to their right was a low cement wall. Behind the two cars rose a steep-covered staircase leading up to a row of attached houses perched along the hillside.

Overton got her single brief look at the man she'd later identify as Mike DeBardeleben as he approached her car, illuminated by his own headlights. As she told Maryland State Police investigators later that morning, he had black hair with a receding hairline, and wore dark-frame glasses. He stood about five-nine or five-ten, weighed perhaps 160 or 170 pounds and was dressed in a blue suit coat, or blazer, and checkered, possibly plaid, pants.

"He walks up and says, 'I'd like to see your driver's license and registration.' I was getting them out anyway. So I handed them out through the window and he takes them and walks back. He was back there a good five minutes or so. Then he comes back and says, 'I'd like for you to get out of the car.'

"I said, 'What for? Why do you want me to get out of my car? What have I done?'

" 'I'd like for you to get out of your car.'

" 'Why? What are you pulling me over for? *What* have I done?'

"Then the thought came to me. 'Don't argue with him. He probably wants you to get out and walk the line to see if you've been drinking.' "

Overton opened her door and was starting to get out when the man told her she could shut off her engine. It was an innocent-sounding suggestion. Just as she turned to reach for the ignition, however, he whipped out a pair of handcuffs and snapped them on her wrists.

"It was *click! click!*" says Overton. "That fast he took my hands behind me. 'What are you doin'?' I asked. 'Why'd you pull me over? I haven't *done anything!*' "

"This car's wanted," is all that he said as he grabbed her manacled wrists, lifted them and pushed her back to his car, which she recognized as a late-model Thunderbird, dark blue. At his driver's-side door, Overton began to resist, screaming and kicking. When he tried to put his left hand over her mouth, she bit him, leaving a wound.

"I'm hollering now. *'You've got the wrong person! Somebody help me!'* When I realized he was trying to shove me in his car, I got louder and louder. *Help me! Help me!'* "

Knoxville was asleep. No one responded.

Overton kept kicking as he struggled with his door, then shoved her across the front seat to the passenger side. Inside, she banged at him with her high heels again and again, trying to prevent him from getting into the car with her. "The whole time I kept kicking and hollering," she says. "Every time he'd reach for the ignition I'd kick his hand off it."

When her assailant at last was able to get the Thunderbird started, Overton repeatedly stalled the vehicle by kicking it in, and out, of gear. "He rammed it into reverse and when he did it jerked and stalled again," she says. "I went out for a minute then and collapsed and I remember saying to myself, 'This is it. I'm gone. I'm not getting out of this.' Then I came to my senses and said, 'You can't let this happen! You've *got* to do something!'

"I took my arms—to this day I don't know how I did it—and somehow managed to get them up and around by the door handle. I reached for it and threw all my weight up against the door and it opened! When it did, it grabbed the cement wall and got stuck."

With the door jammed open and Overton still inside, DeBardeleben managed to restart the car and tried to rock it free of the wall. "It wouldn't let loose," she says. "He gunned it in reverse and I was flung out onto my side." As she fell, the passenger-side door scraped free of the wall, nearly decapitating her as the Thunderbird roared backward. Then he shoved it into drive and hit the gas.

"I got to my knees and heard wheels screaming. He was coming right at me!" Overton saw that she had one desperate chance to avert being crushed under the big car's right front wheel. As he bore down on her, she leaned at an angle into his oncoming fender, using its momentum to bump her up and out of the way, as if she were a crash-test dummy. "There was no other way of doin' it," she says.

Moments later, "I was still on my knees and coming to my senses when I thought, '*Where* did he go?' " She looked across and down Route 180 and saw him circling in the gas station, ready to come after her again. Then Overton looked to her left and saw the familiar covered stairway leading up to the row of houses lining the hillside. If she could reach the stairs, she thought, she might be able to hide.

"I got as far as the second step, and that's as far as

I got. I froze. I couldn't move. I couldn't holler. I couldn't do anything. Then, all of a sudden, I heard this little *eeech!* of tires squealing and I thought, 'Oh my God, he's come back.' "

He had.

"Underneath that staircase was a little area that you could see under. And I could see his feet as he jumped out of the car. I could see exactly what he was doing. He was looking for me, but couldn't see me where I was hiding. All of a sudden he jumped back in the car and I heard the *eeech!* of the squealing wheels again. I got up on my knees and peeked over the side and saw him drive away."

Sheer terror prevented Overton from moving for at least ten minutes, she says. When her motor function at last returned, partially, she crawled on her knees up the wooden stairs to the front door of a family she knew. "When I got to the top," she remembers, "I nudged myself up to my feet. I was standing at their doorway and I just kept banging with my feet and my head because I still could not say anything. Finally, their teen-aged son answered the door, and I just fell into his arms. I remember, falling in and out of consciousness, him hollering to his mother. 'Mom! Mom! Come here quick! It's Dianne Overton. Something's happened!' "

7

Perversions

The Overton case shared with those that preceded it, and most that ensued, a near total lack of useful clues, practical leads, fingerprints or any other physical evidence. There was, as well, no reason yet to connect the attack to DeBardeleben's earlier assaults on Lucy Alexander and Laurie Jensen, despite the similar descriptions of assailant, car, and MO. The Maryland State Police investigators who handled the case had even less cause to be aware of the attack on Elizabeth Mason in North Carolina, or to wonder if perhaps all four assaults were related. There is no mechanism for this sort of interstate, cross-jurisdictional cooperation among police agencies, and very little enthusiasm for it in any event.

DeBardeleben's next known victim was Maria Santini*.

"Wholesome, very wholesome," is how Burlington County, New Jersey, Assistant Prosecutor James A. Ronca describes Santini. "She was very innocent, and innocent looking. Quite proper." Except for her naive quality, the 27-year-old Italian-American mother of two did not at all resemble any of the previous victims. Santini was short with a medium to full figure, Ronca remembers. She wore her dark hair at shoulder length. "She was the kind you'd expect to be a mother and homemaker," he adds. "Into crafts."

Her abduction's particulars, as Santini retold them, also were altogether different, and grotesque. She was a sales clerk at a clothes shop in Willingboro, New Jersey, a small town on the western fringe of Southern New Jersey's Pine Barrens, twenty minutes or so by car across the Delaware River from Philadelphia. At about noon on November 12, 1980, ten days after the Overton assault in Maryland, Maria Santini was alone in the store, listening to the daily Frank Sinatra hour on radio station WPEN, when a slender white male wearing black plastic-frame sunglasses, a dark business suit, and black trenchcoat came through the door. He was carrying what appeared to Santini to be an oversized briefcase, or possibly a portfolio, also black.

She guessed he was 30 or 35 years old and about five-seven, no taller. He had no beard or mustache, but Santini later dimly recalled a small mole or similar mark on his upper lip. His chestnut-brown hair was neatly trimmed and parted.

In a soft, distinctly southern accent he asked if the store manager was in. Santini said no, but that she'd be happy to give him manager Dorothy Beck's telephone number. She turned behind the counter for a piece of paper, then turned back to see a double-barreled sawed-off shotgun leveled at her.

"This is a robbery," the man said. "Open the registers."

"After I opened the registers," Santini later related in her taped statement to Willingboro Township police detectives Donald A. Cramer and James Thompson, "he told me to lie down on the floor behind the counter with my head down on the floor. I laid down and he tied my hands behind me with rope and he tied my ankles together with rope." She wasn't certain, but Santini believed the two lengths of rope were precut, part of a robbery and abduction tool kit the man had secreted either in the carrying case or under his trenchcoat. She did recall that after he bound her, "he walked over to the front door. I don't know whether he was just looking to make sure that nobody was coming in the parking lot, or what he was doing."

The man returned, emptied the $148.55 in bills and coins from the registers and fetched Santini's light blue ski jacket from the back room. "Then," she continued in her statement to the detectives, "he said to me that he was going to take me to a rented house outside [the nearby village of] Browns Mill and rape me. He said that he only wanted sex. He wasn't going to hurt me. And that it wasn't going to be worth it to me to get killed over something like that. He told me quite a few times during the whole thing. 'Don't try anything stupid. I'll shoot you.' "

"You know, you've tied my legs together. How are you going to rape me?" she asked him.

"Don't you worry about that," he replied.

Besides the perversions about to be practiced on Maria Santini, the crime was all the stranger for the fact that it appears her abductor had attempted the same offense, at the same store, thirteen months earlier. According to prosecutor Ronca and detective Cramer, on October 10, 1979, at about 3 o'clock in the afternoon, a previous clerk (coincidentally also Italian-American) had been held up by a white male. She described him as around 40 to 43, about six feet tall, 145–150 pounds, brown eyes, black rim glasses, and straight black hair, parted on the side.

He pulled a handgun on this clerk (whom Cramer describes as dark and pretty, in her late 20s, a bit taller and more slender than Santini) and ordered her into the shop's back room. She refused. So, after rifling the registers, where he found a scant $60, the robber tied her hands and feet with white cotton rope, placed the usual tape gag over her mouth, and left.

Why would he return a year later?

"The robbery was so easy," observes Ronca. "It's pretty deserted and it's near a main road, meaning he can get lost real quick. Maybe he just figured it was an easy place to hit. That makes sense to me."

Detective Cramer guesses otherwise. He believes the clerk's unwillingness to do as she was told is a key to understanding his return. "She said, 'No fuckin' way,' " Cramer opines. " 'I'm not goin'. That's all there is to it!' And he backed down. When he was challenged by a woman he yielded. And I think DeBardeleben came back for her. You know, 'Hey, girl, guess what? Now it's my turn.' He must have been surprised to find Maria there."

The intruder untied Santini's ankles before placing her ski jacket over her shoulders and zipping it up. Then he briskly marched her out the front door to his waiting vehicle, ordering her to keep her eyes averted. The car, she noted, was an old sedan of squarish design, an oxidized green with white (probably primer paint) blotches on it. Inside, the seats were bench-style and upholstered in vinyl. She was instructed to crouch on the passenger-side floor, her head on the seat. The man then covered Santini with a green army blanket.

"Then we just started driving," she told the detectives. "It didn't seem like a very long ride before we got to the house." Along the way, Maria Santini prayed.

She estimated they drove for fifteen minutes before he stopped, ordered her to close her eyes, then took her inside a residence of some sort. Santini remembered he opened the door with a key and took her over a threshold, then blindfolded her with tape before directing her into a gold-carpeted living room, which did not seem to contain any furniture.

He unzipped her coat and told her to lie down on her stomach, her hands still tied behind her. Then he took off Santini's brown oxfords, her burgundy knee socks, burgundy corduroys, and her underpants. As she one day would tell his jury, he proceeded to retie her ankles and added another ligature to her knees. Meantime, "he asked me a few questions. He wanted to know if I'd ever had sex before. I told him, 'Well, I've been married for eight years.' "

Santini hardly looked her age (and did not wear her wedding rings at work lest they catch and snag the merchandise), so the question was not altogether odd. Her abductor told Santini that he, too, was married, the father of several children, and that he had never before attempted anything like this. He was from West Virginia, he said, and worked as a traveling salesman.

Then came his big surprise. "He told me that he was a transvestite and that he enjoyed dressing up in women's clothing. He told me that he was into bondage."

As Santini explained under Jim Ronca's direct examination in court, "He bent my legs up so that my feet were sticking straight up in the air. He tied another rope from the rope that was around my wrist to the rope that was on my ankles."

With that he left the room.

"Did he have anything with him when he came back?" asked Ronca.

"When he came back he was dressed differently," she answered. "He was dressed in women's clothing."

"How could you see that?"

"I caught a glimpse," said Santini. "Because I was laying on the floor . . . I could see as he walked by. He had a skirt on and high heels."

"What did he do when he came back in the room?"

"He knelt down by my legs and he was rubbing the bottom[s] of my feet and my rear end and he was talking some more.

"He said, 'I guess you think I'm pretty strange?' And I said, 'Oh, no!' That was about it."

In the living room he took a half-dozen photos of Santini in various positions. "Did he tell you where he got the idea to do this?" Ronca asked.

"Yes," she answered. "He said that he had seen it in

a magazine and it looked like fun. It was something that he always wanted to try."

When she complained that she was unable to breathe because of her gag, he removed it and placed a cloth gag over her mouth instead. Then he led her hobbling into an adjoining bedroom. She would remember a hardwood floor with wide planks, a small area rug with a floral design on it, and an large old-fashion bureau.

He brought in his camera and flash equipment plus several pairs of women's shoes, which Santini was ordered to wear as he began photographing her again. "I was on my stomach. I was on my side," she told the court. "Different ropes were taken off and added and pictures were taken. Different shoes were put on and off. . . . I can't really recall any specifics except the one position I had so many ropes on me that I couldn't move. I even had a rope from the front of me under my crotch to the back that, you know, the slightest move was painful."

"Did he have a name for that particular position?" asked Ronca.

"I asked him what he was doing and he called it a Chinese Hog-Tie."

Santini said her burgundy velour shirt was removed while she was still in the living room. "He decided he wanted the shirt off," she testified, "but he didn't want to untie all the ropes. So he took the scissors and he cut the shirt, pulled the shirt down and then just unhooked my bra and pulled that down."

"Did he mention anything to you about the different positions and different types of knots that he was trying?"

"He would comment as he would move me, you know, like an inch or alter my position just a tiny bit and he said, 'Oh! That's really good. That looks good!' Then he would go off and take a picture.

"In fact, at one point he took tape and put tape around the top of my arms and the top of my breasts and then underneath. I said, 'What are you doing that for?'

"He said, 'Oh, because it looks so good!' "

Ronca asked, "Were any sex acts performed?"

"He got up onto the bed with me," Santini answered.

"What did he do?"

"He was kissing my breasts and he was rubbing my vagina."

"Were any other sex acts performed then?"

"No."

After a time, her abductor's depraved appetites flagged.

Ronca: "Did he tell you why he stopped?"

Santini: "He said he wasn't getting anything out of it."

She testified that he returned her to the living room and left her there while he changed out of his high heels and skirt—it was a yellow mini, Santini recalled—then came back, untied her and watched, holding a gun he warned her, as Santini reclothed herself except for the ripped velour top. To cover her, he gave Santini a sweaty white turtleneck he'd been wearing.

Back in the car under the blanket, blindfolded and wrist-bound, she was driven around for what seemed to be a half hour. "We made a lot of stops, a lot of turns."

The last stop was down a sandy, overgrown fire road near a cranberry bog in the Pine Barrens. "Because of the way I was crouched on the floor I couldn't get out myself. He helped me out. He told me he was going to let me go now. He explained to me that I was to walk in a certain direction because if I didn't I would end up lost in the woods."

He pulled the damaged burgundy shirt over Santini's head to make a hood, then reached under it and pulled the tape from her eyes. The man also loosened her wrist restraints.

"He asked me if I wanted some money so that I

could make a phone call for, you know, somebody to come get me. I told him, 'No, don't worry about it. I'm sure somebody will help me.' He told me not to move until I had heard him completely drive away."

"How," Ronca then inquired, "would you describe the state of mind that you were in at this point?"

"Scared to death," said Maria Santini. "I thought this was the end, that he took me out in the woods to shoot me."

"Did you remain standing there?"

"Yes, I did."

8

"There's Nobody *That* Good."

Beginning in 1979 with the alias, Frank A. Turner, purchaser of the Multilith 1250 offset press, Mike DeBardeleben, aka the Mall Passer, routinely renamed himself. On March 30, 1980, for example, in his hometown of Little Rock, he registered at a Best Western Motel as Alan Kirk of 5612 Crowley Street in Fort Worth. On April 21, he bought automobile tires in Falls Church as James R. Jones, his primary anonym. Two months later, at the Columbus, Ohio, Holiday Inn he was Michael B. Shelton of Washington, D.C.

December 16, 1980, posing as Thomas R. Curry, 6557 Glendora, Dallas, Texas, he took a room at the La Quinta motel in Indianapolis. The next day in Edmundson, Missouri, he was Mike Shelton once more.

In July of 1981, again in Columbus at a Red Roof Inn, he produced a counterfeit Texas license in the name of Roy Radke, from Austin. In September, he visited a Dodge dealership in Hanover, Massachusetts, posing as Maurice Paquette.

February 23, 1982, brought him as Roger Collin Blanchard to a Drury Inn in Nashville, Tennessee. The same day he passed thirty notes at Nashville's Rivergate Mall. Late that summer, in Little Rock, Robert D. Trombley of 10 Deerfield Drive, Montpelier, Vermont, exchanged his fake Vermont driver's license for an officially issued Arkansas license, listing his address as 5517 MacArthur Drive. Then DeBardeleben-as-Trombley purchased a handgun, later found among his possessions.

On August 17, he was Paul Donnelly of Burlington, Vermont, and stayed at a Regal 8 Inn in Madison, Wisconsin. Over the next few days, sixteen Circular 7215, 7373, and 7404 notes were recovered from Madison-area merchants. Before the local banks knew they had a problem, Donnelly was Roy Sledge, staying at a Best Western in Kansas City. In October, in Birmingham, Alabama, he'd become John P. Martel of Omaha, Nebraska, and was passing his twenties at a furious rate.

Altogether, the Secret Service ultimately discovered that DeBardeleben had planned, prepared, or used twenty-eight such aliases. By the end of fiscal 1982, he also had stung businesses and banks in forty-four states for more than $130,000. The Mall Passer finally had begun to irritate—and to embarrass—the Treasury Department. "We made him a top priority," recalls Joe R. Coppola, who through much of the Mall Passer investigation was Special Agent in Charge (SAIC) of Headquarters Counterfeit Division. "Deep in my heart I really wanted to nail this guy. There's nobody *that* good."

A major complicating difficulty in any counterfeiting case is that most forged bills aren't discovered until they make their way, via commercial and savings banks, to one of the various FRB (or "Fed") banks around the country. There the dollars are stacked into Currency Verification and Counting System machines, automatic devices that examine the bills for dirt, damage, and wear, sort them by denomination, count them, and check them for the magnetic toners in the printing ink that tell the sensors if a note is genuine.

"Then they get kicked out into what are called audit trays," says Greg Mertz, who first joined the investigation as a rookie in the Indianapolis field office. "The counterfeit gets picked up there, and is mailed to the Secret Service office with the name of the DI, or depositing institution. The Fed can put you onto the DI, but when a bill's discovered there your chances are slim and next to none of tracing it.

"If, for example, you get it from the bank and go back to where he passed it, Walgreen's, and you say, 'Mr. Walgreen, you made your afternoon deposit of $10,500 two weeks ago on the fourteenth. Can you tell me who gave you this twenty-dollar bill out of that $10,500?' He'll look at you as if you're on drugs.

"But every once in a while someone will take the bill and look at it and think, 'Boy, this bill's not real!' They've never before had a counterfeit. So then they'll just think, 'Naahhh! This isn't counterfeit!' All the same, they do look again at the person who passed it, and they make a mental image. He's made an impression and they may remember him. Every once in a while you get a hit like that."

After the first Mall Passer description, provided by the Donut Palace clerk at the Florence Mall in July of 1979, it would be almost two years before the Secret Service turned up another witness who could offer what seemed to be a reliable recollection of the suspect. She was a clerk in a Burnside, Minnesota, shopping center. On June 24, 1981, DeBardeleben handed her one of the sixteen Circular 7215 notes he passed in Burnside that day.

"She was suspicious of the note," recalls Joe Bergeman, who was rotated into the Counterfeit Division during the investigation. "When she looked at it closer, and wanted to talk to the person who passed it to her, he was gone. She called the police and took them out to the parking lot where she saw him driving away, waving and smiling at her. She got a good look."

The clerk described a white male; about 35, six feet tall, 170 pounds, blue eyes, short black hair "with a touch of gray," light skin, wearing wire-rimmed glasses. His car was late model, dark blue. A second witness was positive the vehicle was a Thunderbird.

Three days later and a thousand miles away in Aurora, Colorado, a Denver suburb, DeBardeleben passed a new variant on his 7404 edition twenty-dollar bill, and was remembered again. "The passer," according to this witness, was "a white male, late 30s, six feet tall, thin build, brown hair, thin silver wire-rimmed glasses."

From these and other descriptions, the Secret Service produced a series of composite drawings, which then were distributed to field offices in every area the Mall Passer was known to have hit—meaning most of the country. If the treasury agents couldn't crack the case with finesse, there always was the blunt force approach to investigation.

"I remember Larry Sheafe, who then was Joe Coppola's boss," says Mertz. "He told us to take this one composite and the description of the bills and to go to *every* mall in our district, which meant every mall in the state of Indiana. 'Go to every store and show every manager this composite drawing and description of the bills.' And we did it."

As Secret Service agents scoured America's malls, their reports back to Washington provided a cumulative portrait not only of the Mall Passer's physical appearance, but also his M.O., *Modus Operandi,* and habits, too. DeBardeleben usually was neatly clothed, if not tastefully or expensively so; the Mall Passer often wore polyester. He seemed to employ disguises; generally beards, mustaches, and wigs. It appeared that he might wear makeup and may sometimes have dyed his hair, or put a rinse in it.

DeBardeleben tended to avoid male and older female clerks, preferring instead to pass his bills to younger women and girls he sometimes distracted with conversation as they rang up his purchase. One time, a clothing store security guard grew suspicious as DeBardeleben, carrying a large shopping bag, browsed a men's socks display. The security man, trained to be alert for shoplifters, relaxed his vigilance when the suspect selected a pair or two, then strolled casually over to a young clerk to pay for them with what turned out to be a 7373.

Nothing caused greater consternation within the Secret Service than the Mall Passer's seemingly ghostlike ability to hit a mall in Jacksonville, Florida, for example, while the very same day his funny money rained into store registers 425 miles and at least seven hours away by Interstate in Mobile, Alabama. Some agents thought he was a trucker, while others, noting the enormous distances he was moving in very brief periods of time, assumed they were looking for a frequent flyer; a salesman perhaps, a commercial pilot maybe or—it occurred to more than one of the investigators—a present or past Secret Service agent. "It was disturbing to think that maybe you were looking for a friend, a rogue agent or a former agent," remembers agent Jim Rich, then of the Fort Worth office. "But I'll admit I was worried that someone involved with our agency was doing this. We did have a number of agents who were extremely good printers. This was the reason that some of them were hired; they were experts and had good backgrounds. They could go undercover, be put into a counterfeiting operation because they could talk the talk and walk the walk, so to speak."

9

Dr. Zack

JUST BECAUSE I'M <u>THINKING</u> ABOUT [MURDER] + WANT TO DO IT
DOESN'T MEAN I <u>HAVE</u> TO! <u>BUT,</u>
  —I <u>CAN PREPARE</u> FOR IT—
  —I <u>CAN</u> BE <u>READY</u> FOR IT—
  (JUST IN CASE THE <u>OPPORTUNITY</u>
  PRESENTS ITSELF— + EVERYTHING'S
  PERFECT!)—BUT, I WON'T <u>COUNT</u>
  ON IT. I'M NOT <u>REALLY</u> GOING TO
  DO IT— (<u>UNLESS</u> CONDITIONS ARE
  PERFECT—ACTOR FOLLOWS
   THE "SCRIPT")

April 27, 1982, was a mild spring day in Bossier City, Louisiana, next door to Shreveport on the Red River, about twenty miles from the Texas border. It was humid, as usual, but the high temperature under partly cloudy skies would be a tolerable 79 degrees. Breezes at ten to fifteen miles an hour teased through Bossier Parish's abundant pasture grass and dark green magnolias.

Shortly after eight that Tuesday morning the sales staff at the storefront office of Normans Realty on Meadowview Drive in Bossier City was holding its daily meeting when a male, who identified himself only as "Dr. Zack from Midland," telephoned the office to ask insistently, and by name, for agent Jean McPhaul, a petite and attractive native Alabaman who'd been selling real estate in Bossier City for

about five years. The dark-haired, green-eyed Mc-
Phaul, forty years old and recently separated from her
husband, Richard, was wearing a tasteful red suit and
white blouse that day. At first she declined to leave
the meeting. But when Dr. Zack kept phoning, asking
for her by name, she took the call, spoke briefly with
him, then headed out the door in a hurry. Dr. Zack,
she said, was looking for a new house in the area, and
was eager to purchase same soon. Money was no object. McPhaul added that she was to meet this intrigu-
ing sales prospect at the Bossier Sheraton Motel, five
miles away.

Jean McPhaul was next seen in her 1980 white-and-
gray, four-door Pontiac Phoenix pulling into the small
sales office parking lot at GreenAcres Place, a new
subdivision of mostly $100,000 to $300,000 houses,
plus some more expensive residences, then thinly
sprinkled over a flat tract of rust-red river-bottom land,
laced with drainage bayous, a few miles east of Bossier
City. With her was a male whom she left sitting in the
Pontiac passenger-side seat as she went into the office
to select the houses to show him.

Tom Kennedy, a building contractor, was at the
GreenAcres sales office that morning. He'd later recall
catching sight of McPhaul's companion as he exited
the Pontiac and walked around a bit. At one point, said
Kennedy, he and the man were no more than ten feet
from one another. According to a Bossier City police
report, Kennedy described him as a

W/M, approx. 5'10", 150 lbs., 40–45 years of age,
with premature gray hair with some natural color.
KENNEDY said his hair was neat like a military
cut. He said his face was long and thin with sunken
cheeks and appeared as if he had his false teeth out.
KENNEDY said the man's nose was long and thin
with some type of deformity. He said he was pale and
thin, like he had just been in a hospital. KENNEDY

said he had no facial hair or indication of a heavy beard.

Bernadette Willadson, a secretary at the GreenAcres office, also saw the client with Jean McPhaul, albeit not as closely as had Tom Kennedy.

McPhaul chose five houses to show her customer that morning, then drove off with the keys, a cup of coffee, and Dr. Zack. Shortly thereafter, a GreenAcres office employee remembered that the location of the lockbox on one of the houses McPhaul intended to show had been changed. She drove out into the development in search of McPhaul, whom she found standing outside her car in front of one of the houses. Dr. Zack, inside the car, raised a newspaper over his face as this woman approached.

She was the last person to report seeing Jean McPhaul alive.

Norman Hood, owner and boss at Normans, later told Shreveport/Bossier *Times* reporter Lee Ivory that he didn't start to worry about McPhaul until after two that afternoon. Unaware of just where she intended to take her mysterious customer, Hood and another realty agent drove over to the Sheraton where they found McPhaul's Pontiac parked around in back. The vehicle was empty, save for a pair of McPhaul's shoes—the ones she had worn to work that day. The Pontiac also was unlocked, a bit of apparent carelessness that was totally out of character for Jean McPhaul. "She's a conscientious lady," Hood told Ivory.

Norman Hood checked back with his Meadowview office to learn they'd just heard from GreenAcres Place; Jean McPhaul had appeared at about 10:30 that morning, checked out five sets of keys and had yet to return. At this, Hood contacted the Bossier police, and then telephoned McPhaul's daughter, Karen.

"I was at home for some reason," remembers Karen Bodden, who was twenty-one, married and about to become a mother herself. "Her boss called me and asked if I'd heard from Mom. I said, 'No.' It was strange for her. I mean, she called in all the time."

Bryan Douglas ("Doug") Payne, thirty-three at the time, was among the first Bossier City police officers to respond to Norman Hood's call from the Sheraton. Payne, an amiable, easygoing Shreveport native, son of an oil-field worker, had been on the force for six years, the last two as a homicide detective.

He was not at first persuaded that harm might have come to Jean McPhaul, although he did order a surveillance unit to watch her car overnight. "I was thinkin' maybe she got friendly with this guy," he says, "and they went off to his room to spend the night together or something. Maybe they were out partying."

The surveillance passed without incident. Next morning, Detective Payne visited the Normans office on Meadowview. "Everyone there said, 'This is not like her. She should have called in.' "

In the interim, McPhaul's estranged husband, Richard, a bus driver, had returned from a road trip. "I called him," his daughter Karen remembers. "I said, 'Dad, they can't find Mom.'

"He said, 'Well, she probably went out of town.'

" 'Dad, you don't understand. She calls me if she's going out of town. I haven't heard anything from her.' So Dad got kinda scared. He came over to the house."

Doug Payne then personally visited Karen Bodden that morning, and was unambiguously informed of how seriously Jean McPhaul appreciated the potential hazards of her profession, which was why McPhaul always checked in, reliably, every few hours. "Her daughter reinforced that this was way out of the ordinary for her mother," Payne says. "At that point, we knew something was very wrong."

The previous afternoon, Norman Hood retraced Jean McPhaul's probable itinerary with Dr. Zack around GreenAcres Place. Hood looked for the Realtor in each house she expected to visit, and found nothing save for some unusual-looking wads of insulation on a hallway rug at 424 Highland in the tract development, a shingle-roofed, brick-and-board structure designed somewhat in the style of a Creole (also known as coastal) cottage. On Wednesday morning after interviewing Karen Bodden, Doug Payne and his partner, Glen Sproles, drove out to GreenAcres Place to search the houses once more.

"We went up there and opened cabinets, drawers, closets," remembers Payne. "Everything. Then we came to this third house and started doing the same thing."

Payne also noticed the wads of insulation "of the type you blow into the attic. Five or six little pieces, tightly rolled, as if somebody had gotten the insulation on their clothes and brushed it off. We said, 'We *sure* better check up in this attic.' " Norman Hood already had, but not thoroughly. "Well, I pulled the ladder down and Sproles stepped up ahead of me," recounts Payne. "I'm walking up behind him and we're talking and looking for the light. He finds the switch up there, turns it on and says, 'Oh shit! She's here!' "

Doug Payne squeezed past his horror-struck partner up into the cramped attic where he, and Sproles, stared for a moment, stunned. Six feet away, lashed to a rafter brace by means of a ligature pulled tightly around her throat, was Jean McPhaul. Her eyes still were open, her knees were bent at about a thirty-degree angle, and her shoeless feet just touched the floor. She was other-wise fully dressed and drenched in blood from two deep puncture wounds to her heart.

There was no sign of a struggle. As Doug Payne re-constructed the murder, Jean McPhaul must have will-ingly climbed up into the attic and may have had no warning before the killer garroted her with a three-foot length of stitched denim—possibly a woman's belt or sash—that he had brought with him.

"It appeared," says Payne, "that she was strangled

first, jerked up against the rafter's brace, tied off, and then he stabbed her over the back from behind. Then he walked around in front of her and stabbed her again." The killer cleaned his bloody blade on McPhaul's white blouse over her left breast. "We could tell perfectly where he wiped it off."

Otherwise, he left no trace of himself. The slippers Jean McPhaul wore so as not to track mud through the house were found wedged into the tank of a downstairs toilet. Her purse never was recovered. At autopsy, Coroner George McCormick confirmed what seemed evident from a look at the dead woman. She had not been sexually assaulted in any way; all her clothing was in place.

Cause of Death: Strangulation and knife wounds.

Motive? "That was our biggest problem," says Payne. "There was no motive. Normally you have a body with bullet holes in it or whatever, and there's been a robbery or a rape or a fight. Here we had a real estate agent who showed a house to a doctor and we find her standin' up lookin' at us with a rope tied around her neck and two stab wounds in her heart. No reason for it."

Once again, the FBI was asked to consult. "The motive for the murder," opined agent J. Michael Watson, "was the murder itself."

[The killer] was experiencing a great deal of stress prior to the murder. . . . This type of stress may have been caused by the loss of a loved one, such as his mother or wife and children. This could occur either by death or divorce. His anger was clearly directed at a "woman," and McPhaul was picked by him specifically. The subject has a good education and may have some college background. He is not living with a woman now, but has been married in the past, probably more than once. He did not know the victim prior to the murder, but planned out his crime against victim one or more days in advance. The subject has a previous history of mental illness, and may have been hospitalized for such mental problems, later diagnosed as paranoia and antisocial behavior. The offender will not live in the general area of the killing, and left victim's car at the Sheraton to throw police off. He may have stayed at a nearby motel. He kept the victim's purse as a souvenir of the crime and he will, in all likelihood, keep possession of the purse. He will be described by those who know him as a very private person ... He will have sporadic employment in his past. He will have few, if any, close friends, male or female. He will, in all likelihood, be a white-collar worker, if employed.

<u>Post Offensive Behavior</u>

I do not feel that his behavior will be radically altered as a result of the murder. He may be slightly calmer to those who come in contact with him. He will probably strike again using generally the same M.O., but he will wait until the stress factors again build to a point he can no longer tolerate. This may take weeks, months, or even years.

The fact that Dr. Zack had asked for McPhaul by name initially suggested to the police a personal acquaintance, which is commonly true in murder cases. However, Doug Payne also established that the victim's photo had appeared in a local Normans newspaper ad, and that she had personally passed out literature at a real estate promotion, held at a Shreveport shopping mall, several weeks before her murder. Dr. Zack, probably a stranger according to agent Watson's profile, easily could have known McPhaul's name.

Her macabre slaying dominated the local news for weeks, and attracted a torrent of tips to the Bossier police. According to a *Times* article by reporter Ray Waddle, one caller was certain the killer worked for a local bus company (McPhaul's estranged husband Richard was a bus driver). "Another," wrote Waddle, "said the suspect can be viewed every night as an anchorman on a cable TV news show."

In the end, only one caller had anything useful to share. On Thursday the 29th, Bossier City detective Bill Carroll visited an aged Shreveport rooming-house proprietress, a Mrs. DeMoss, who recounted a visit of two days before. Just before noon on the 27th—about the time police believed Jean McPhaul was murdered—Mrs. DeMoss noticed a white male, approximately forty years old, about six feet tall and 150 pounds, parking what she took to be a gold, late-model Toyota down the street from her house. He then approached on foot.

At the door she noted a couple more details: short brown hair, parted; gray eyes; dark blue pants and a light shirt; tan briefcase of good quality leather; small hands, pasty skin; and, as the police report put it, "he was also wearing a big heavy ring with a good-size setting in it (like a class ring)."

He introduced himself as Dr. Zack from Mobile, Alabama (Jean McPhaul was born in Bay Minetee, Alabama, thirty miles from Mobile), and said he was interested in renting a room for himself, his wife—whom he specifically referred to as Mrs. Zack—and their three-year-old daughter. "He said," the report continued, "he had been laid off by the government. He said he did respiratory diagnostics and was going to sell his hospital equipment and had an appointment at Schumpert Hospital to show his line."

After the inquiry, DeMoss told Carroll, Dr. Zack left and did not return.

Despite the lack of physical evidence, the Bossier City police seemed confident of their witnesses. "If we can just get a hold of the suspect we should have enough evidence now to convict him," Lieutenant Scotty Henderson, chief of detectives, (told) the *Times* on Friday, April 30.

It wasn't too many days later that Henderson's optimism suddenly seemed well-founded. As Doug Payne laboriously pored over the thousands of names of those registered in area motels at the time of the murder, "I ran across a guy at the Sheraton who was from Midland, Michigan," he says. "Of course, at the time all we had was Dr. Zack from Midland. So I did a little background on this ol' boy and found he was workin' for a company whose name I'd appreciate you not mentioning.

"I got to talkin' with a police officer up in Michigan and I said, 'My suspect used the name of Dr. Zack. Does Zack ring any bells for you?' He said, 'Sure, Zack Construction Company.' So I say, 'Check to see if this guy *knows* anyone named Zack.'

"He comes back again and says, 'Well, he's got a next door neighbor named Zack.' And I said, *'All right!!!* Man, this is lookin' good!!' And he had stayed at the Sheraton.

"Anyway, I got to checkin' and I find that he rented a car in Monroe [about 60 miles east] and drove to Shreveport and got on a plane and went on his merry way someplace else. So I went and got the car and checked the mileage on it. The mileage was just enough miles to get from Monroe to the Shreveport airport, no more. I said, 'Hell! They went out to GreenAcres in her car. So we wouldn't even have had a tenth of a mile difference there.'

"We get the car and start goin' through it and found a tube of lipstick in the front seat. I got in touch with one of her best friends and said, 'Look, I've got this lipstick. Tell me, is it familiar?' She said, 'Yup! It's the same brand and same color that Jean McPhaul wore.'

"I'm just goin' berserk! I said, 'We've got this bastard now! We have him in the area. He stayed at the motel where we found her car. Had a lipstick in his car that matched what McPhaul wore. He came from Midland. His next door neighbor's name is Zack.' And I'm just goin' ape shit! I said, 'Hey, we've *got* this sonuvabitch now.' "

Payne also had issued a nationwide appeal for any police jurisdiction with an unsolved Realtor murder to contact him. As he later recalled, he received reports of a least seventy-five such homicides. The detective then went to a map where he plotted these murders against known installations of his suspect's employer. "I started sticking in these pins and *damn*!! Every city there was a plant we had real estate homicides that were close. I went to Scotty Henderson and said, 'Look, I've got to go to Midland, Michigan. We've got this guy now!' So Sproles and I take off."

Payne recounts how he befriended a security man at the suspect's Midland employer. "We said, 'We have got to find out more about this guy without him knowin'. We need to get into his office and see what he's got in there.' So he says, 'Okay, this is what we're gonna do.' "

The plan was for Payne and Sproles to toss the office under cover of night. "We couldn't spend a whole lot of time in there," he continues. "So we jerk a lot of the stuff out, run back to the motel and spend hours going through all the stuff. Then we had to sneak back in to get all the stuff back before daylight!

"We spent the next day goin' through it. From his travel vouchers we know where he's stayin' and everything."

At the same time Payne and Sproles were trying to piece together the evidence in Michigan, they called back to Bossier City where other officers were dispatched—belatedly, it seems—to reconstruct the suspect's movements on April 27th. That's when the compelling circumstantial case against him collapsed.

"There was no possible way," Payne recalls, shaking his head. "He wasn't even close. There were like forty different people who could testify where he stopped and ate and everything. It was just completely out. You talk about a sinking feeling, you know? I was ready to put him in the electric chair."

10

Foos And Mertz

Wednesday afternoon, April 28, 1982, just hours after officers Payne and Sproles discovered the murdered Jean McPhaul, Mike DeBardeleben was 800 miles away in North Carolina. By nine o'clock that night he'd hit the South Park Mall in Charlotte, and the Eastridge Mall, situated on a low rise next to Interstate 85, in neighboring Gastonia, where he passed a total of thirty bills for a $600 gross return. Among his targets were old favorites such as the Waldenbooks outlet at the Eastridge Mall, and some new victims, including a nearby Holiday Inn.

He got away clean—again—but the Gastonia police investigation, together with a canvass conducted by agents Paul Albergine, Al Lowe, and Robert Turner of the Secret Service's Charlotte field office, developed a group of nine store clerks and other witnesses with strong memories of the Mall Passer. Bob Turner, the service's coordinator of counterfeit investigations in Charlotte, perceived that these witnesses' recollections might be compared, contrasted, and combined to produce a more detailed and accurate Mall Passer sketch. To that end, Turner engaged a local artist named James S. Rucker to attempt a composite composite, so to speak, from these witnesses' written statements, as well as the original drawings they did with a police artist. The result was a color pencil portrait of a pallid, middle-aged male, neatly groomed and bespectacled with a distinctively long nose.

Four months later, as the Secret Service's various investigative initiatives to catch their man were flowering and faltering in frustrating succession, agent Dennis Foos arrived at WFO from his most recent posting, the Seattle field office. Foos was assigned to the Criminal Squad, which was responsible, among other things, for all counterfeiting investigations in the Washington area.

As a Secret Service agent, Dennis Foos makes a good Hamlet. "I'm a bit overcautious and a bit of a procrastinator," he says. "I'll say, 'We need to do this, but I don't want to jump on it without some more research.' I can be too careful." His close colleagues emphasize a different attribute, Foos's native good humor. "Denny by nature is an agreeable person," says Greg Mertz. "You could piss on his leg and I swear he wouldn't get mad."

Foos was born in Albany, California, in 1946, and was raised in Seattle, where his father, a Navy veteran, worked as a cab driver. Foos graduated from high school in 1964. Two years later, he joined the army. "I guess I was one of those what-can-I-do-for-my-country? types," he explains. "I wanted to fly helicopters in Vietnam."

However, while still in basic training at Fort Ord, near Monterey, California, Foos was invited to join the White House Communications Agency (WHCA), an inter-service technical group that sees to all White House and presidential communications needs. Says Foos, "I thought to myself, 'Vietnam or Washington, D.C.?' All things considered, Washington, just sounded like a better choice."

At WHCA, "I ended up sort of their logistics guy. When the President travels, WHCA goes out in advance to set up his communications; radios, telephones, you name it. My job was to get the people and equipment to where they had to go. It was challenging, really. In fact, I got a medal for it."

Foos, who married the former Mary Schlag of Alexandria, Virginia, while at WHCA, was discharged from the army a buck sergeant in April of 1969, and departed with his wife and their infant daughter for Seattle where he had indistinct thoughts of getting into real estate. In the back of his mind, however, were ideas of a radically different career choice, the Secret Service, notions gradually fostered by his daily contact with agents while working at the White House.

As a result, in Seattle, "I just plain changed my mind about real estate," he says. On a visit to the local Secret Service field office, Foos learned that the Treasury Department was about to expand the responsibilities of its uniformed White House police force to include protection of foreign embassies in the capital, formerly a Metro Police responsibility.

The realignment presented an opportunity for Foos to join the Secret Service while he pursued a de facto requirement for becoming an agent, his college degree. The newly renamed Executive Protective Service hired him as a uniformed officer in April 1970. Along with standing post, walking footbeats, and working car patrols on Embassy Row, Foos led what he recalls were "a lot" of public tours of the White House, and was trained as an original member of the service's first counter-sniper team.

Four years later, he became the first member of his family to finish college when he earned a degree in Justice Administration from the District's American University. Following graduation, he was accepted as a Secret Service agent-trainee.

During the 1976 campaign, Foos protected President Gerald Ford's daughter, Susan. In 1978, he was sent to San Clemente as part of Richard Nixon's protective detail. A year later, the agency relocated him to Seattle, where Foos remained with his family until 1982 when, with strong encouragement from Mrs. Foos, her husband answered a call for volunteers to relocate to Washington, D.C.

At the time, he knew next to nothing about the Mall Passer, who's westernmost excursions had been to California. With his new assignment in August of 1982, however, the Mall Passer would begin to occupy Foos; first as a distraction, then an annoyance and, in the end, an obsession he would share with Greg Mertz and the third member of their team, Mike Stephens.

On October 20, 1982, one of the Mall Passer's notes came into WFO from D&H Parking at Washington's National Airport, a significant location if the Mall Passer indeed was a pilot, as some agents guessed. Agent Foos was assigned the D&H "run-out."

"In a simple, basic run-out," he explains, "you go back to the people who took the note and ask them if they have any information at all. Generally, they'll say no, and that's the end of that. I had very little expectation that something would come of this run-out. A parking lot at National Airport? They're going to be able to tell me which car that bill came from? No way. However, this *was* a Mall Passer bill, and we were grasping at anything."

Foos pursued the lead with due diligence. When it led nowhere, he decided that National would be a good place to show around the new Rucker sketch from Charlotte. It depicted the Mall Passer in wire-rimmed glasses and wearing a diagonal-stripe tie.

At the Butler Aviation facility, a one-armed man behind the counter said to Foos, "Yeah, that looks like Joe." The counterman called over another employee. "Hey, look at this!" he exclaimed. "Isn't that Joe?" The other man agreed. Joe, they both said, flew aircraft for a Roslyn, Virginia, company—Dennis Foos's next stop.

"I showed the people at this company the composite and they said, 'Holy cow! That's Joe our pilot.' They pulled out a picture of their pilot and it looked as if it had been traced from our drawing. He was even wearing the same tie!

"So this is what you'd call a layover, everything identical. We put guys on the company airplane with him, flying around surreptitiously. Unfortunately, we were barking up the wrong tree. Eventually, we got the records of where the plane had been and who was flying it and he was never in the right spot. To make a long story short, it was a washout."

In early September of 1982, Foos was joined in his windowless seventh-floor office at 1800 G Street by Greg Mertz, newly arrived from the Indianapolis field office.

Mertz was born in Fort Wayne, Indiana, where three preceding generations of Mertz males had made their livings as woodworkers. His great-grandfather built violins by hand. His grandfather and father both were cabinetmakers. As a kid, Greg also worked summers for the family residential contracting company. But there seems never to have been a question of him becoming a fourth-generation carpenter.

Greg Mertz is a born cop.

He first experienced what he calls the "adrenaline high" of police work early one morning of his seventh grade year in school as he was pedaling his newspaper route. "I saw two guys burglarizing a little dairy store," he remembers. "So I raced home and called the police—I was so excited I forgot to give them my name—and then I raced back and hid in the bushes by the store. I waited and then all of a sudden I saw the police cars—no red lights, no sirens, no nuthin'—swooping down on the place, just like something on TV! A planned raid! And then I heard a cop on a PA system say, 'Come out with your hands up!' Or something like that. I was fascinated."

Mertz's boyhood role model was actor Efrem Zimbalist, Jr.'s character on the Sunday night *FBI* television series. "I remember saying, 'I'm gonna be a federal agent.' "

When he graduated from Indiana University with a criminology degree in 1975, Greg, like Dennis Foos, became the first member of his family ever to earn a college degree. From 1973 to 1977 he was a campus cop at the university. For the next four years he was a Fort Wayne police officer; first in uniform and then on the narcotics and vice squads. He married in 1975, and fathered two children; a daughter born in 1977 and a son born in 1981, the year Greg Mertz joined the Secret Service and thus fulfilled his personal sense of destiny.

Dream achieved, Mertz was soon acquainted with certain of the job's less glamorous aspects. His first major protection assignment was Ronald Reagan.

"It was for the World's Fair in Knoxville," he says. " 'Man, this is *big* stuff,' I said, 'I'm gonna protect the President of the United States!' "

When he arrived in Knoxville in suit and tie for his assignment, Mertz was given a querulous once-over by a senior agent. " 'No one told you to dress soft for this?'

" 'Dress soft?' I thought to myself. I didn't even know what he was talking about.

" 'You were supposed to wear casual clothes.'

" 'Uh, nobody told me that.'

"He says, 'Oh well,' and reaches down on the ground for a pair of fisherman's hip waders. Then he pointed and said, 'Your post is about a hundred yards into that tunnel over there. Here're your hip waders and here's a flashlight. Don't let anybody in that tunnel.'

"So I go over and I walk back and forth in two feet of water in this tunnel for like six hours, sloshing around in my coat and tie, thinking, 'What the—?' "

Mertz became familiar with his senior office partner's piece of the Mall Passer case by virtue of proximity. Over his first few months at WFO, the young agent also helped out Dennis Foos from time to time. Then came the Apple Blossom Mall caper in Winchester, Virginia.

After fielding a call from the mall, indicating they'd been hit by the Mall Passer, Mertz drove out to Winchester to investigate. He found a woman cab driver there who remembered being summoned to the small local airport, where she said a man emerged from a blue and white airplane asking to be taken to the Apple Blossom Mall. The driver then told Mertz how the fare had instructed her to leave him at one end of the mall, and to pick him up at the other end fifteen minutes later. She did, she said, and then returned him to the airport where he flew away.

The cab driver's recall was poor, so it was arranged through the Service's Special Investigations Squad to have her hypnotized. In her trance, the cab driver remembered the aircraft had two engines, one on each wing, and that the props were four-bladed. She described how many windows she saw, and their configuration, and recalled the airplane had three wheels, one under each wing and a third in the rear. She could not summon the tail number, except to vaguely see a set of figures with an N after them. There was no way to ascertain their order.

Two further avenues of investigation suggested themselves. One was for Greg Mertz to visit the Smithsonian Air and Space Museum in search of an airplane expert who might be able to make something out of the cab driver's description. The second course was to ask the FAA to check it's records for tail numbers corresponding in any way to the digits remembered by the cabbie. The FAA in reply said it had no such capability. So agents Mertz and Foos borrowed the microfiche listing tail numbers for *all* aircraft in the U.S. and Canada, together with a machine to read them.

At the Smithsonian, Mertz's expert said that no

plane ever built answered the description he was provided, but if someone shifted around the wheels, then it looked a good deal like a Beechcraft King Air, A–200. Back at WFO, the two agents searched the FAA files for A–200s bearing one or more of the numbers. "We were far from convinced that what she'd given us was accurate," remembers Foos. "And we knew they were out of order."

Foos and Mertz nevertheless had labored on, meticulously scanning thousands of small-type tail numbers until they found one blue-and-white Beechcraft King-Air A–200 with two or three of the correct tail numbers. Long shot though this seemed, they were intrigued to see what sort of suspect all the hard work had turned up.

"Can you tell us who owns this particular plane?" Mertz asked a Beechcraft executive.

"Sure," said the official, "I believe it's the Reverend Jerry Falwell."

Another dead end.

11

The Collar

Christmastime 1982, the spreading flood of Mike DeBardeleben's fake twenties reached even to Santa Claus at a mall in Springfield, Virginia, south of Washington, D.C. Yet even at this dispiriting juncture in the country wide manhunt there was cause for hope.

After many months of fruitlessly searching for a predictable pattern in the Mall Passer's apparently random travels, the treasury agents were beginning to discern a logic to his movements. In Washington, Dennis Foos noticed that periodic clusters of passes were being made locally, not necessarily in malls, and that a disproportionate number of these were made at area Food Giant stores. The pattern suggested to Foos that the Mall Passer lived in the Washington area, or that Washington and northern Virginia were some sort of crossroads in his trips.

In Charlotte, agent Frank Hancock plotted three years of Mall Passer activity in his state, and in a memo to headquarters offered several bold prognostications: Among them, that it was "highly probable" the Mall Passer would return to Charlotte in January and in April of the coming year. Hancock got his first guess wrong; the Mall Passer hit South Carolina in January. But his projection for April was right on.

On Monday, April 25, 1983, agents of the Charlotte field office revisited the Eastridge Mall in Gastonia, where they distributed fresh copies of the Mall Passer sketch and alerted both store personnel and the mall security staff that the Mall Passer might strike again locally at any time. Three days later—and exactly one year since the Mall Passer last had hit the Eastridge Mall—Mike DeBardeleben, clad in gray corduroys and a blue-and-gray knit pullover, walked into the Eastridge Mall's B. Dalton Bookseller store. Manager Dean Huey noticed the middle-aged shopper, and asked him if he needed any help. Not yet, De-Bardeleben replied, he was browsing. After a few moments, he selected from the shelves a $3.95 paperback, *Singles,* by Jacqueline Simenauer, and brought it to the cash register, where DeBardeleben asked Huey to hold it for him while he went to get some money. It was about 7:40 P.M.

Twenty minutes later, according to the bookstore manager, the lone shopper returned, proffering for payment a very suspicious-looking twenty-dollar bill. Huey, trained by B. Dalton to recognize counterfeit money, didn't like the faded look of the note, especially when he compared it to the sharper-hued bills in his till. Nevertheless, he accepted the twenty, rang up the sale ($4.11, including tax), counted out the customer's change and then watched the man exit the store with his purchase.

As DeBardeleben walked away, Dean Huey considered again and decided to follow him. At the front of B. Dalton's, Huey looked right and left and saw nothing. But just as he was turning back, he espied the man across the way in the K. and K. toy store, standing in line to make another purchase.

The more Huey saw of DeBardeleben the more certain he was that the Mall Passer had returned, and the more cautious Huey became lest he betray his suspicions. Huey busied himself straightening books and tables at the front of Dalton's, while continuing his surveillance of K. and K.'s across the way. When his suspect did emerge, the bookstore manager watched him stroll down the corridor toward his next target, JC

Penney's. At that, Huey rushed for his store phone to summon security guard Ray Harold Barker. It looked as if the elusive Mall Passer was about to be caught.

And he probably would have been, save for a stroke of surpassingly poor luck. Dean Huey excitedly dialed Ray Barker's pager number, unaware that the portable device wasn't working: Barker's pager had been broken during a scuffle the previous day. Huey rang the guard persistently for five minutes, then gave up and decided instead to dispatch a B. Dalton clerk to personally locate Barker. More time lost. Once he was found, Barker hurriedly radioed a mall-wide security alert and relayed Huey's description of the suspect.

Among those who received the alarm was Barbara Alexander, a security console operator inside the television surveillance facility at Matthews–Belk department store. Alexander immediately began to hunt for the Mall Passer on her eleven black-and-white television monitors. Within a few moments she spotted the man as described by Barker. DeBardeleben was completing a purchase in the Matthews–Belk stationery department. According to procedure, Alexander then relayed the message to Achwha Dean, a plainclothes detective working the floor of the store, telling Dean the Mall Passer suspect's description and his whereabouts.

DeBardeleben moved on into the personal care department, where he bought a cosmetic case from clerk Dawn Oatman. Barbara Alexander at her television monitors could see Achwha Dean shadowing the suspect, and she took the opportunity when he stopped to purchase the case to zoom in for a close-up look at him. By now it was around 8:10 P.M.

The Mall Passer walked on from Matthews–Belk's personal care department to the adjoining toy section, where he finally sensed, or detected, the surveillance. Outwardly cool to that point, he suddenly seemed jittery as a first-time shoplifter to John Eric Fortenberry, a clerk in the toy department. "He was very nervous, shaking," Fortenberry later testified in court. "I thought he was going to steal something."

Achwha Dean, struggling within herself to quell an inexpressible fear of her anxious quarry, gamely tracked DeBardeleben as he moved through the store. The unarmed detective followed him from Fortenberry's cash register into the sports department, and then finally out the Matthews–Belk door under a sign which read, "I-85 Parking." Outside, Dean watched the Mall Passer hurry across the parking lot to a long, low-slung, light-colored, beat-up two-door vehicle of indeterminate age and manufacture. He backed out of the lot, trying to protect his tag number. But Dean was able to catch it—North Carolina plate RYP 87—as he turned to make his short dash to the mall exit onto the eastbound lanes of I-85.

According to agent Bob Turner, DeBardeleben doubtlessly saw the Gastonia police roaring west to the mall on I-85 that night as he headed east. Subsequent investigation revealed his destination was a Rodeway Inn, about twelve miles east on I-85, where the Mall Passer spent the night as Maurice R. Paquette, 82 Albion Street, Wakefield, Massachusetts, an identity he'd first used 2½ years earlier while car-shopping in Massachusetts.

A check with the North Carolina State Department of Motor Vehicles indicated, to no one's surprise, that tag number RYP 87 was hot. On October 16 of the previous year, after hitting the nearby Eastland Mall, DeBardeleben had grabbed the tag in a Winn–Dixie parking lot from a '74 Black Camaro owned by Ronald A. Fischer of Charlotte.

The news of his narrow escape from the Eastridge Mall quickly was broadcast to Secret Service field offices throughout the southeast and mid-Atlantic states. Although there was no reliable way to pinpoint exactly where the Mall Passer would hit next, many field offices once again dispatched agents to visit their local malls, distribute the sketch, describe the Mall Passer's product, and discuss with mall merchants recommended procedures should the elusive counterfeiter come to town again.

Similar regional mobilizations had occurred before in the case, and had netted the Secret Service zilch. But this time there was an air of expectation in the field offices, as well as in Washington. Some agents believed that the Mall Passer was losing his edge. Why else would he have risked passing his product to an adult male—Dean Huey—something he rarely, if ever, had done before? Moreover, his near brush with capture in Charlotte did not drive him into hiding, as had similarly close calls in the past. Three days after fleeing the Eastridge Mall, he was papering the Lenox Square Mall in Atlanta. The following weekend brought him to the Columbia Mall in Columbia, South Carolina. On May 11, he hit the Fairgrounds Square Mall in Reading, Pennsylvania. Some days after that he struck the malls of Lynchburg, in southwestern Virginia.

An appearance in Lynchburg usually meant that the Mall Passer was outbound from the Washington area, headed in one of two directions. Either his itinerary would take him south from Lynchburg on State Route 29 into North Carolina (as it did in April, bringing him to Charlotte) or he would swing west at Lynchburg onto I-81 (as he had, most recently, in July of 1982), which he'd follow past Roanoke and down through Tennessee and Arkansas toward Dallas and Fort Worth.

It was against this latter possibility that in early May agents from the Secret Service's Knoxville field office visited the so-called Tri-Cities of eastern Tennessee; Bristol, Johnson City, and Kingsport. All three communities lay adjacent I-81 near the Virginia border, and all three were among the Mall Passer's past targets.

Again, the agents canvassed the Tri-City malls store by store, handing out their posters and urging vigilance.

This time, the legwork would pay off.

At about 7 o'clock on Tuesday evening, May 24, 1983, DeBardeleben appeared in the Johnson City Mall, where at a T-Shirts Plus outlet he purchased a blue and white billed hat for $3.25 from clerk Melissa Cloyd. He gave Cloyd a bogus twenty and a quarter for the hat, and received $17 in change. Forty minutes later he was at the Miracle Mall, also in Johnson City, where he passed thirteen more notes, all 7373s and 7404s.

At 8:40, twenty miles away at the Fort Henry Mall in Kingsport, he walked into B. Dalton's and asked clerk Donna Cooper if the store carried Kingsport city maps. She replied that they did, and pointed out the map rack on the wall. He selected one, placed it on the counter, then told her he'd be back in a couple minutes. "I am going to get the money from my wife," he explained. Approximately five minutes later he returned to pay for the map, and a copy of *Newsweek*.

From a later investigative report:

> The purchase price of the magazine and the map came to $3.20 and he produced a $20 bill plus 20 cents in change. Upon examination of the bill, Ms. Cooper stated that it looked strange and she then checked the numbers on the bill with the bill descriptions left previously. . . . She also inspected the composite drawing. . . . She stated that this individual bore a marked resemblance to the composite drawing. Ms. Cooper then told the individual that the bill was possibly "bad" and that it matched a list of "bad $20s." She then asked him if he got the bill in change somewhere. The man looked up and around to the surrounding stores and stated that he got the bill at the National Shirt Shop, which is located just across the mall from the B. Dalton Bookstore. Ms. Cooper told him that she

would call the shirt shop to tell them and he said, "My wife took it in change," and then continued with an explanation and attempted to pay her with three $1 bills. During this time she held the $20, thus preventing him from taking it back, and she then called the police. While she was on the telephone he further stated, "Let me go get my wife. Do you see her standing by the phone?" and pointed toward the National Shirt Shop. At this time Ms. Cooper stated that he left the bookstore in the direction that he had pointed and Cooper did not see him again.

Minutes later, Criminal Investigator Harold E. Gilreath of the Kingsport police department arrived at B. Dalton's. Together, he and Cooper telephoned agent T.J. Bondurant, head of the Secret Service field office in Knoxville, 130 miles to the west. It was 8:57 P.M.

Bondurant, excited to hear that the Mall Passer was in his territory, first thought of sending Knoxville agents Jones ("Pete") Allison and Jim Burch directly to Kingsport. Then he thought again. Bondurant believed from past experience that the Mall Passer was heading west on I-81, and that his likely next target would be Knoxville, probably the next day. If so, Bondurant reasoned, the prudent move would be to send junior agent Burch alone to Kingsport the next morning, while Bondurant and the more experienced Pete Allison would go ahead as already planned to work an undercover food-stamp fraud case. In the afternoon, when the Mall Passer customarily stirred to action, Bondurant and Allison would be deployed in two Knoxville malls, waiting for him. T. J. Bondurant sensed that Wednesday was going to be his lucky day.

At two o'clock on the afternoon of the 25th, Bondurant was in place at the West Town Mall in West Knoxville, while Pete Allison headed south for the newly opened Foothill Mall. "I was thinking," Bondurant candidly recalls, " 'Of course, *I'm* going to be where he is. *I'm* going to make this collar. Just to be safe, I'll send Pete down to cover this other mall.' "

Pete Allison arrived at the Foothills Mall at approximately 2:45 P.M. After visiting several stores and the mall security office, Allison made a final stop at Waldenbooks, where he introduced himself to manager Donna Meador and her assistant, Denise Clegg. "Oh, I'm familiar with this guy," said Meador when Allison showed her the Mall Passer sketch. "I saw this when I worked at a Waldenbooks in Memphis. In fact, I've seen this flyer so often that I know I'd recognize this guy the moment I saw him. I won't have any problems recognizing him."

Allison went on with his canvass, and Meador went back to work. Then, just minutes later, she looked up to see in amazement, the bespectacled Mall Passer, standing there alone in the corridor. "I *know* that's him!" Meador said to herself. "And he's coming in here!"

Before he did, she whispered to her assistant, Denise Clegg, who slipped into the bookstore's back room and dialed the police and Secret Service. Meador meanwhile sold the Mall Passer a paperback. She accepted his counterfeit twenty and carefully tucked it aside. Meador then watched in secret as DeBardeleben sauntered out of Waldenbooks and into Kay-Bee Toys next door.

Agent Allison heard the alarm in his car outside the main mall entrance. Adrenaline pulsing, Allison hit the pavement at a sprint. Holding a police radio in his right hand and grasping his .357 in its cross-draw holster with his left, the agent burst through the mall doors, blew past the startled personnel at a mall security station and dashed on another fifty yards to Waldenbooks.

"He was just in here!" Donna Meador exclaimed to him. "He just left! The security people are following him!" Allison radioed a request for help to the

Maryville police, and then raced back to the mall security station where he learned that Lieutenant Ron Duffin of the mall security force, whom he'd met only an hour before, already was shadowing the suspect.

Duffin followed DeBardeleben from Kay-Bee Toys to the large fountain at the Foothills Mall's main intersection, then up and down another corridor before the Mall Passer caught on to the tail. At that moment, agent Allison joined Duffin, who pointed out the suspect, about twenty yards away and hurrying from them toward a section of the mall that was still under construction. Allison quickly radioed the Maryville police again, informing them of the Mall Passer's location and direction, then gave chase with Duffin.

DeBardeleben by this time had broken into a full run. With Allison and Duffin in full pursuit, he cleared the doors and darted left only to encounter two very large and imposing Maryville policemen, Sergeant Mike Johnston and officer Phil Keeble.

"He proceeded to tell them that he'd already been cleared by these guys behind him and pointed to us coming out the exit," says Allison. "He tried to walk by them, so they slammed him up against a car.

"He says, 'Look, guys! I'm all right! They cleared me!'

"I'm on the radio telling them, 'Hold that guy! Don't let him go!' and Lieutenant Duffin was hollering at them, too. 'Don't let him go!' Of course, they had no intention to. That guy wasn't going *anywhere*."

PART
TWO

12

Enigma

Exultation at the Mall Passer's dramatic capture quickly turned to peeved frustration as the sullen suspect refused to talk, and then to uneasiness and dread when his true identity was established via fingerprints the next morning. For agent Mike Stephens, mere mention of DeBardeleben's name provoked dark memories of the suspect's 1976 arrest, troubled recollections he now shared with agents Foos and Mertz.

Stephens recalled that DeBardeleben was nabbed outside his house at 1201 South Columbus Street in Arlington. The next morning, Stephens led a search of the residence. The search team, a half-dozen agents in all, entered the house through the front door, Stephens in the lead. Indistinct voices filtering down from an upstairs radio as the team picked its way through DeBardeleben's dark, dusty living room, a chaos of randomly discarded clothing, cardboard boxes, and a few pieces of cheap furniture. "It was a total mess," as Stephens describes it. "It was obvious he just threw stuff all over the place. The kitchen was even worse, a total wreck."

Up a very narrow and twisting staircase to the second floor, Stephens discovered two closed rooms, a bath between them, on a short hallway. The radio was playing behind the bedroom door on his right. His handgun drawn, Stephens tried the knob, pushed the door opened and tried the wall switch.

Instantly, a movie projector clicked on, flooding the

opposite wall with the black-and-white glare of an explicit XXX sex flick. "It scared the hell out of me," says Stephens.

Once he shut off the film projector and switched on a lamp, the agent found himself standing in an airless den, rank with the stench of sweat, cigarette butts, and moldering, half-eaten sandwiches. Various articles of male clothing were strewn around. Several empty soda bottles lay on the floor. The walls were covered with amateur pornographic photography.

There were stacks of five-by-seven cards with females' names, addresses, measurements, and brief physical descriptions written on them. There were dildos, whips, vibrators, pills, handcuffs and rope, as well as audio recordings (cassette and reel-to-reel) of everything from television shows to phone-sex conversations. On DeBardeleben's unmade queen-size bed, covered with filthy sheets, Stephens saw several sex magazines, many devoted to bondage and anal intercourse. Under the pillows were a .38 revolver and a 9mm automatic, both loaded. In all, the Secret Service would recover five handguns in the house, together with an astonishing 3,500 rounds of various caliber ammunition.

"We've got a very peculiar guy here," Stephens said to no one in particular as he turned from the fetid bedroom to the second upstairs door, which was padlocked tight. One blow from a sledgehammer took care of the lock, and allowed the door to swing open, revealing to the agents, in dim outline, their mission's major objective, DeBardeleben's printing plant, a Multilith 1250, with counterfeit money and aluminum printing plates lying on the floor around it.

The successful search for DeBardeleben's plant and plates—his inks and other paraphernalia were recovered from the kitchen—essentially sewed up the 1976 counterfeiting investigation. The Secret Service had secured the physical evidence. With testimony from several witnesses, the case was solid and certain to result in a conviction.

For Mike Stephens, however, the March morning search at 1201 South Columbus had raised more questions than it answered. Secret Service agents are accustomed to dealing with aberrant, sometimes violent and often wildly irrational cranks and would-be presidential assassins. But Stephens never had encountered a subject who was, as he puts it, so *peculiar.*

Then there was the interview that Stephens and agent Art Gallow conducted with DeBardeleben's estranged wife. Caryn, then 24, about five-six, chesty, with long black hair and dark eyes, spoke haltingly, often in a whisper, throughout the interview. To Stephens, she had the sleepless look of the haunted.

Gently as possible, he mentioned the pornography, sex devices and weapons found at 1201 South Columbus. Caryn stiffened, tears starting in her eyes. "She was extremely nervous," Stephens recalls. "Then I asked, 'Are you aware of any other crimes your husband may have committed? Specifically, sex-related crimes?' She broke down and sobbed, 'He will kill me! He will kill me!' Her lawyer interrupted at that point, advising Caryn to answer no further questions from us about her husband's possible crimes."

Stephens also recalled for Foos and Vezeris the story of Phillipa Voliner*, a Memphis, Tennessee, bar dancer who was savagely pistol-whipped in 1975 by a man calling himself Eugene Baker. Voliner identified DeBardeleben as Baker, Stephens explained. In a coup of both determination and luck, Stephens proved that DeBardeleben owned the 1973 AMC in which Voliner was attacked. Nevertheless, a local prosecutor declined to press the case. Reason: "She was a hooker, an unsympathetic victim." says Stephens. "Too hard to convince a jury to convict."

Saturday, May 28, 1983, four days after DeBardeleben's arrest in Knoxville, an exhausted agent Greg

Mertz sat sorting through DeBardeleben's belongings seized earlier that evening at LandMark Mini-Storage. Saturday was Mertz's final night as a duty officer, and he knew it was going to be bumpy. He had slept but six or seven hours since the case broke on Wednesday, and not at all since Friday. As the early hours of Sunday, May 29, crept slowly by, he fought to stay awake, sitting on the floor of his office, sorting through the piles and piles of paper seized at Landmark, looking for some clue to the location of DeBardeleben's plant.

By about four that morning, he'd found a number of receipts, filled out to various of DeBardeleben's aliases, from storage facilities around northern Virginia and in other states, as well. Mertz, Foos, and Stephens already had discussed how what they knew about DeBardeleben suggested he might have led several parallel lives. The stack of storage receipts hinted at a network of stashes to coincide with these identities.

Musing on this possibility in the middle of the night on the floor of his office, surrounded by silence, Mertz let his bleary gaze rove to one of the audiocassette tapes seized at Landmark. It was marked "Caryn."

"When I first saw it," he recalls, "I remembered her name from the 1976 investigation and her connection to DeBardeleben's old counterfeiting operation. 'Maybe,' I thought to myself, 'there's something on this tape that's going to lead me to an additional location.'

"At this point I'm really tired. And you know, when you get that tired, things don't click like they should. Your reactions are slowed down. I took the tape, still thinking about the counterfeit, and pushed it into my Dictaphone. Immediately I hear a woman screaming, *'what are you going to do to me?!!'* "

Next, Mertz heard a male grunt, *"Huh?"* The tone was completely emotionless.

"No!!" the woman screamed again. *"What are you*

*going to do to me!? Please! Please tell me!! Please tell
me!!! What are you doing! Tell me!!!!!"*

"*C'mon,*" the man drawled, irritated.

"*Oh please don't do it again!*"

"*You gonna be a cry baby? Huh?*"

She whimpered. "*No, I won't.*"

"*All right.*"

A pause.

"*Please!*" the woman screamed again. "*Untie my
hands! Please, Mike! Don't fuck me in the ass! I
wouldn't do something like that to you! Don't fuck me
in the ass!!!!!*"

Greg Mertz punched the stop button on his Dictaphone. "It was like the *Twilight Zone,*" he remembers.
"It didn't register right away. It was like, 'Am I *really*
hearing what I'm hearing?' I was just totally dumbfounded."

The tape, a half-hour long and edited in places, quite
clearly depicted Mike DeBardeleben torturing and sodomizing his wife, Caryn. DeBardeleben forced her to
beg for the pain and humiliation. He giggled as she did
so.

"*Please let me die,*" Caryn pleaded. "*Let me die. Let
me die. Let me die.*"

"*Calm down. You gonna calm down?*"

"*Why can't I die? Why can't I die,*" Caryn went on
in high-pitched singsong. "*Why can't I die? Why can't
I die? Why can't I die?*"

"*My mother died.*"

"*I wish I were her! I wish I were her and not me! I
wish I were her, oh God! I want to die! Why don't you
do it?*"

Greg Mertz shut the machine off a second time.
"You know," he says, "as a police officer I'd seen dead
bodies and interviewed rape victims. I wasn't the most
experienced cop in the world, but I wasn't a rookie.
This mortified me. I really was mortified, totally per-
plexed. 'What *is* this? Where did it come from?' He

was cold and calculating. No emotion at all. Not one iota of sympathy, and not even very much anger in his voice. He was torturing his wife in a businesslike fashion."

The agent recalls sitting stock-still for perhaps ten minutes before he was able to stand. "I put the receipts on Denny's desk and scribbled him a short note about the tape, something like, 'Listen to this.' Then I went home."

Sunday morning, May 29, Dennis Foos arrived at WFO to find on his desk a sheaf of DeBardeleben's storage-facility receipts left there hours earlier by Greg Mertz. Foos also found the "Caryn" audiotape and Mertz's terse note, "Listen to this." He did, and the horror of what he heard unnerved him. "It gave me the willies," he says.

By this time, the Secret Service had put together a sketchy portrait of DeBardeleben. They knew that he had been married five times, and that he was born March 20, 1940, in Little Rock, Arkansas, the second of three children in the family of James Mitchell DeBardeleben, an army officer and civil engineer, and Mrs. DeBardeleben, the former Mary Louise Edwards. Both parents were native Texans.

The first entry on DeBardeleben's rap sheet was a felony arrest for carrying a concealed weapon, at age sixteen, in Albany, New York. He subsequently was arrested several times on charges ranging from theft to sodomy to attempted murder and kidnap, but had served prison time only twice; 1962, in Texas, for a parole violation, and again in 1976 on his first federal counterfeiting beef. The rap sheet also disclosed the first of many anomalies that came to characterize the investigation. Because a clerk had misunderstood "expired" on a parole form to mean "deceased," the National Crime Information Center had believed DeBardeleben dead since 1978.

More curiouser still was the interstate maze of mul-

tiple, intersecting identities and paper addresses that
DeBardeleben maintained with obvious, painstaking
care—a network of "cutouts" worthy of a spy ring.
From Albany, for example, resident agent Michael
F. Reilly reported that 1927 Central Avenue, the address DeBardeleben gave as J. R. Jones when he registered the 1971 Chrysler in New York, was the Skyway
Motel, a low-end hostelry known to the local police for
its unsavory clientele. A second Albany address, 1723
Central Avenue, which was found among the jottings
seized in DeBardeleben's Alexandria apartment,
proved to be that of Colonie Answering Service, which
he'd used as a mail drop. Kathy Smith at Colonie recognized DeBardeleben's photo as that of the man she
knew as J. R. Jones, and said the customer had asked
that his mail be forwarded to an address in Alexandria.
WFO agents Bob Finan and Keith Stauffer then visited
the Alexandria address, which turned out to be Cynthia
Potter Associates, yet another answering service and
mail drop.

Similarly, Baltimore Field Office agent Paul
Rakowski checked out Optikon Electronics in Glen
Burnie, Maryland, Jones's putative employer, and discovered this address was that of ATS, Arundel Telephone Service. Dot Radulovich, head operator at ATS,
told Rakowski that her records showed Mr. Jones had
set up the Optikon account on October 30, 1982, the
same week he'd rented L-517 at the Oakwood Apartments (and indicated Optikon as his employer on the
apartment lease application). Radulovich further noted
on Jones's card that he'd previously opened another
account, under the name Jones, listing 1735 Central
Avenue in Albany as his address.

The pile of handwritten telephone numbers seized at
DeBardeleben's apartment ranged from a weather report service to a cab company to a pornographic recording in New York City, plus several numbers for
telephone answering services and mail drops. Some of

the numbers belonged to prostitutes, including "Tara," a local hooker who recognized DeBardeleben's photo as that of an anonymous john whom she had serviced on four or five occasions at various places around Washington and northern Virginia, including two motels in Arlington and, within the past ten days, at apartment L-517. Tara said the sex with DeBardeleben was never strange. He spoke often to her of his drug use, especially his fondness for speed and coke. DeBardeleben also had told Tara that he was a professional thief with a prison record but said nothing specific about his crimes, nor did he ever mention counterfeiting.

Many of the seized notes were shorthand physical appraisals of women he apparently encountered at random. After listing a license number, a typical note read:

> Brown Dodge Challenger
> 5'3" Blonde
> Big Tits! ****
> Nice Ass! ***
> Pretty Face ****

Another note listed a name, Nora Thomas,* a rating:

> 16? 5'10" 140
> Blonde Face 5* Ass 3-4*

and a telephone number and address. Agent Don Flynn visited the teenage girl:

> [She] could not identify the defendant as anyone known to her. However, she recalled an incident some time in the past when during a visit to a Holiday Health Spa facility in Falls Church, Va., an older white male struck up a short conversation with her regarding the facility. [She] could provide no further description

of the man nor any reason why the defendant would
have her name and address.

The Richmond, Virginia, field office, working with
the state Department of Motor Vehicles, turned up a
second address in DeBardeleben's name, 1913
Hileman Road in Falls Church, the gray bungalow
where he'd printed his counterfeit. Dennis Foos drove
out to the house, which he discovered unoccupied.
Next door, neighbor David Peoples told Foos that
DeBardeleben had lived at 1913 from May 1979 until
his eviction in late 1981. Peoples also remembered a
woman named Barbara Abbott,* a schoolteacher from
Maryland, who was introduced to Peoples as DeBardeleben's wife.

According to Peoples, his former neighbor was for
the most part quiet and secretive. He kept his shades
drawn, and often received late-night visitors.
DeBardeleben, who told Peoples he was a hair dresser
by trade, often disappeared for weeks at a time in a car
Peoples remembered as dark blue, with decorative
portholes—the '77 Thunderbird.

After Plantation Realty evicted DeBardeleben, much
of the stuff the realty agents found inside the house
was hauled out and dumped near the curb. Peoples remembered his neighbors sorting through the junk.
They found a lot of skin magazines and dirty pictures,
he said. There also was photographic equipment, including an enlarger, chemicals, paper, trays and a print
dryer. But what was *really* curious, he said, were all
the socks, at least 150 pairs of black men's dress socks,
still in their bags with tags attached.

"What was all that about?" Peoples asked.

Taken together, these few known fragments of
DeBardeleben's life suggested a covert world of extraordinary complexity, filled with violence and dark
corners. As Foos left WFO that Sunday morning,
headed out to resume his canvass of storage facilities,

it occurred to the agent that, so far, the more the Secret Service knew about DeBardeleben the less they understood him. He was becoming a deeper and deeper enigma to them, a malign question mark. Meanwhile, they still had no idea where he'd hidden his press and plates.

Foos gave some of DeBardeleben's receipts to agents Stephen Caruso and Roland Maye, who began calling the storage companies. Their first lead of the day turned out to be a dead end. Ackley Payne, the manager of American Storage in Fairfax, Virginia, advised Roland Maye that a J. R. Jones of Albany, New York, had leased locker #61-D from an indeterminate date through the preceding November. Mr. Payne knew nothing more about Jones.

Then paydirt. Agent Caruso contacted Maud H. Ward at Private Storage of Manassas, on Balls Ford Road in Manassas, Virginia, the famous Civil War battleground. Mrs. Ward told Caruso that J. R. Jones, an employee of Optikon Electronics in Albany, New York, currently was leasing locker C-75 for thirty dollars a month. Jones was paid up to the end of May. According to the sign-in sheet Mrs. Ward consulted, Jones, who drove a 1971 Chrysler, had made frequent visits to C-75 since he first rented the locker in June 1982. His most recent entry was for May 23, just two days before the Mall Passer's capture.

Dennis Foos heard the news on his car radio. As he returned to WFO and his typewriter, where he'd knocked out the case's fourth search warrant affidavit in four days, Foos put a call into Mike Stephens at home. He described for Stephens the contents of the "Caryn" tape and notified him of the impending Manassas search.

Stretch Stephens was a practical choice to bring into the case. A veteran agent who'd joined the Secret Service in 1971, he was more familiar with DeBardeleben than anyone else and had made it clear he'd like to take part in the new investigation.

A St. Louis native, Stephens attended tiny Olivet College, near Lansing, Michigan, where the future agent played varsity basketball and was editor of the school newspaper. He considered becoming a veterinarian—his father had been a general surgeon in St. Louis—but by graduation had decided on journalism as a career, and enrolled in the graduate program at the University of Missouri in the summer of 1970.

That July, he married a St. Louis girl, Mary Linda Peskorse. In August, the Selective Service sent him an induction notice. Healthy, willing to serve, Stephens was so certain he'd pass the physical and be drafted that he quit school to spend some time with his young wife before appearing for his physical—which he failed.

"It was my left knee," he says. "I had hurt it playing football my senior year in high school. It was mystery to me why they considered it a problem. Frankly, I couldn't believe it. I mean, my wife had driven me down to the induction center at six in the morning and was back home, crying on her bed, when I called about two o'clock and said, 'Come back and get me.' "

He began that autumn to think of joining the Secret Service (his brother Lou, a St. Louis policeman, later became an FBI agent). Mike sold life insurance while his application was being considered. "It was," he says, "the most miserable year I ever had, even though I was pretty good at it."

From his first posting, Memphis, in 1971, Mike Stephens was moved in 1974 to the old WFO, located in the Potomac Electric Building on Pennsylvania Avenue. Three years later, after the first of his three daughters was born, he was assigned to the White House protection detail, and stayed there until '81, when he was sent to the Detroit field office as an Intelligence Squad supervisor. At the time of the Mall Passer's arrest, Stephens just had transferred back to WFO, where he was made a supervisor in the Special Investigation Squad.

By early afternoon on the overcast Sunday, another search team had assembled in suburban Manassas, about twenty-five miles due west of downtown Washington. Included in the group were Foos, Caruso, Mike Musgrave, Bob Gundel, Mike Stephens, technicians Ratliff and Spires and, briefly, Al Buskirk, SAIC of the Washington Field Office.

The agents immediately opened C-75's orange door to find, at last, DeBardeleben's partially dismantled Multilith 1250. The machine was standing in one corner under a small mountain of junk; cheap clothing, some chairs and a dented lampshade, a mattress, a clock radio, plastic bags and cardboard boxes. Mixed with this debris were his plates and inks, assorted other counterfeiting gear, and $207,700 in counterfeit twenties; again, variously incomplete.

Celebration should have been in order. The Secret Service had won again. They had their suspect behind bars and his plant suppressed. Case closed—ordinarily. "We were elated about that," says Mike Stephens. "But I remember that our feelings were very mixed, like we all sort of looked at each other and said, 'This isn't going to be so easy.'"

Inside the Manassas locker, the searchers also found six handguns: three .22 Derringers, a .45 Colt Commander semiautomatic, a Smith & Wesson .38 revolver, and a Browning .25 semiautomatic pistol. There was a quantity of knives, razors and cutting tools, women's underwear, seven more license plates (all stolen) as well as a number of stolen women's driver's licenses. DeBardeleben had kept a generous supply of white adhesive tape in the locker. Here and there were wadded balls of the stuff, with hair stuck to them. He stored hundreds of pages of handwritten notes, the usual collection of smut (sample titles: *Nude*

Bondage Fantasies and *Shaved Bondage*) and an extensive library of books ranging from pop psychology to true crime to a volume entitled, *The Big Brother Game: Bugging, Wiretapping, Tailing, Optical and Electronic Surveillance, Surreptitious Entry. HOW TO STOP IT OR DO IT BACK!*

Rain showers ambushed the search team just as the bulk of this material had been pulled outdoors from the crowded locker. Concerned lest potential evidence be harmed or destroyed, Dennis Foos ordered a U-Haul truck brought to the site. When it arrived, approximately two-thirds of C-75's contents were loaded into the truck. It was driven to the Washington Navy Yard that afternoon, where the seized material was kept under lock until Tuesday, May 31, when it was brought to WFO for processing.

The enormity of that task seemed overwhelming. In all, the three Virginia searches had yielded 144 cardboard boxes of potential evidence, not counting the press itself and some of the larger items from Manassas. Nor was it lost on the Secret Service agents that counterfeiting—the crime for which they'd assiduously chased the Mall Passer for four years—probably was among his less serious offenses in a criminal career the dimensions of which seemed almost limitless.

Under normal circumstances, case agent Foos would now coordinate disposition of the case, organizing the evidence and working with the U.S. Attorney's office to build the counterfeiting case against DeBardeleben. Again, this was no usual case.

"It was apparent that this would be too much for one person to handle," explains Foos. "So I asked Jane Vezeris for help. She said sure, and gave me the name of an excellent agent, a guy I highly respect. She picked him because he was a detail man. But I had Greg in mind when I went to see her. He knew the case and he's a good detail man. But Greg will also jump up and go kick down a door in a second. So I told her I actually wanted Greg and she said fine."

Another twist in the improbable case was how it had developed backward and inside-out. Most law enforcement investigations—such as the initial Mall Passer investigation—are launched in response to a crime, or series of crimes, and proceed—ideally—toward identification and apprehension of the wrongdoer. Precisely the opposite occurred once the Mall Passer was caught and identified. The Secret Service knew that they'd undoubtedly caught a major felon. But counterfeiting aside, who was going to uncover the broad range of crimes that their evidence strongly suggested he'd committed?

There would be no easy resolution to that question. The Secret Service's official responsibilities began and ended with the Mall Passer case, which had been successfully completed. Moreover, Secret Service agents are untrained in the investigation of crimes outside their Treasury Department purview. With this in mind, in early June of 1983, Jane Vezeris informally approached the FBI.

"We didn't know what we had," she says. "We just knew we had a room full of stuff, and we didn't know what to do with it. So we contacted the bureau and explored it with them. 'Look, we've got a whole bunch of stuff here. You might be interested. We really can't tell you what crimes were committed, but we kind of think it's this, and we kind of think it's that.'

"They said, 'Sounds nice. When you come up with something, let us know.' "

The Bronx-born Vezeris, née Bisacquino, a 1974 graduate of New York Law School, was one of only a handful of women then serving as Secret Service agents. She had arrived at WFO from the Headquarters Legal Affairs office just two days before DeBardeleben was caught, and was temporarily on loan as ATSAIC— Assistant To The Special Agent In Charge—from the

Special Investigations Squad to the Criminal Squad, in which capacity she was agents Foos and Mertz's immediate superior.

Vezeris says she is sympathetic toward the FBI's reluctance to step into the case. "If I was on the other end of that call I know I would have done the same thing," she explains. "We really didn't give them a lot to go on, so I can't fault them."

Since it was clear, based on DeBardeleben's known travels as the Mall Passer, that a national investigation would be necessary, and since the only logical alternative agency to conduct that inquiry, the FBI, had declined to intervene, Jane Vezeris raised the subject of pursuing the investigation themselves with agents Foos, Mertz, and Mike Stephens, who was doing his best to insinuate himself into the case.

"It was obvious that Mike had a strong interest," she recalls. "Dennis was the case agent. And Greg was brought in because he'd immediately started rolling with the case. The four of us sat down and started talking."

Out of these discussions in early June came the idea to approach Al Buskirk. "Give us a little time," Vezeris asked the SAIC. "We'd like to work on this and see if we can come up with what this guy was involved in."

It was an entirely unorthodox proposal. From time to time in the past, the Secret Service had formed investigative teams and strike forces. But as far as anyone could remember, the Service *never* had wandered outside its turf in this way. Nevertheless, Al Buskirk gave his blessing for Vezeris to take her proposals to the Acting Assistant Director, Joe Carlon.

Jane Vezeris, by reputation cautious and constitutionally incapable of rash action, took Dennis Foos to her meeting with Carlon, utterly confident of Carlon's blessing. "I knew Joe well," she says. "I knew he wouldn't need a lot of convincing to do the right thing."

What Vezeris had not anticipated was the drop-in attendance of the Secret Service director himself, John R. Simpson, 56, who walked into Carlon's office during the briefing and stayed to listen. Simpson, from Boston, was a twenty-one-year veteran of the Secret Service and had been named its director in 1981. Sober-sided and fatherly, he was, says Vezeris, "very conservative. I remember at staff briefings he might say something like 'Damn!' and then would instantly apologize to me. Very straitlaced."

Which is why Vezeris had her misgivings when it came time to play the "Caryn" tape with its subject's anguished screams and DeBardeleben's sadistic demands of her. "I could tell that the tape made him very uncomfortable," Vezeris says. "And clearly, it disturbed him to hear what we thought DeBardeleben was involved in."

Vezeris and Foos do not remember the director asking either of them any questions, or saying much of anything during their presentation. But when it was over he stood, recalls Vezeris, and addressed himself to his acting assistant director. "Give them whatever they need," Simpson said, then turned to Vezeris and Foos as he left the room. "Do whatever you think you must do."

13

KRK

Coming as it did on the eve of another presidential campaign—a quadrennial headache for the Secret Service with its precedent claims on the agency's resources—Director Simpson's sudden, decisive, and open-ended endorsement of an ad hoc DeBardeleben investigative task force, to Mike Stephens, was a high-minded, even noble, action. "I'm very proud of it," he says. "We may not have had any choice, but the director said, 'Let's do the right thing.'"

It was an equally proud moment for Dennis Foos—but a nervous one, too. "I remember thinking, 'God! I *hope* we're not barking up the wrong tree. Something better come out of this.'"

Not much would until the agents devised a means of organizing the evidence they'd seized. "We just had massive amounts of raw data looking at us," says Greg Mertz, "boxes and boxes. Then we were faced with the question: What the hell are we going to do with all this stuff? How are we going to disseminate the information? And how are we going to act on it?"

Making sense of the evidence would be as much a challenge as imposing order on it. DeBardeleben's hundreds of pages of handwritten notes, for example, varied from crude, typewritten attempts at composing his own porn (sample: *"GET YOUR BACK DOWN BITCH! TILT YOUR ASS UP!!! he shouted as he pushed brutally on her trembling little waist ..."*) to home recipes for methamphetamines (principal ingredients: ether and the cotton stuffing from Vicks inhalers), hand-drawn monthly calendars outlining his counterfeiting schedules, disquisitions on his poor health and dozens of detailed scripts for every occasion—from wheedling drugs from doctors to bank examiner scams.

A hand-lettered example:

HELLO, MRS. _____? THIS IS MR. BENSON FROM THE BANK. DID YOU JUST RECENTLY MAKE AN $800 WITHDRAWAL FROM YOUR SAVINGS ACCOUNT?

YOU DIDN'T!! ARE YOU SURE, MRS. _____??

MRS. _____, ON OCTOBER 14TH $800 WAS WITHDRAWN FROM YOUR SAVINGS ACCOUNT, AND YOU SAY YOU DIDN'T MAKE THIS WITHDRAWAL?? (EXCITED CONCERN!) MRS. _____, IF YOU DIDN'T MAKE THIS WITHDRAWAL, SOMEONE HERE AT THE BANK IS TAMPERING WITH YOUR ACCOUNT!!!!!

MRS. _____, WHAT DO YOUR RECORDS SHOW AS THE BALANCE AS OF THE 14TH?—YES, MA'AM, I'LL WAIT.

YES, THAT CHECKS WITH OUR RECORDS HERE BEFORE THIS WITHDRAWAL WAS MADE, BUT MRS. _____ IF YOU DIDN'T MAKE THIS WITHDRAWAL SOMEONE HERE AT THE BANK HAS ILLEGALLY WITHDRAWN $800 FROM YOUR SAVINGS ACCOUNT.

FIRST OF ALL, DON'T WORRY ABOUT THE MONEY, MRS. _____, BECAUSE THE BANK WILL MAKE IT GOOD, BUT WE CERTAINLY WOULD LIKE TO FIND OUT WHO THIS PERSON IS!!—AND I'M SURE YOU WOULD, TOO!

MRS. _____, WOULD YOU BE WILLING TO COOPERATE WITH US TO TRY AND CATCH THIS PERSON?

NOW IF YOU DO HELP US AND WE'RE ABLE TO MAKE AN ARREST, YOU'D RECEIVE A $1,000 REWARD. BUT MRS. _____, YOU COULDN'T TELL ANYONE ABOUT IT. THIS INVESTIGATION MUST BE KEPT CONFIDENTIAL, AND YOU COULDN'T TELL ANYONE THAT YOU WERE WORKING WITH US. IF YOU DID WE WOULDN'T BE ABLE TO CATCH THIS PERSON. YOU CAN KEEP A SECRET, CAN'T YOU, MRS. _____? AND YOU DO WANT TO COOPERATE WITH US?

O.K., NOW HERE'S WHAT I WANT YOU TO DO:

I WANT YOU TO COME ON DOWN HERE TO THE BANK.

I WANT YOU TO <u>WEAR GLOVES</u> AND MAKE A WITHDRAWAL OF $4,800—YOU <u>DO</u> HAVE A SET OF GLOVES DON'T YOU, MRS. _____? YOU SEE WE WANT TO GET THE <u>FINGERPRINTS</u> OFF THE MONEY, YOU UNDERSTAND ABOUT <u>FINGERPRINTS</u> DON'T YOU, MRS. _____? YOU SEE, IF WE CAN GET A GOOD SET OF FINGER-PRINTS, WE'LL BE ABLE TO MAKE AN <u>ARREST</u>, BUT WE DON'T WANT TO GET <u>YOUR</u> FINGERPRINTS MIXED UP THE WITH PER-SON'S WE SUSPECT.

O.K. NOW WHEN YOU GET DOWN HERE TO THE BANK, JUST HAVE THE TAXICAB <u>WAIT</u> OUTSIDE FOR YOU. WE'LL BE WATCH-ING YOU, SO JUST COME IN THE BANK AND GO TO THE FIRST TELLER ON YOUR LEFT. BE SURE TO WEAR YOUR GLOVES, AND MAKE A WITHDRAWAL OF $4,800 IN <u>CASH</u>.

NOW, IF <u>ANYONE</u> HERE AT THE BANK SHOULD ASK YOU <u>WHY</u> YOU'RE MAKING THIS WITHDRAWAL, JUST SAY IT'S FOR <u>PERSONAL</u> REASONS, AND YOU'D RATHER NOT DISCUSS IT.

NOW, THE TELLER <u>MIGHT</u> TRY TO GIVE YOU A CASHIER'S CHECK, BUT I WANT YOU TO <u>INSIST</u> ON <u>CASH</u>—TELL HER YOU WANT THE $ IN <u>100 DOLLAR BILLS</u>—YOU SEE, MRS. _____, THIS WAY WE'LL HAVE <u>ENOUGH</u> BILLS TO GET A <u>GOOD</u> SET OF FIN-GERPRINTS.

NOW AFTER YOU <u>MAKE</u> THE WITHDRAWAL, GO ON BACK HOME IN THE TAXICAB, AND WAIT FOR ME TO CALL. PAY THE TAXICAB FARE, AND I'LL REIMBURSE YOU FOR THIS LATER.

NOW AFTER YOU GET HOME, I'LL SEND LT. JOHNSON FROM THE STATE POLICE OUT TO YOUR HOUSE, AND HE WILL EXAM-INE THE $ FOR FINGERPRINTS.

NOW, ARE YOU <u>SURE</u> THAT YOU UNDERSTAND ALL OF THE DIRECTIONS, MRS. _____? WOULD YOU <u>REPEAT</u> THEM BACK TO ME SO I'M SURE YOU <u>DO</u> UNDERSTAND?

O.K. FINE. NOW I'LL CALL THE TAXICAB IN ABOUT 15 MIN-UTES. DO YOU THINK YOU CAN BE READY BY THEN? O.K.— NOW BE SURE TO WEAR YOUR GLOVES, MRS. _____ O.K. I'LL CALL YOU LATER. GOOD-BYE.

(CALL BACK IMMEDIATELY)

MRS. _____, THIS IS MR. BENSON AGAIN. I JUST WANTED TO TELL YOU THAT WHEN LT. JOHNSON COMES OUT TO YOUR HOUSE TO BE SURE TO ASK HIM FOR HIS IDENTIFICATION SO YOU KNOW THAT HE'S THE RIGHT MAN.

NOW THE GUILTY PARTY <u>MIGHT</u> TRY TO KEEP YOU FROM <u>MAKING</u> THE WITHDRAWAL IN ORDER TO <u>COVER UP</u> THEIR CRIME. ONE OF OUR VICE-PRESIDENTS IS A SUSPECT ALSO, SO IF THIS HAPPENS IT'S <u>IMPORTANT</u> FOR YOU TO IN<u>SIST</u> ON <u>MAKING</u> THE WITHDRAWAL AND TO <u>INSIST</u> ON <u>YOUR</u> RIGHT TO <u>PRIVACY</u>. JUST SAY THAT AFTER ALL IT'S <u>YOUR</u> AC-COUNT, AND IF <u>YOU</u> WANT TO MAKE A WITHDRAWAL FOR <u>PERSONAL</u> REASONS YOU HAVE A RIGHT TO DO SO, WITHOUT HAVING TO EXPLAIN WHY—IT'S REALLY NONE OF THEIR BUSINESS.

Another of DeBardeleben's scripts, also hand-printed in block letters:

HI—

MY NAME IS RICK, AND I'M WRITING THIS LITTLE NOTE TO YOU BECAUSE I'M <u>TOTALLY</u> IMPRESSED BY YOU—SINCE THE DAY I SAW YOU AT MERCHANTS, WHEN YOU GOT YOUR CAR FIXED.

IS IT <u>TRUE</u> BLONDES HAVE MORE FUN??

I COULDN'T RESIST STARING AT YOU, AND WHEN YOU SMILED BACK AT ME THAT WAS IT! AND I'VE REGRETTED NOT STARTING A CONVERSATION WITH YOU UNTIL YOU WERE DRIVING OUT OF THE PARKING LOT—

<u>BUT</u>!—I NOTICED YOU DRIVE DOWN PAXTON STREET, SO I THOUGHT YOU MUST LIVE IN AN APT. IN THAT DIRECTION.

UNFORTUNATELY, I HAD TO LEAVE TOWN THAT EVENING ON A BUSINESS TRIP FOR TWO WEEKS—I HAVE RETURNED RE-CENTLY, BUT JUST NOW HAVE BEEN ABLE TO DRIVE DOWN HERE AND LOCATE YOUR CAR.

I HOPE YOU DON'T FIND ME PRESUMTUOUS [SIC], BUT WHY DON'T YOU CALL ME UP AND LET'S TALK ABOUT THE WEATHER??

(HO! HO! HO!)

RICK (AFTER 10:00 P.M.
WEEKNIGHTS)

DeBardeleben drew up lengthy itineraries of the sort discovered in the search of his car in Knoxville, plus lists of the materials he intended to take with him. *"Plenty of rpe (nylon) Belt with "O" ring for waist,"* read a representative example. *"Wraparound shades, rubber bands, "Ladies" trenchcoat w/hood (dark blue-black), K-Y (in car?) cameras (man) + floods, rainy + weekend best, I-bolts, Buzzer/alarms, "panties" to tear, makeup, eye shadow, lipstick, hair curlers, nail polish, enema bag, SAY "ORIGINAL STATEMENTS!!, plenty of spd. + downers + smoke for her! (+ laxatives!)"*

The agents found scrupulously compiled address and telephone directories for hundreds of bank executives in Northern Virginia and Maryland. DeBardeleben's notes included each individual's name, title, home address, names and ages of family members, descriptions of family vehicles, surveillance notes and, in some cases, annotations such as "30K" or "40K" and "excellent," "fair," and so on.

Then there were his endless, bizarre plans.

1—BUY 5 ACRES IN W. VA. MOUNTAINS

2—RENT BULLDOZER + DIG MYSELF "BASEMENT"

3—SIDE OF HILL, SOFT DIRT (NO ROCKY GROUND) PLACE SMALL SELF-CONTAINED TRAILER, COMPLETE WITH A/COND, HEAT, POWER, ESCAPE EXIT—THAT CAN BE COLLAPSED IN A HURRY—WITH MOTORCYCLE OR? AT END OF TUNNEL— HIDDEN

4—BUY LAND UNDER OTHER OUT-OF-STATE NAME—JR?—WITH ANS. SER FOR ADD.

5—BUY TRAILER + PLACE WITHOUT ANYONE ELSE KNOWING.

6—ROOM FOR PR, PLACE TO PARK CAR HIDDEN OR ACCESSIBLE BY MOTORCYCLE (EASIER TO HIDE)

The writings revealed DeBardeleben's intense self-absorption, expressed on paper as self-analysis. *"Here I am,"* read one note,

> —*depressed as to best*
> —*course of action—filled with doubt.*
> —*not great amount of physical stamina*
> —*extreme hostility toward women*
> —*artistic nature—creative desires*
> —*intelligent*
> —*dislike authoritarian work situations (rigid boss, hours, etc.)*
> —*low in capital*
> —*beautician/hairdresser?   yuk!*
> >   *1—long hours on feet*
> >   *2—around women all day*
> >   *3—have to please women*
> >   *4—placed in position of subservience to women.*

There was a tincture of savage, undifferentiated misogyny in almost everything DeBardeleben wrote. But as Foos, Mertz, and Stephens read through his notes, it was obvious that the object of his purest malevolence—and most rabid fantasies—was his fourth wife Caryn, who usually appeared in the pages as "C."

"I really want what I thought I had with C.—a relationship," he wrote.

> *But the rel. I had with C. wasn't what I thot it was—it's was S/M. I took responsibility, made decisions. She was dependent, "obedient," etc. But this is not "closeness" but a way to avoid closeness. She was a*

*"better looking" girl than I was a "guy" but she
didn't realize it at 1st / also she was just a 'Hi
Class—camouflaged 'HOOKER' = no __real__ feelings. . . . . . By "fooling" me it not only destroyed my
image of her but of 'ideal. rel. also.' . . .*

Elsewhere, *"she __never really loved me__ but only __used
me__ . . ."*

And, *"I don't want to k. C—I want to punish her—
F.I.A.H.—make her cry, crawl, beg. . . . . ."*

. . . *before I can do C., I want to do* SMB/KRK. . . .
. . . __REPAY C.__
. . . __ALTER BASIC NEEDS:__
1   HUNGER (+ THIRST) - (+ AIR)
2—SLEEP (speed)
3—COLD (+ WATER) (+ICE)
4—NOISE

__DEVICES:__
*1—WHIPS, DILDOS, HCFs, CEILING HARNESS: UPSIDE DOWN,
    IN WATER ETC.*
2—A.H. HARNESS: SUSPENDED SHOULDERS
3—A.H. PLATFORM: AT CORRECT ANGLE TO HOLD IN PLACE
*4—2 HANDLED BROOM DEVICE TO A.F. WITH DILDO WHILE
    34½*
5—PHOTO AND TAPE EQUIPMENT
6—"THE BIGGIE"!!!

__SCRIPT/SCENARIO__
*1—TELL ME ABOUT THE PAIN: NECESSARY? WHY? DESCRIBE
    IT: DETAILS, MORE DETAILS . . . . HOW DOES IT
    FEEL—I DON'T KNOW, IT'S NOT HAPPENING TO __ME__!! CON-
    VINCE ME THAT YOU __LIKE__ IT!*
2—TELL ME HOW YOU FEEL HUMILIATED, DEGRADED . . . . . .
3—. . . . . .TELL ME HOW YOU LIKE FOR ME TO BITE YOUR TITS

SLAP YOUR FACE, SMACK YOU IN THE ASS, MAKE LOUD SURPRISE NOISES.

4—BITE OR CIGAR OR WHIP AT MOMENT OF EJACULATION.

5—HAIR: PULL AS MANE: SAY "ARF", "BOW-WOW" "NEIGH"

6—SAY ORIGINAL STATEMENTS . . . ."

DeBardeleben frequently wrote in ciphers and codes, most of which were quite simple. It was obvious from context, for example, that "C" was Caryn, that "sir" was shorthand for siren and "hcf" code for handcuffs. Other notations, including "fas" (for Fastin, an amphetamine) or "POMOS"—Post Office Money Orders—were somewhat more obscure.

In case there was something of potential value in the coded entries, the task force forwarded dozens of pages to the FBI for cryptanalysis. The bureau experts detected a couple of transposition ciphers, rudimentary encryptions in which notations are written backward and are sometimes abbreviated (Example: KRF = FRANK). They also concurred in most of what the Secret Service agents already had surmised about DeBardeleben's other alphanumeric entries.

"KRK," the bureau agreed, probably meant kidnap, rape, kill, while an "SMB," from context, no doubt stood for sado-masochistic broad (or bitch). "FM" was funny money. "BB" was Black Beauty, slang for another type of amphetamine. "Gn" was short for gun. "BL," "BLD," "BLDE" and "BLNDE" all meant blond. And AF, one of DeBardeleben's more common acronyms, stood for ass fuck.

The disagreeable responsibility for the classification, storage, and retrieval of these notes, as well as for cataloging the rest of the evidence, was entrusted to Greg Mertz. There was logic to the decision; of the three agents, Mertz was the most orderly thinker and possessed a genuine talent for detail work. The agent himself explains another reason for the choice: his junior status.

"Hey," he says, "I was the FNG."

FNG?

"Yeah, FNG. Fucking New Guy. FNGs always get the worst assignments."

Mertz also was the only one among the three who had any practical experience with the investigation of violent crime. "I remember at the start Stephens and I had to ask Greg what a ligature mark was," says Dennis Foos.

The task force knew that they couldn't simply send out a description of what they'd found, and what they suspected DeBardeleben had done, then wait for cops from around the country to come to Washington to dig through their 144 boxes of evidence. So Mertz devised a more manageable way to make the material available to local law enforcement.

He made a list of twenty evidence categories: guns, female clothing, maps, miscellaneous notes and newspaper articles, jewelry and so on. Then he emptied each box, photographed each item in it, assigned each to a category and then returned it to the box. "That's all I did twelve hours a day for four months," Mertz says. "It was horribly boring. Cataloging and categorizing and taking pictures. I had to put on rubber gloves so I wouldn't contaminate anything that could be used as evidence down the road.

"But it had to be done. If you later came to me and asked, 'Which boxes contain books?' I could say, 'Boxes nine, fourteen, twenty-nine' and so forth. Then we'd get the pictures of the books out and if one seemed significant, we could go to the box and actually retrieve it. That was our recall, or memory system."

All documents of every sort—from DeBardeleben's notes to gas receipts to the several residential real estate brochures recovered during the searches—were formatted onto legal-length sheets and photocopied. A group of business cards, for example, would be combined onto one sheet, as might two or three telephone bills.

Mertz then stamped each document with a Rapid-Print number and placed it in an envelope. Each corresponding photocopy was stamped with the same Rapid-Print number, then was bound into a two hundred-page notebook. In this way, approximately fourteen thousand separate bits of paper of all sizes and shapes and relative importance to the investigation were reduced to thirty-seven uniform volumes.

From these books would come the agents' computerized data bases. After consulting with Jane Vezeris's husband, John, also a Secret Service agent who, at the time, was himself working on the computerization of the Secret Service's Master Criminal Index, the task force acquired an Apple computer and data-management software, which they had customized to their unique requirements.

Mertz and the others realized that they'd amassed such an immense trove of raw data—notes, receipts, calendars, bank records, telephone numbers, names and, of course, the service's extensive and detailed records of the Mall Passer's movements—that if properly organized this information could tell investigators a great deal about DeBardeleben.

Once Mertz had completed the Rapid-Printing, a squad of data-entry clerks was needed to get all the material into the computer, more personnel than could be conveniently shifted from their regular jobs at 1800 G Street. Since such sensitive material could not be entrusted to temporary office help, the only answer was to import clerks from the various field offices.

They were brought to Washington in rotating shifts; two clerks for two weeks, one of them working at the computer from eight to four each day, and the other from four to twelve. Their instructions were to record just about everything they saw on the photocopies— names, numbers, addresses, dates, towns, highways, etc.—and to enter them separately in any one or all of a dozen so-called fields, or formats: Date, City, Hotel/ Motel, Name and the like. The clerks also transcribed every word of DeBardeleben's writings, which were placed in a Free Text field. It required ten weeks, sixteen hours a day, for the clerks to work through the hundreds of thousands of entries. The result was a digital abstract of DeBardeleben's life, massively annotated.

If a police department in Texas, for example, wished to know where he might have been on September 23, 1981, Greg Mertz could look at a computer run and answer the inquiring agency: Albany, New York. On Rapid-Print #02003 he'd find a bill dated that day, made out to J. R. Jones, from Albany Auto Repair. The computer also would indicate that on Rapid-Print #03639 there was a 9/23/81 receipt from the Skyway Motel made out to Jones.

How about April 14, 1982? According to the computer, DeBardeleben-as-Maurice Paquette was a patient that day at Providence Hospital in Mobile, Alabama. July 10 of the same year? Sorry, a blank.

Did he ever stay at the Motel 6 in Pensacola, Florida? Yes. Four times apparently. And always as Alan Kirk. The Playboy Club in Buffalo, New York? Why yes. Mr. Paquette was there on November 12 and 13.

Did the surname Parker appear in his writings? Yes. In his notes there are references to a Barry, an Evelyn, a Josephine, a Margaret, and a Sheila, including phone numbers and addresses. Deborah Adams? No, but there's a Debbie Adams along with a telephone number.

How many times does the word "fraud" appear in his writings? Twelve. "Caper"? Seven. "To kill," or "killing"? Four.

14

A Break

Dennis Foos, who did most of the memo writing for the team, sent an initial arrest Teletype to all Secret Service field offices on May 26, the day after Pete Allison apprehended DeBardeleben at the Foothills Mall, and followed it with a second Teletype on June 3, in which the field agents were first formally notified that the erstwhile Mall Passer they'd chased since 1979 appeared to be "an accomplished con artist and may be involved in fraud, forgery, or sex-related crimes of a violent nature."

Days passed, and although there was plenty of telephone and telex traffic back and forth with the field, nothing of substance came to light. "Ah!" Dennis Foos thought aloud one day in the drab seventh-floor office set aside as task force headquarters. "I *sure* hope we're not wrong about this guy."

Mertz and Stephens said nothing.

On June 14, a federal grand jury in Knoxville indicted DeBardeleben on six counts of passing and possessing counterfeit currency, two counts of firearms possession by a felon, and one count of carrying a firearm during the commission of a crime. At the arraignment, he fired his court-appointed attorney, William Hotz, and hired local criminal defense lawyer James A. H. Bell, known familiarly as Jim Bell. An August date was set for Federal Judge Robert Taylor to hear arguments over Bell's contentions that most of the evidence against his client should be suppressed. Barring a setback at the suppression hearings, Federal Prosecutor Charles Fels had an open-and-shut case against the defendant.

The news from Knoxville heartened Dennis Foos, but only moderately so; the task force's mandate was to uncover far more serious crimes than counterfeiting. On June 16, he placed a routine follow-up call to Linda Johnston at Landmark Mini-Storage. Foos wanted to know if some bags of loose clothing the searchers had left behind was still there and intact. With the focus of the investigation now on sex crimes rather than counterfeit, the paper bags' contents took on new potential meaning.

Over the phone, Johnston explained to Foos that J. R. Jones had fallen in arrears on his storage-space rent. So after the May 28 search, she went back into #230 to see if there was any property left that might fetch a few bucks. A quick inspection of the several bags remaining in the locker canceled that hope; most of them contained old clothes and nearly valueless counterfeit proceeds, pot holders and pet collars and the like. Johnston said she also found a small black case containing a dildo and, as she later testified in court, a very specific sort of erotica.

"Some of the sex magazines were perverse," she said under oath. "It wasn't just male and female. Doing things like that is fine, but like it was between guys, you know, gay stuff. It's just things like that that stick out in your mind."

She also found a bra and a pair of women's black stretch pants, inside of which "there was underwear, women's underwear that looked like they had semen on them and blood on them and just nasty looking."

Where on the garment?

"The main back part . . . the butt part of it was full of blood."

And where, asked Dennis Foos, thinking that the

stained underwear might provide crucial serological evidence, had Mrs. Johnston put these items?

Oh, Johnston told him, she'd thrown them in the trash.

His funk deepening, Foos turned to his stack of phone messages, which included one from Harold Bibb, the Secret Service resident agent in Shreveport, Louisiana. Pondering, according to his recent custom, what else might go amiss that day, Foos returned the call, fully expecting Bibb to bear more bad news.

He could not have been more mistaken.

Harold Bibb apprised Foos of the still-unsolved 1982 stabbing murder of Bossier City real estate agent Jean McPhaul. Then Bibb shared an epiphany.

"I was sitting there at my desk looking at DeBardeleben's picture," he told Foos. "I said, 'You know, I've seen this guy somewhere before.' I sat there for fifteen minutes, wondering, before I said, '*I* know where it was. He looked just like the guy who killed Jean McPhaul!' "

Bibb, who lived at GreenAcres Place, three blocks from the house where Jean McPhaul was murdered, explained to Foos how he'd compared DeBardeleben's photo to the published sketch of "Dr. Zack," and how Bibb also pulled his Mall Passer file to see if DeBardeleben had been through the Shreveport–Bossier City vicinity at the time of McPhaul's murder. It looked as if he had. Just before the April 27, 1982, killing, the Mall Passer had struck to the west in Tyler, Texas, off Interstate 20, which continues east directly through Bossier City. The day after the murder, of course, DeBardeleben was in Charlotte, North Carolina, at the Eastridge Mall where he nearly was caught.

The conversation ended with Dennis Foos cautiously optimistic that here, thank goodness, was his devoutly desired break. A few days later—after determining that a Louisiana license plate found among the dozens in DeBardeleben's possession had been stolen January 30, 1982, from a 1974 Chevy in Bossier City, less than a mile from the Sheraton where McPhaul met her murderer—Foos spoke by telephone with Detective Doug Payne of the Bossier City police department. Payne, who'd been briefed by Harold Bibb, told Foos that he very much would like to look through the seized materials at WFO. Among the interesting evidence Payne had turned up in his initial investigation, he added, was a receipt from a Motel 6 in Shreveport, made out to a James R. Jones, and dated April 23, 1982, four days before the McPhaul murder.

Payne also mentioned that the ligature found around McPhaul's neck was made from stitched denim, and looked as if it might be the belt to a woman's garment. Her killer clearly brought it with him and maybe, just maybe, the rest of the dress could be found in the evidence. Likewise, the murderer apparently had kept McPhaul's purse as a souvenir of the homicide. There were women's purses recovered at the two storage facilities. Finally, McPhaul had been stabbed. Doug Payne wanted to take a look at Mike DeBardeleben's knife collection. After some negotiation back and forth, it was agreed that he'd come to Washington, D.C., in early July.

Foos and Mertz and Stephens made sure the detective felt welcome. "There was nothing I asked for that I didn't get," says Payne. "I remember I called back to [his boss] Scotty Henderson and said, 'You're not gonna believe these guys up here! These guys are federal agents and they actually work! They work the streets! They're out at night doin' stuff that we do back home!' Until I got there I really didn't believe that Secret Service agents did all that they do. It shocked me."

Unfortunately, a positive first impression was about all that the trip achieved. After rummaging in the partially sorted evidence boxes for two days, Payne concluded that his best chance of cementing the case would be through his three witnesses; Tom Kennedy, the contractor, and Bernadette Willadson, the secretary, both of whom saw Dr. Zack in Jean McPhaul's car at GreenAcres that day, and Mrs. DeMoss, the Shreveport rooming-house keeper of whom Dr. Zack inquired about vacancies.

Discovery of the McPhaul case did have a tonic effect on Dennis Foos's nerves, however. "That one broke the ice," he recalls. "It felt good to know we were on the right track." Likewise, a surprise second part of Doug Payne's story served to persuade Foos, Mertz, and Stephens that, if anything, they'd so far *under*estimated Mike DeBardeleben's capacity for evil.

In the process of searching for crimes similar to his case, Payne told the agents, he'd contacted police detectives in Barrington, Rhode Island, who were working on a murder uncannily similar to the McPhaul slaying, the 1971 murder of fifty-two-year-old Edna Macdonald, also a real estate agent. The known details of the two cases were so alike, he said, as to make them layovers—meaning that if Mike DeBardeleben was a killer, he'd been at it for at least twelve years, maybe much longer.

According to what the task force members later learned directly from Barrington police detectives Louis Gelfuso and Gary Palumbo, in early April of 1971 a man variously identifying himself as Charles Murray, Peter Fuller, Peter Rogers, and Peter Morgan began appearing at real estate offices in and around Barrington, an affluent, predominantly white bedroom community of approximately twenty-eight thousand residents, about a forty-five minute rush-hour commute southeast of Providence, the state capital.

Witnesses described a smooth-shaven white male, five-eight to five-ten, 165–175 pounds. He kept his dark hair neatly combed, with long sideburns. "Well dressed," read a later wanted poster bearing the suspect's Identikit likeness,

> neat, expensive, conservative business suit, wearing glove on right hand, carrying and/or wearing white raincoat. Alleges to have wife and three children, gives impression of good education ... States he may be relocating from the New Jersey area and is a traveling business person.

Louis Gelfuso, now retired, remembers that homicides then were rare in Barrington, one every fifteen years or so. Now and again the police would handle an accidental shooting and the odd suicide. But in an upscale and highly transient community such as Barrington, where no fewer than sixty to seventy houses were unoccupied at any one time, housebreaking was by far the local crime of choice.

Gelfuso reports that suspect Murray–Fuller–Rogers–Morgan visited properties with several Barrington-area Realtors in April of 1971, supposedly shopping for a house when, in fact, he was shopping for a victim. He told the Realtors he was interested in seeing newly built, unoccupied dwellings, preferably colonials, in the $40,000 to $50,000 range. "He was probably alone at some point with all of them," says Gelfuso. "But with the younger ones he never placed follow-up calls or made follow-up visits. I think he was in search of a particular type, a particular look and a particular personality. And the *only* one he seriously followed up on was Edna Macdonald."

Edna Macdonald, known as Terry from her mother's maiden name, Therrel, was married to Barrington businessman John G. ("Jack") Macdonald and was the mother of his four children: John ("Chip"), 23, a serviceman stationed at Okinawa; Lynn, 22, who lived at home; Debbie, 19, who'd recently moved to Boston, and Sue, the baby of the family at 17, a senior in high school.

Terry was a sturdy five-four, 140 pounds, with hazel eyes, blond hair turning to gray, and an earnest, open smile that seemed genuine—and was. "Mom was just a very unsuspecting, very trusting person," says her daughter, Lynn. "She always looked for the good in people. She was always positive about them."

On the morning of April 2, 1971, a Friday, Peter Morgan arrived unannounced at Child's Realty, where Terry worked, and spoke for a while with the agent. Mrs. Macdonald entered Morgan's particulars on a half-page office file form. According to her notes, Morgan was from Union, New Jersey, had a wife and family, needed three bedrooms, specified "NEW houses—not usual Colonials—" and was willing to pay as much as $60,000. It appears that Terry Macdonald showed Mr. Morgan one or more possibilities that morning.

April 27, Hope Davidson at Child's received a person-to-person call from Morgan, purporting to be in Nashua, New Hampshire, who asked for an evening appointment with Mrs. Macdonald two days hence. He said he'd meet her at the Sheraton–Biltmore Hotel in Providence at five on Thursday, the 29th.

Under lowering skies a soaking spring rainstorm was on the way—Terry Macdonald climbed into her 1970 Pontiac (vanity plate: T E R) at about four-thirty that Thursday afternoon, and headed north for Providence. Norman Fugnand, night doorman at the Sheraton–Biltmore, would later tell the Barrington police that Mrs. Macdonald appeared in the hotel lobby around five o'clock and remained there for about an hour, waiting for a Mr. Morgan, whom she asked Fugnand to page, without results.

At approximately ten of six, Terry telephoned the Macdonald family house at 28 Tiffany Circle in

Barrington to tell her youngest daughter, Sue, that Peter Morgan was nowhere to be found. She was about to give up and come home. If, in the next few minutes, Morgan called looking for her, Sue was to take down his location. Ten minutes later, according to a Barrington police investigative memo written the following morning:

> . . . the mother called again and stated that she had found the man as she was driving off; he was at a different entrance to the hotel and had hailed her down and that she would be showing him some new houses in Barrington.

Terry's husband, Jack, was in Chicago on a business trip that night. So it was only her daughters, Sue and Lynn, at home for dinner as they waited for Mom to finish up with Mr. Morgan. Lynn Macdonald, who like her brother Chip and sister Debbie, was engaged to be married later in '71, remembers that her mother had promised to go shopping with her for bridesmaids' gifts.

Just before eight, a steady rain now pelting down, Terry Macdonald turned her Pontiac into the driveway at 28 Tiffany Circle and jumped out. Peter Morgan remained seated on the passenger side where Sue Macdonald, casually glancing down through the shutters of her upstairs bedroom, could just make out his form as he sat there, quite still, in what she recalls were dark-colored trousers. Sue Macdonald never saw his face.

"This'll be quick," Terry told Lynn, who irritably reminded her mother that she'd *promised* to take Lynn shopping that night. Mrs. Macdonald grabbed a flashlight and a measuring tape and was quickly on her way out the door again. "I'll be right back" she assured her daughter.

She wasn't.

Since Thursday was a school night, Sue Macdonald was in bed early. Lynn began worrying about her mother as nine and then ten o'clock passed with no sign of her. Because of the weather, Lynn feared that perhaps Terry had been in a car accident.

By midnight, she had called both the Providence and the Barrington police. "I didn't get the sense they felt it was urgent," she says. Then she awoke her sleeping sister. "She told me Mom wasn't home yet," says Sue. "I said, 'Oh, don't worry about it! Mom probably met up with some friends.' "

Neither daughter for a moment considered any more ominous explanations for their mother's failure to return home. "In Barrington, Rhode Island," explains Sue, "I don't think any of us would have thought of foul play."

At two that morning, Lynn roused Sue again, and for good that night. "Sue," she said nervously, "we've got to do something." The young women telephoned the Macdonalds' nearest family friends, Jim and Lynn Swett, who came directly to the house. Jim Swett started making early-morning calls, trying to locate Jack Macdonald in Chicago and also to get a line on who this Peter Morgan might be.

According to Louis Golfuso, the official search for Terry Macdonald did not get underway in earnest until midday on Friday, after most of the obvious and innocent explanations for Terry Macdonald's disappearance had been checked out and discarded. It didn't take long to find her.

Early that afternoon, Hope Davidson at Child's Realty provided the police with a list of the three houses Mrs. Macdonald might have intended to show Peter Morgan the previous night. Detective Robert Casale checked one of the residences thoroughly, found nothing, then moved on to the second house, at 24 Heritage Road in Barrington, a brand-new, two-story, clapboard structure not yet landscaped, and still lacking electricity. The address was no more than a five-minute drive from the Macdonald house on Tiffany Circle.

Mrs. Macdonald apparently had taken with her the only available key to the locked house. The landscaping crew at work on the yard when Casale arrived there also had no means of access to the house. After peering through its windows and seeing nothing but an empty interior, Casale walked across the street to 20 Heritage Road, the residence of Dr. Richard Pease and his family. At that time, the Peases were the only family on the street. Dr. Pease, who knew Terry Macdonald, told Casale he'd seen her arrive at—and leave—24 Heritage in the company of an unfamiliar male late the previous day. "I kind of relaxed on that house for a while," Casale recalls. "It appeared that she'd been there, but left."

Casale, who'd gone on duty at eight o'clock Friday morning, worked on other parts of the investigation until about eighty-thirty that night, then returned to the police station in the company of Reverend Bernard Norman, a Catholic priest and police buff who acted as a sort of unofficial chaplain to the Barrington police department. Though Casale was tired, he was bothered that he hadn't been able to get inside the Heritage Road house, or the third residence on his list. "I just felt uncomfortable going home," he explains. "I needed to look *inside* those two houses to feel as if I'd taken care of my assignment the way I should have."

Casale telephoned the builder of 24 Heritage Road at his home in West Barrington and asked if he perhaps had a key to the house. The contractor said that he did, and agreed to give it to a policeman who was to fetch it and bring it to Casale on his way to reinvestigate the house. "I said to the chaplain, 'C'mon. I have two houses to check out and then we'll go get a coffee or something.'

"So I meet the cop on the road. He gives me the key, and we go to Heritage Road. The reverend and I each had a flashlight, and we checked out the first floor real thoroughly. I mean, we looked up in the chimney, looking for anything we can find.

"Then we got around to the kitchen, and found a stairway there; one side to the basement, the other to the upstairs. The reverend headed down, and I headed up. I was halfway up the stairs when I heard the reverend make this horrifying groan. He didn't say anything, he just kind of groaned. I turned around, pulled my gun out and came running downstairs.

"I saw him standing at the bottom of the stairs with his head cradled in his hand. I'm saying, 'Norm, Norm, what's up, what's up?' He's just kind of moaning and groaning, not really saying anything intelligible.

" 'What's the matter!'

"Without turning his head, he pointed back to the opposite side of the house. I turned around and scanned where he was pointing with my flashlight. The first time, I almost passed her over. It looked like a pile of rags. I didn't recognize it as a body. Then the second time I had to focus on it because it just wouldn't click that there was a human being."

The murdered Terry Macdonald, completely clothed, was lying on her back near the far wall. A length of cord, looped around an overhead pipe, had been secured to her neck, which was hoisted a few inches off the basement's dirt floor in what experts in aberrant crime recognize as a "display" posture.

"Of course I went running over there and sure enough, it was her," says Casale. "It was the first body I'd ever found, and it was an awful experience. It was like, 'This can't happen here. This is Barrington, a nice town. This kind of horrible, horrible crime just doesn't happen here. It's unthinkable.' It was years before I could drive by that house again without shuddering."

15

"David, Do What He Says."

The task force's contacts with the Bossier City and Barrington detectives initiated a deluge of what ultimately were two hundred inquiries from investigative agencies around the country. Agents Foos, Mertz, and Stephens soon were amazed at the volume of unsolved murders that cops everywhere were trying to clear.

On June 20, agent Michael Shannon, the Secret Service resident agent in Grand Rapids Michigan, began working with detective Frank Whitaker of the Kalamazoo police on an unsolved prostitute murder. In early July, the Owensboro, Kentucky, police offered four open homicides for consideration. In neither jurisdiction could DeBardeleben be connected to the crimes.

Late in June, agent Rick Johnson in the Rochester, New York, field office briefed local FBI agents Bill Dillon and Gene Harding on the case. Both bureau agents were then working a recent, baffling murder in Greece, a Rochester suburb, near Lake Ontario, and both were eager to hear more about Mike DeBardeleben in connection with their investigation.

As Dillon and Harding explained to Johnson, their case began on Wednesday night April 13, 1983, when 36-year-old David M. Starr, manager of the local Columbia Savings Bank, drove his gray, 1978 Chrysler Cordoba home to 98 Applewood Drive in Greece to find his 42-year-old house mate, Joe Rapini, sick with a 101 degree fever. Rapini, who worked as a blood chemist at nearby Park Ridge Hospital, suffered chronically from a vascular disease that often kept him home from work. This day, Joe Rapini's usual head and chest pains were accompanied not only by the fever, but by diarrhea and vomiting, as well. He could keep nothing in his stomach. So, instead of going as usual to weekly choir practice at the local Aldersgate Methodist Church that night, David Starr called Rapini's personal physician, Dr. Hal Parmalee, and arranged with the doctor to bring his ailing friend to the emergency room at Park Ridge. They arrived at the hospital at 6:30.

Parmalee examined Rapini, ordered blood and stool tests, then told David Starr that his companion required an upper GI examination, which could not be performed until Thursday. There was no need to hospitalize Rapini overnight, Parmalee continued, but the doctor did administer an injection, which Starr assumed was some sort of sedative. Rapini was moderately groggy when they reached home at about 9:30.

Starr noticed nothing unusual in the neighborhood, nor their house, as he pulled the Chrysler into the garage next to Rapini's light brown Plymouth Duster. He secured the garage door, then unlocked the door leading into their kitchen. With Rapini just behind him, Starr stepped into the kitchen, where he felt a light breeze blowing across the room.

One glance revealed a kitchen window had been broken. A second look revealed who'd broken it. Standing in the hallway, faintly illuminated by a ceiling light over the stove, stood an intruder. He was pointing a gun at Starr and Rapini. "Don't move," the stranger said steadily. "Down on the floor. You're going to be in a bank robbery."

David Starr yelped in terror.

The banker was sufficiently composed, nevertheless, to remember his robber-ID training at Columbia Savings. He tried to fix in his mind an impression of the man, from head to toe. Although Starr wouldn't have long to look, and the light was not good, he later was able to describe to detectives a ski-masked male, 35 to 40 years of age, roughly six feet tall, 170 pounds, probably white, wearing a dark jacket over a white shirt or T-shirt, and dark pants. His weapon was a blued-metal handgun that he held in the two-handed police-style, arms extended, feet apart.

Speaking slowly and softly, the solitary gunman ordered Starr and Rapini into the adjoining family room, where he handcuffed both men's wrists behind their backs. David Starr would not directly see the man again that night. "Subject," read a subsequent FBI report, "stated that if they cooperated they would not be harmed, but if they did not do what they were told that subject would kill them."

"David," said the thoroughly frightened Joe Rapini to his friend, "do what he says."

With both victims securely in his power, the intruder asked where they kept their bed linen; he wanted to cover their heads with pillowcases in order to safely remove the ski mask. David Starr, followed by Joe Rapini, rose to his feet and led the man upstairs where they waited, still handcuffed, their faces against the wall, as he opened the linen closet and removed two cases. All three then returned downstairs, where the man permitted his hooded hostages to sit together on the family room couch.

He told Starr that he wanted at least $70,000, that the money should be in five-, ten-, and twenty-dollar denominations, and that there should be no tricks if the two friends valued their lives. He explained further that he'd done plenty of robberies and kidnaps in the past—enough to get him two hundred years of jail time if caught—and that he'd done jail time and had no intention of doing any more.

The scheme, as he outlined it, was simple. Rapini would be driven to an undisclosed location and held there until the ransom was paid. If everything went smoothly, Joe would be left unharmed in an automobile trunk where passersby surely would discover him—if he made enough noise. David Starr, for his part, was to enter the bank in the morning, collect the cash, then deliver the money as per handwritten instructions he'd receive later. Their captor drilled Rapini and Starr on these particulars several times before he was satisfied they understood their roles.

He next marched Starr downstairs and handcuffed him to a post, then returned to the first floor where he dictated several notes for Rapini to record in his handwriting. This required approximately fifteen minutes, after which he brought Starr upstairs again and allowed him a cigarette and a glass of Coke as they reviewed his instructions once more. The kidnapper also had found a roll of masking tape. Before returning Starr to the basement once again, he ordered him to gag himself and wrap his head with it, using the entire roll. It was now 11:30.

As David Starr sat alone in his basement, handcuffed, his head swathed in masking tape, he listened to the garage door open and close. It would be two hours before he heard another sound—the kidnapper returning for him through the sliding glass kitchen door. "Subject immediately came downstairs and removed the handcuffs," the FBI report continued.

> Subject then took Starr back to the first floor level of the house. Subject instructed Starr to remove the masking tape and pillowcase. . . . Subject allowed Starr to have a cigarette and something to drink and discussed with him what he was to do. Starr noted that the subject was not as calm as he had been earlier in the evening. Subject appeared to be less patient . . . Subject also stated to Starr, "I hope you don't panic like Joe did. We are having a hard time with him. He didn't want me to leave because he was afraid the other guy would kill him."

* * *

At about 3:00 A.M. the gunman directed David Starr out to the garage and into his gray Cordoba. They drove a short distance together before he stopped the car and ordered Starr to get out. Per the extortion plan, the banker was to walk back to his residence, retrieve the Cordoba, then drive himself to a parking lot across from Columbia Savings. There he'd wait for 8:30 and the opening of the vault. Once Starr had gathered the ransom, he was to look under a planter in front of the bank for further instructions.

David Starr did precisely as he was told, arriving at the appointed spot opposite the bank at 3:30 A.M. Fifteen minutes later, a small, white two-door automobile with what Starr took to be a woman at the wheel cruised past him. He saw what appeared to be the same car at about 5:00 A.M. and again at seven that morning.

Eighty minutes later, Starr walked into the bank, ready to collect the money the moment the vault opened. Working swiftly as he explained the situation to his stunned staff of tellers, he was able to collect $37,900 in twenty minutes, and was on his way out again, warning the others to do nothing until Joe Rapini called to say he was okay.

At 8:45, he read the note left for him in the planter. It directed Starr on a northerly course to the Ontario State Parkway where he was ordered to stop and retrieve a second message from his trunk. This note—in Joe Rapini's hand, as was the first—directed him to go west on the parkway. Driving on, Starr believed he again saw the small white car, its headlamps on, driving in the opposite direction. He took a left at Townline Road as indicated in the second note, and then proceeded another fifty feet until he came upon a burnt-out house on a garbage-strewn lot, with an old washing machine standing in the front yard near the road. It was next to the derelict appliance, according to his instructions, that David Starr left the ransom payment.

He immediately returned to the bank, arriving back in his office at 9:15. Approximately nine hours later, the police found Joe Rapini's Duster abandoned in the parking lot of a large apartment complex not far from 98 Applewood Drive. Joe Rapini was discovered in the trunk. He had sustained a severe beating about the head and face. But the cause of death was a .32-caliber bullet through his heart, one of two .32-caliber slugs recovered from his chest. Each had been fired from a different handgun. Subsequent forensic examination of the Duster's interior indicated that Rapini probably had been killed while sitting in the front passenger seat, and that three .32-caliber rounds were fired inside the vehicle, one of them into the dashboard. Further, it appeared that Rapini had been shot somewhere else, and then was driven, already dead, to the parking lot where he was found.

Although there had been suspects developed in the case, FBI agents Dillon and Harding immediately focused on Mike DeBardeleben, whose interest in banks and bankers was well established. He also fit David Starr's general physical description of the Rapini suspect, owned a ski mask that had been recovered by the Secret Service and, in his Mall Passer mode, had traveled extensively across upstate New York.

At Dillon and Harding's request, the task force consulted its extensive Mall Passer files and found that one of DeBardeleben's twenties was dropped at a drugstore across the street from David Starr's Columbia Savings Bank branch on May 26, 1981. Fifteen days later, the Greece Police Department gathered a fistful of the bills from local merchants. On April 11, 1983, two days before the Rapini murder, DeBardeleben passed another bogus twenty at a Gold Circle Store in Cheektowaga, New York, a western suburb of Buffalo, about seventy-five miles southwest of Greece.

The Secret Service provided the FBI agents a photo of DeBardeleben. A teller at Columbia Savings reportedly recognized him. "I have a little problem confirming that," says agent Harding of the FBI. "Let's just say it's not inconsistent." Harding adds that there is other, so far undisclosed, evidence that further suggests DeBardeleben's culpability for Joe Rapini's death. "He's definitely a prime suspect," says Harding.

The ransom money has never been recovered.

16

Moe

Mike DeBardeleben's father, also known as Mike, was born in 1906 in Georgetown, Texas, just north of Austin, and was raised in Brownsville, Texas, across the Rio Grande River from Matamorros, Mexico.

A stocky five-seven with a stiff bearing, reddish hair, and florid complexion, the elder DeBardeleben entered Texas A&M University at College Station in 1924, where he earned mostly C's and B's and a few A's on his way to a Bachelor's degree in civil engineering in 1928. Two years later, A&M awarded him his master's degree, also in civil engineering.

With the onset of the Depression, the young engineer took a job with the Texas Bureau of Public Roads in Fort Worth, where he met Mary Louise (known as Mary Lou) Edwards, a vivacious, five-four, 26-year-old legal secretary with twinkly hazel eyes, dark-blond hair and a come-hither shape. Young Miss Edwards was an eyeful.

And she cared deeply for him. "Mary," says her older sister, Evelyn Beal, "was just crazy about Mike. When they were going together they had an awful lot of fun. They went dancing every Saturday night. She was real happy then."

Evelyn Beal pauses. "You know, some people just ought not to get married. My sister should have stayed single. She and Mike were so different. She liked to have fun. He was a more serious type. He expected a wife to have dinner on the table at a certain time. He wanted the house immaculate, the children all washed and scrubbed. Mary wasn't that kind. She wasn't too interested in things like that."

Against Evelyn's better judgment—"They didn't ask me," says Beal—Mary Louise Edwards married Mike DeBardeleben in 1934. They started their family four years later in Little Rock, Arkansas, with the birth of a daughter, oddly named Michael Linda, who would be known as Linda. At 4:36 A.M. on Tuesday, March 19, 1940, after an extended labor, Linda's little brother, Mike, also was born in Little Rock. The DeBardelebens' third and last child, Ralph, was born twenty-one months later.

"I never did think my sister was just really happy after that," recollects Beal.

"Mike and I (and my brother, Ralph) had parents with problems," his sister Linda explained in a 1976 letter to J. Richard Faulkner, Jr., DeBardeleben's federal probation officer.

My mother, 10th and last child, lost her mother at birth and her father at 11. She was raised by many different relatives and her stepmother, but never felt loved. She wanted to be a "good mother" to her children but felt so unloved herself she could give us little confidence. She was an excellent stenographer and could play piano by ear and draw portraits quite well but she was never a good housekeeper or cook. She was happier at work in an office than at home. She drank periodically when pressures were too much for her and during these times we had no mother. (Fortunately, we had a live-in maid until I was 5, Mike 4.)

My father had a demanding mother and a strict upbringing and stuttered all his life. Before he went to college he had taken a speech course which taught him to control his stutter unless he was tired or under stress. His inability to express his feelings coupled with his high standards for himself and his family made everyone miserable (including himself). It was difficult to please him—he seldom praised anyone but would criticize often. Consequently, his wife and children were made to feel inadequate no matter how hard they tried to live up to his standards. . . . It makes me sad to know my parents never achieved a happy marriage, nor understood their children—they just didn't know how to solve their problems. . . .

Mike was a child with strong feelings and a temper like his Father . . . He played hard and enjoyed things intensely. He also wanted things his way. Because he was not as obedient as I, Mike was severely punished . . . He was made to sit in a corner for long periods. He had his head held under water to "cool him off" (which must have terrified him). He was spanked and he was switched with sticks—all before he was old enough to go to school or even know what was expected of him. My parents held my behavior up to him as an example. They labeled him a "bad boy" and would expect the worst from him.

Soon after Pearl Harbor, DeBardeleben, senior, took a second lieutenant's commission in the army and was posted to Washington, D.C., for the duration. According to his daughter, it was at this time that he realized his wife Mary Lou wasn't simply a periodic tippler. She was a sot. As a consequence, Lieutenant DeBardeleben began an affair with a woman in his office—Mrs. DeBardeleben knew of the liaison—and he considered a divorce. "However," wrote Linda, "my father felt strongly that a natural mother would love her children better than a stepmother—so he decided to stay married."

Mary Lou DeBardeleben kept drinking; at home alone, with another woman in the neighborhood and in taverns, which she sometimes visited with little Linda in tow. Her husband moved the family to Austin, Texas, in 1945, and then shipped to the South Pacific for nine months where he took part in the post-World War II U.S. atomic testing program.

"We were most neglected then," reported Linda of life in Austin.

"My mother was often drunk. I tried in a limited way to take care of my brothers. My memory isn't too clear, so I don't know how Mike was affected. I know I felt very alone. I walked to school, came home and fixed my lunch or took money for a school lunch while my mother was in bed. I would cook a few simple things for us like pancakes. Sometimes my mother took us to bars with her. I later learned she had affairs with men she met there. When my father returned and discovered the situation, he was so embarrassed he felt compelled to move. He reenlisted into the army and we went to Camp Campbell, Ky.

In 1949, DeBardeleben, by then a major and a battalion commander, transferred with his family from Kentucky to Frankfurt, West Germany. In 1950, he was promoted to lieutenant colonel and moved again, this time to The Hague in the Netherlands, where he served two years as a military advisor at the U.S. embassy.

"My two brothers never got along well," reported Linda,

but I had fights with them as well. I can remember taking up for Ralph only because he was younger and Mike was stronger ... Because we were not close to other Americans in Holland and couldn't speak Dutch we stayed close to each other, which was a disadvantage. When there are three children, one of them usually gets left out. Mike was left out a lot.

* * *

Her brother Mike's recollections generally conform to Linda's. "From an early age," he wrote Faulkner,

> I can recall wanting to please my parents but being frustrated by some of their unrealistic demands. While Linda and Ralph would seek escape from the turmoil of our early family life by playing outside for extended periods, I preferred to be alone in my room, with my artistic [interests]: drawing and sketching ships, cars, designs and cartoons. I derived much inner satisfaction at being able to express myself artistically, but my parents seemed to discourage me from developing this interest, probably because they felt it to be impractical in terms of a possible future profession. Thus I concentrated my efforts in more 'practical' directions, and while in school excelled academically ... until my sophomore year when I neglected my studies and began my 'acting out' behavior at age 16.

In 1953, Lieutenant Colonel DeBardeleben, 47, retired from the army and accepted a position with the Commerce Department's Federal Bureau of Public Roads in Albany, New York. His older son enrolled at Philip Livingstone Junior High School in Albany where his marks were excellent. As a second-semester eighth grader, for example, Mike received a 92 in English, a 95 in Social Studies, a 93 in Science, 89 in Algebra and a 79 in Spanish. His classroom deportment scores were high, as well. His marks for Appearance were perfect, and nearly so for Courtesy, Home Study and Initiative & Effort. His Reliability, by contrast, was uneven, and his report card suggests problems with Self-Control.

Then came high school.

"Matters got worse," wrote Linda. "Mike was threatened and beaten up by boys at school.... [He] must have stopped trying to please my father about the time that I went off to college [1955]. I lost track of what was happening."

According to his parents' later sworn complaint, in 1956 Mike DeBardeleben committed the first of what were to become routine physical assaults on his mother, whom he called Moe. Both his father and mother would tell authorities they feared their son was capable of murdering them.

On Saturday, September 8, 1956, Mike and a pal drove to Bennington, Vermont, where the teenagers purchased a .22-caliber Harrison & Richardson Model 922 revolver, and a .22-caliber Astra Auto Pistol, plus some ammo. It is unknown what the two boys intended to do with these weapons, but on Friday the 21st, at about 4:00 P.M., police patrolmen William Scheidel and Charles Shutter responded to a telephone complaint of gunfire in a wooded vicinity of Albany, where they arrested 16-year-old Mike DeBardeleben for carrying a concealed weapon. This was the first entry on his rap sheet.

The following May 13, 1957, a Monday, at 8:45 in the morning, he almost collided his '51 Chevy Coupe with a vehicle driven by Albany policeman George Lynch. DeBardeleben may, or may not, have intended to hit Lynch; details of the incident are lost. The encounter, however, did result in a second rap sheet notation: Reckless Driving.

For his mug shot he wore a leather jacket, dark-rimmed glasses, and a bored sneer.

When DeBardeleben also was expelled from Peter Schuyler High School that spring, his parents readily agreed to a then-common prescription for delinquent youth—the military. According to the arrangement, their son pleaded guilty to a reduced charge in the reckless driving case, and paid a small fine, while a local judge dismissed the previous autumn's gun charge altogether. In return, on June 26 Mike DeBardeleben joined the air force and was shipped to Lackland Air Force Base in Texas for his basic training.

Airman DeBardeleben's military career was brief. After basic, he was transferred to Scott Air Force Base in Illinois where, in March 1958, he was court-martialed for a variety of offenses ranging from wearing "Improper Insignia and Improper Uniform" to disorderly behavior. Sentence: Two months in the stockade and $155 in pay forfeited.

In June, DeBardeleben again was cited, serially, for "Unauthorized Absence from Bed Check," "Breaking Restrictions" (twice) and being "Disrespectful to Superiors." Besides more time in detention and another fine, he was ordered to visit an air force psychiatrist. The doctor's report described

> a verbose young man of superior intelligence who gave an extensive history of repetitive acts of [an] egocentric and antisocial nature dating back several years. He has developed a maladjustment principally in terms of character and behavior in which he approaches interpersonal relationships with a self-centered suspicious attitude that leaves little room for consideration of others, for pangs of conscience, or for profit from his mistakes. His character and behavior disorder makes the prognosis for sustained satisfactory military service extremely guarded.

In August, DeBardeleben was discharged from the air force "Under Other Than Honorable Conditions" and moved to Forth Worth where his parents had bought a small, two-bedroom ranch-style tract house at 3920 Spurgeon Street. His sister Linda long since had left home. Shortly after Mike's arrival his younger brother Ralph dropped out of high school, left his parent's house, and joined the army.

Mike was 18, nearly grown to his full adult height, six feet, and weighed about 160 pounds. His hair was a somewhat darker brown than the irises of his even-set, myopic (20/225) eyes. His complexion was pale, and he had two distinguishing marks, a small mole on his upper left lip and an irregularity at the bridge of his nose, a souvenir of boyhood nasal surgery.

DeBardeleben lived at home and worked for a time at various jobs, from pumping gas to selling men's clothing, but he made it clear that he considered long-term gainful employment beneath him. "He was a timid little boy when he was really young," said his aunt, Mrs. Beal, "a sweet l'il ol' kid. When he got a little older, I remember he could be very charming and I also remember him telling me that he did not intend to work hard for a living. 'I'm not gonna get an old job from eight to five,' he said. 'I'm going to have money when I grow up.'"

In January of 1959 DeBardeleben enrolled at R. L. Pachal High School in Fort Worth, and was expelled in March. In August he married Linda Wier, a Fort Worth teenager. They separated three weeks later.

On October 5, 1959, at approximately 3:30 A.M., DeBardeleben and an accomplice attempted to rob the Ecco Service Station on East Rosedale Street in Fort Worth. With his partner waiting at the wheel of their car, DeBardeleben pulled a paper bag over his head and approached the night-shift attendant, 29-year-old Henry Swearengen, pistol in hand. "Swearengen," reported the *Fort Worth Star-Telegram,*

who had been robbed three times before, told police he knew what was coming and started to take his money out of his pants pocket. The would-be robber apparently thought the attendant was going for a gun and fired through a plate-glass window at Swearengen, jumped back into his car and fled. Pieces of the bullet pierced Swearengen's jacket but he was uninjured.

The other youth confessed his and DeBardeleben's complicity in the failed holdup when the pair was arrested two weeks later for a string of auto thefts. Some of the cars had been stripped for salable parts. Others were vandalized. One, a brand-new Corvette, had been shoved into Fort Worth's Lake Benbrook. Police divers found it in twenty feet of water. DeBardeleben was sentenced to five years probation in the case.

That November, his premature baby daughter was stillborn at Northwest Hospital. By Christmas, Linda Wier DeBardeleben had seen the last of her husband, who in the meantime had begun wooing a pretty 17-year-old high school girl, Charlotte Weber,* the eldest of three daughters in the family of a Fort Worth railroad engineer. Blue-eyed, five-five, with dark brown hair and not a lot of common sense, Charlotte fell in love with Mike DeBardeleben. "I was enthralled," she says. "I really, really was at the time. He was a very beautiful man, a handsome young rebel, something to pursue, something to make into the ideal husband, settle down with him and do whatever you're supposed to do for the rest of your life."

Charlotte also recalls Mike's abundant vanity, the time he spent in front of mirrors, adjusting his look, sometimes highlighting it with makeup, using eyebrow pencil. "He was very careful about his appearance," she says, "especially his hair. He was combing it all the time. Mike was a person who *hated* the idea of growing old."

His parents still feared him. "He lit fires in his room," she says. "He kicked doors in. He knocked the walls in. These were things his mother and daddy would tell me. But they weren't trying to turn me against him in any way. I had the impression from his family they were looking for somebody to take him off their hands, and I don't blame them."

The Webers disliked Mike even more. "My daddy *detested* him," she says. Charlotte nevertheless became pregnant by DeBardeleben in her parents' house in March 1960, the night of her senior prom. On June 9, 1960, she and Mike were married, also at her parents'. The couple's first home was a garage apartment at 3127 Lubbock Street in Fort Worth.

Charlotte soon was acquainted with Mike the family man. "He immediately lost interest in me," she says. "He was not abusive, though. I don't want you to think he was. And I don't want you to think that he wasn't abusive because he had any feelings for me. It was just that he didn't care one way or the other whether I existed. So I went back to my parents."

Their daughter, Bethene,* was born on December 12, 1960, and for the next several weeks, at her father's insistence, Charlotte and the baby lived with her in-laws on Spurgeon Street. She describes Mary Lou DeBardeleben as frumpy and forlorn. Moe had red-dyed hair, a ruined figure, mottled, parchmentlike skin and the lost look of the hopeless alcoholic in her sad, brimming eyes. Charlotte pitied the older woman, who seemed pathetically intent on trying to please her ill-tempered boy. "She always tried to get along with Mike," says Charlotte. "She showed me how to fix eggs sunny-side up, the way he liked them."

Weber has no recollection of ever actually seeing Mary Lou DeBardeleben intoxicated, or even taking a drink, although "Mike and his father were always accusing her of it," she says. "I think the only time I ever saw them in cahoots was when they ganged up against her, accusing her of drinking—pushing her toward it, really, I think. If she tried to assert herself, or become anything but the odd person out, it was always thrown in her face. 'Well, we need to go look for Mama's bottle.' I remember Mike once saying he was going to go up on the roof looking for Mama's bottle.'"

Mike abandoned Charlotte and the baby, then came visiting one more time. "He came over to the house," Charlotte recalls. "My mother was upstairs. I think

Bethene was asleep in her bassinet. So we got to messing around, and that's all it took. Our second baby girl was conceived in the back room on a tacky old red velvet sofa."

Charlotte was forced by her parents to give up her second daughter for adoption, "because I couldn't afford to keep her." In September 1961, Charlotte and Mike DeBardeleben finally were divorced.

A month earlier, 19-year-old Ralph DeBardeleben, home on leave from the army, drove his car to a church parking lot, ran a hose from its exhaust into the sealed interior, and turned on the engine.

Evelyn Beal remembers that Ralph signaled his imminent self-destruction. "My sister Mary had a friend who was worried about him," she says. "He talked to her. He wouldn't talk to Mary. And she said, 'You better watch out. There's something bothering Ralph.' Mary said, 'Oh, that's foolish. There's nothing serious about it.'"

Ralph DeBardeleben was not the only suicide in the family. His father's sister, Cherelle Patterson, a schoolteacher and mature mother of three, would also take her own life. Mike DeBardeleben later blamed Ralph's death on the same dysfunctional home life that he believed had shaped him. "My younger brother," he wrote to Richard Faulkner, the probation officer,

was an introverted, sensitive, withdrawn person who reacted to his early emotionally deprived childhood and family instability with apparent total conformity to his environment.

Evidently, his inability and/or unwillingness to show anger or rebellion, caused his emotions to become so withdrawn and "bottled up" that following a severe depression he experienced while in the army, he committed suicide. . . .

Although I have sought to understand the reasons for his suicide and can point to his difficulties with . . .

rigorous paratrooper training along with the rejection of a girlfriend as possible reasons, I suppose they were merely catalysts for his final act.

In retrospect, I feel that Ralph was just emotionally so crippled by his early environment that he simply could not cope with the adversity of life without some professional assistance, which he never received. At the time, none of us were knowledgeable or perceptive enough to recognize his need for support, until it was too late.

On Sunday, August 13, 1961, the *Fort Worth Press* ran this account of Ralph DeBardeleben's death:

SOLDIER, 19, ENDS LEAVE BY TAKING OWN LIFE A 19-year-old soldier, who told his teen-age sister he wasn't going back to the Army when his leave was up, kept his word yesterday by taking his own life. Ralph DeBardeleben, on a 12-day leave from Ft. Benning, Ga., was found in his parked 1956 car by patrolman B.N. Bliss. . . . DeBardeleben was due back at Ft. Benning next Wednesday. He had been staying at a motel during his leave due to an argument with an older brother. He told his . . . sister Friday night that he wasn't going back. . . .

17

Sociopath

In 1961 and '62, Mike DeBardeleben made several attempts to resume his education. Beginning in the summer of '61 when Texas Christian University in Fort Worth granted him a special dispensation to enroll without a high school diploma, he alternatively attended TCU and North Texas State University in neighboring Denton, with indifferent results. He took business courses, some English, and a smattering of other subjects including French and psychology. After two years, Debardeleben was a second-semester freshman with a D+ average. Then, in September 1962, his probation on the auto-theft sentence was revoked and Mike DeBardeleben found himself doing hard time in the Texas state prison at Huntsville.

Incarceration worked no evident improvements in his character. After eight months in Huntsville, DeBardeleben was paroled into the custody of his parents, who had relocated again, to Arlington, Virginia. The DeBardelebens undoubtedly were chary of allowing their violent and bitter son back into their presence. They soon had concrete reason for wishing he'd remained behind bars.

According to a complaint that his father filed with Arlington County authorities in late March 1964, Mike terrorized his parents from the moment he arrived home. He was, reported the senior DeBardeleben, obsessed with carnality in various manifestations, and had been for some time. His insatiable sexual appetite led Mike to hookers, from whom he'd contracted gonorrhea. He demanded money, special food and clothing, said his father, as well as a movie projector so that he could screen pornographic movies in his room as he recovered from a series of illnesses, including hepatitis, mononucleosis, and prostatitis.

This bout of illness apparently signaled the onset of chronic ill health, especially a painfully recurrent case of colitis, that would devil DeBardeleben throughout his adult life. It also marked the beginning of his outward physical deterioration, a galling affront to his towering vanity. Though barely into his mid-twenties, pain and sickness—doubtlessly exacerbated by drug dependency—began inexorably to hollow DeBardeleben's eyes and to line his face. His smooth complexion turned chalky and pitted. His torso withered. In time his gait, once almost a swagger, would slow to the tentative shuffle of the persistently unwell.

As he convalesced, Mike diverted himself by reading psychiatry and psychology texts and by photographing nude models. If either of his parents raised an objection, he threatened their lives, especially that of Mrs. DeBardeleben, who remained a special target of her son's verbal and physical abuse. According to her husband, Mike once menaced Moe with a letter opener, and another time with a hatchet. It was the night that he went after her with a razor that his father finally summoned the county sheriff. A few days later his son was sent to Western State Hospital in Staunton, Virginia, for psychiatric observation.

At Staunton, where DeBardeleben would spend forty-five days under evaluation, the professional staff found no evidence of organic pathology, depression, or psychosis. One senior psychiatrist would recall the patient's unwillingness to accept responsibility for his behavior, as well as DeBardeleben's startling claim—in light of his history—that he was considering a career in clinical psychology.

This doctor, who interviewed DeBardeleben a few days before his release and after his father dropped assault charges, concluded—as had the Air Force psychiatrist—that his patient was not mentally ill. Mike DeBardeleben, thought the physician, was antisocial and a sociopath and therefore probably not a likely candidate for psychotherapy. Jail, noted the psychiatrist, might be the most appropriate setting for DeBardeleben.

On May 16, 1964, his father drove out to the hospital to take his son home.

Four months later, Mike married again; this time to an elfin beauty, nineteen-year-old cosmetology student Wanda Faye Davis, from rural Tazewell, in extreme southwestern Virginia. Faye Davis had come to Washington, D.C., in flight from the oppressive small-town mentality of Tazewell. According to her daughter, Lindsey*, Faye's intense distaste for life in Tazewell manifested itself in a recurrent dream. Ma and Pa Kettle would chase Faye to a cliff where she'd jump rather than be caught by the hillbillies. "That was her idea of Tazewell," says Lindsey. "She was *dying* to get out of there."

Agents Foos and Stephens found Faye, who had returned to Tazewell with Lindsey in the early 1970s, and was living there in a trailer with her daughter, then thirteen. Faye at one time had been the unblemished embodiment of innocent loveliness. However, though not yet forty, she long since had lost the rare comeliness and remarkable figure of her youth. Puffy and lumpy, she looked physically spent to Foos and Stephens. A local state trooper had told them that Faye worked from time to time as a truck stop hooker, although she insisted in the interview that she was employed as a nurse, and that was how she supported herself and her daughter.

It was clear from the outset that Faye, too, had been a victim. Her story shocked and revolted Foos and

Stephens, who asked if she would repeat it under oath. With considerable apprehension born of a terror that her incarcerated former husband could somehow avenge himself on her and Lindsey, Faye agreed to answer a subpoena.

"When I met him I had just turned nineteen," she testified. "Emotionally, I was probably fifteen or sixteen. He was very sophisticated, very nice looking, very well dressed, very flattering. I had never met a man like this. I had never been in a nice restaurant. I had no insight in dealing with people like him. I believed everything I was told. At that time, I believed everybody was good and honest and that you could see a crook on the street and that you would recognize him. I believed this."

Soon after the wedding, Faye continued, "He gradually led me into taking nude photographs, and then they became worse and worse and worse. He eventually had pictures of me engaged with him in various sex acts. He had pictures of me tied up and him hurting me."

Once his young wife was thoroughly compromised, DeBardeleben proposed she assist him in his "Mr. Benson" bank examiner scam. "I didn't want to do it," Faye explained. "He told me then that he would send the pictures to my family and to my hometown. I was very young. I was very gullible. I believed him. Therefore, after a lot of talking and a lot of coercion and a lot of threats to me, I did agree."

As Faye explained it, the flimflam would begin in a new town with scouting trips through older residential neighborhoods—"not ultra rich or ultra poor," she said, "but older, nice," areas where DeBardeleben could reasonably expect to find a lot of widows. They'd mark down the street names, then head for the public library where Faye culled the city directory for names of women who lived on those streets. Next, she would telephone them.

"I could find out whether or not these people were elderly, whether or not they were living alone, whether or not they had someone they counted on for advice," Faye said. "These elderly ladies were quite often lonely. They would talk to you forever if you let them. They volunteered a lot of information. I could even find out what bank they banked at, quite often."

Out of these conversations, her husband would select the likeliest marks, and make his calls to them two or three days later. If he succeeded in persuading one of the older women actually to withdraw her money and then go home to wait for him, "within ten or fifteen minutes Mike would knock on her door. He was dressed up in a business suit. He would flash a badge and ID that said 'Federal Bank Examiner.' Nobody ever examined that very closely."

According to Faye, the bank examiner jobs began in late 1965 and continued for approximately eighteen months. She guessed they pulled between twenty-five and thirty of the scams altogether, in several states. On the average, the take was about $1,200, but varied from as little as $800 to as much as $3,500.

Faye also was familiar with far darker deeds. In 1966, DeBardeleben, along with Faye's cousin, was charged by the Prince George's County, Maryland, police with the assault, sodomy, and kidnap of a young girl. The assault charges were later dropped; at trial DeBardeleben and his co-defendant were found not guilty of the other counts.

"The reason they were acquitted," Faye remembered being told by Mike's lawyer, "was because the girl did get into the car with them willingly. . . . The jury just took it all together and because they didn't think the girl was kidnapped they just acquitted them on all of it."

"Did your husband ever talk to you about desiring to actually kill women?" she was asked.

"Yes," Faye answered. "This was his big thing in

life. He hated his mother tremendously. To him, all women were whores, sluts, tramps. They asked for what they got, and they deserved what they got. His greatest thing that he could have ever thought about was to abduct a woman, torture her, have various sexual activities go on, strangle her and watch her die, or blow her brains out with a gun. Then he would hide her so that if she was ever found there would be no evidence of who had done it and it would be the perfect crime."

In April 1969, Faye continued, she was Mike's accomplice in a kidnap-extortion. She testified that for two months her husband had surveilled Edgar W. Smith, Jr., an American National Bank branch manager in Wheaton, Maryland. DeBardeleben recorded Smith's comings and goings from the family residence at 3707 Fairly Street in Wheaton, as well as Smith's work routine at the bank. On Friday, April 25, Mike was ready to strike.

That morning, he stole a set of license plates and placed them on his car. Faye was dispatched to a Giant Food Store parking lot adjacent to the bank and told to keep an eye out for Smith. If everything went according to plan, he told her, the banker would pull into the lot at about two o'clock and place a brown paper bag beneath his car. Faye was to recover the sack, then meet Mike at a prearranged location.

At about 1:30 that afternoon DeBardeleben knocked on the Smiths' front door, and was greeted there by the banker's wife, Mary. He flashed a silver badge, told her that he was a U.S. Secret Service agent and "that he wanted to talk to her about her husband and some things that were going on up at the bank," said Faye. "She let him in."

Inside, DeBardeleben pulled a gun on the frightened woman, locked the front door and threw her to the floor, where he handcuffed her and covered her mouth and eyes with adhesive tape. A moment later Mrs.

Smith heard him telephone someone he called "Joe," with instructions to proceed as planned.

DeBardeleben then telephoned Edgar Smith at the bank, announcing himself as "Dr. Freeman from Holy Cross Hospital." When Smith, who knew no such physician, came to the phone, DeBardeleben was brutally abrupt. "Listen," he told the banker, "we got your wife in a motel and we will kill her if you don't do what I say. Take $60,000 from the bank to the Wheaton Library and put it in the men's room."

He removed the tape from Mary Smith's mouth and put her on the line. "Honey!" she sobbed, DeBardeleben's gun at her throat. "They have a gun and are going to kill me if you don't give them the money!" Smith asked where his wife was being held, but there was no answer. All DeBardeleben would say is that the money better be in the library men's room within seven minutes.

Smith dropped the phone and raced over to Irene Hagen, his head teller.

"Gimme $60,000!" he shouted.

"You must be kidding," Hagen replied.

"Gimme $60,000! They have my wife in a motel and they are going to kill her!"

Hagen had just half that amount, which Smith grabbed. He scooped another $4,000 in twenties from teller Suzanne Kershner's cash box, then bolted out the door to his car, where he discovered an envelope that Faye had stuck in the window. "Disregard Previous Instructions" it read. Inside, a second message instructed Smith to reach beneath his car where he'd find a brown bag in which he was to deposit the ransom. The note further directed that, instead of the library, Smith was to drive around the corner to the Giant Food Store parking lot, position his car in the lot's very center, place the brown paper bag of money beneath the vehicle, and walk away.

While he was doing so, back at 3707 Fairly Street

DeBardeleben dragged Mrs. Smith into the kitchen and barricaded her there before leaving the house. Though blinded, gagged, and handcuffed, Mary Smith managed to struggle outside to the street where a neighbor came to her aid.

Faye meanwhile retrieved the money and rendez-voused with Mike. They drove southwest for hours across Virginia, past Tazewell into the mountains around Marion, a tiny burg just off I-81 near Virginia's Hungry Mother State Park. "There was a little shed on the left-hand side of the road," Faye testified. "It was visible from the road, but it was sort of set down underneath the road. We took the money into that little shed and we dug the ground up and buried it in glass jars."

"Do you know if Mr. DeBardeleben ever successfully retrieved that?"

"I know he got $8,000 from it at one time. I don't know if he ever got the rest. I would imagine that he did."

"While you were married to DeBardeleben, did he ever talk to you about law-enforcement agencies, about his feeling that he could never get caught?"

"He really thought he was omnipotent, that he was God. He thought all law-enforcement agents were turkeys and ignorant and that he would outsmart anyone of them, especially local police. . . . These were local yokels to him. The FBI and Secret Service held no threat to him. He wasn't afraid because he was smarter and slicker than they were."

"Did he arm himself?"

"He carried guns constantly. He had what I call an arsenal. He was never without a handgun, never. He had German Lugars, a .357, .38 Specials, Browning automatics, .22 pistols. And not just one of each! He had several of each kind and probably some that I cannot even remember."

Faye told of DeBardeleben showing her photos he'd

taken of women as he sexually abused them. When she threatened to go to the police, "I was tied to the bed. Sexual atrocities that I will not mention to you were performed upon me. It even hurts to think about it."

She recalled cutting her wrist in one attempt to get away. "I was hysterical," she testified. "I begged the doctor to call the police. I begged them not to send me home with Mike. I told them what would happen. My husband was very glib . . . The doctor sent me home with him.

"You don't know the meaning of being beaten up. I am not talking about somebody taking their fist and beating you black and blue. We are talking about things being done to you that you wouldn't believe."

"How did you finally end up getting away from Mr. DeBardeleben?"

"It got to the point where I didn't really care what happened to me anymore, and I didn't care what happened to him. But the real turning point was this: I got pregnant and we were living on South Columbus Street at the time. He pushed me down the stairs, and I had a miscarriage.

"It wasn't very long after that until I got pregnant again. My husband wanted me to have an abortion, which I would not do. I left him. Being pregnant and going to be responsible for somebody else seemed to be all I needed to get away from him. I no longer cared about the pictures. I was very much afraid of him physically, but I was not really afraid of him emotionally anymore. He had done about as much damage to me mentally as he could."

Faye discovered her second pregnancy shortly after the Smith extortion case. She was granted a Mexican divorce in August of 1969 and bore her full-term baby girl, Lindsey, at George Washington University Hospital in Washington, D.C., on Friday, January 2, 1970. "I went back to work very soon after she was born," Faye testified. "At one point he came to my apartment and

I [wouldn't] let him in. He pushed his way in and he tried to rape me. He would have done so had I not screamed loud enough to rouse the manager of the building who banged on my door. Mike stopped what he was trying to do, and he left. He did come back to the apartment a few times after that with his new wife to see the baby."

DeBardeleben had begun pursuing his fourth wife, Caryn, even before Faye left him. He first accosted the schoolgirl on a suburban Virginia street, asking directions to the community pool. From that moment on, says her attorney, Greg Murphy, of Alexandria, DeBardeleben was a constant presence in Caryn's life, expertly manipulating the impressionable girl.

That autumn, the beginning of Caryn's senior year, he left roses each day in her car, and paid her the constant, courtly attention with which naive high school girls such as Caryn have no experience and little defense. Still, says Murphy, his client successfully resisted DeBardeleben's advances until the following spring, when Mike was seriously injured in a motorcycle accident. Confined as he was with several broken bones to a rented hospital bed, his helplessness touched Caryn.

Although her parents (like Charlotte Weber's) had issued stern warnings that she should stay away from him, Caryn and a friend took turns caring for DeBardeleben. When her mother finally ordered her to avoid DeBardeleben entirely, Caryn, upset, secretly visited him anyway. Expert at exploiting weak moments, DeBardeleben then posed marriage (which he'd already proposed several times before) as the only answer to the impasse. On July 10, 1970 at age eighteen, Caryn became the fourth Mrs. James Mitchell DeBardeleben II in Silver Springs, Maryland.

Her husband returned to college again, spending a semester at George Mason University, where he took courses in philosophy, history, government, and elementary Spanish, in which he earned an A. Meantime, as Greg Murphy tells the story, DeBardeleben systematically subjected Caryn to the same degradation and duress he'd practiced on Faye, stripping the girl of her self-respect and isolating her from her family.

By then he had the process thoroughly thought through—and commited to paper. "If he is to come out a winner," DeBardeleben wrote,

[a man] *must be aware of all this:*
—*Get his satisfaction early*
—*Isolate her contacts with others*
—*Don't let her make* _any_ *decisions*
—*Don't her acquire any skills (working, driving, social skills, etc.)*
—*Don't let her have any power (bank accounts, ownership, inside information—material for blackmail.)*
—_Never_ *trust her completely*
—*Don't "enlighten" her with knowledge (especially of psychology)*
—*Always remember that the relationship is* _temporary_ + *likewise prepare to "cut her loose" before she does it to you*
—*Set the "price" higher than needed at first; whip, infidelity, extreme humiliation—then gradually reduce to keep at an adequate level.*
—*Actively seek a "new" partner when she begins showing signs of rebellion.*
—*Make her more dependent: drugs? Live in country, no phone (or hidden—for my use only) no drivers license, no books (except fantasy) no fancy clothes, no doctors.*
—_Never_ *show weakness, guilt or insecurity.*

In time, DeBardeleben coerced Caryn, as he had Faye, into becoming his accomplice in crime. Faye, who left the Washington area for Richmond, Virginia, testified that she saw the DeBardelebens intermittently

Outrageous, cruel and inhuman: Mike DeBardeleben
in mug shots from 1966, 1976, 1980, and 1983.

The DeBardeleben Family, Christmas 1953.

Mike and his mother ("Moe"): A "textbook case" of love-hate.

DeBardeleben's high school arrest photos.

ABOVE: Mike with Charlotte and their first daughter, Bethene.

LEFT: Wanda Faye Davis, the third Mrs. DeBardeleben. "To him," she testified, "all women were whores, sluts, tramps. They asked for what they got."

Terry Macdonald: A fatal resemblance to Moe?

Jean McPhaul: She and the other realtors were DeBardeleben's perfect victims.

Elizabeth Mason: Near death from strangulation, she underwent an out-of-body experience.

Lori Cobert-Hubbard: "I was going to do whatever it took to survive."

Mike "Stretch" Stephens was determined to put DeBardeleben on death row.

Dennis Foos was an inveterate worrier. "God," he thought early in the investigation, "I hope we're not barking up the wrong tree."

Greg Mertz, the junior member of the task force, was also the only one of the three with experience investigating violent crime.

Willingboro, New Jersey, police detective Don Cramer bucked his own department, and the prosecutor's office, to pursue DeBardeleben.

Detective Doug Payne's efforts led to a capital indictment in Bossier City, Louisiana. However, DeBardeleben would never be tried for killing Jean McPhaul.

The Secret Service seized 144 cardboard boxes of evidence from DeBardeleben's two mini-storage lockers. Along with stacks of hard-core pornography, women's bloodstained clothing, and a huge volume of handwritten notes, the agents found handguns, drugs, stolen license tags, hundreds of roadmaps, and carefully sorted quantities of the suspect's counterfeit twenties.

Artist James S. Rucker's definitive Mall Passer sketch, completed one year before DeBardeleben's ultimate arrest.

Mike DeBardeleben, in an unaccustomed pose, at the Lewisburg Federal Penitentiary in 1990. He has 365 years yet to serve.

Then–Treasury Secretary Jim Baker presenting department awards to agents Stephens, Mertz, Foos, and Jones ("Pete") Allison, who collared DeBardeleben near Knoxville, Tennessee.

in the early 1970s. "He came down there with his wife," she remembered, "and he bragged he was involved in the bank examiner's game again, and that his wife was his partner. She tried to get him to shut up. She was very nervous. She was very upset. I felt real sorry for her."

PART
THREE

18

A Sleazy Guy

Friday, August 5, 1983, Mike Stephens initiated the search for Caryn with a call to her attorney. He told Greg Murphy that DeBardeleben had been rearrested and that Caryn's ex-husband appeared to be a serious suspect in a number of atrocious sex assaults. As Stephens spoke with Murphy, he summoned Caryn in his mind's eye, remembering from seven years earlier her wild agitation at the mention of sex crimes. The agent was not surprised to hear from Murphy that Caryn was seeing doctors, and still was in precarious psychological condition. "Frankly," he says, "it would not have surprised me if Murphy had said, 'Oh, she committed suicide three years ago.'" Stephens at the time did not disclose to Murphy the content—or even the existence—of the "Caryn" audiotape.

Greg Murphy (Stanford '69, University of Virginia Law School '72) recalls that he had only just hung out his shingle in 1975 when Caryn's family came to him for help. They explained she had an abusive husband from whom Caryn recently had fled, and that they wished Murphy to handle both her divorce and a secret relocation for the frightened woman.

Murphy, though a young lawyer, already was handling several cases that involved extreme interpersonal behavior. Unusual clients were usual for him. One estranged wife had alleged she found her husband fornicating with a German shepherd. Another woman divulged to Murphy that she'd fellated a top local law-enforcement official in the expectation of winning leniency for her recently incarcerated husband. Still a third woman, also a client, was the battered spouse of a wealthy area business leader. She'd repeatedly attempted suicide leaps from the Memorial Bridge over the Potomac River. Years later, Murphy would represent John Wayne Bobbitt, the Manassas resident whose penis was surgically reattached after Bobbitt's wife, Lorena, severed the member with a kitchen knife. Greg Murphy is well accustomed to the uglier side of human nature.

Caryn DeBardeleben, though patently terrified of Mike, had been reticent to disclose to her lawyer the real reasons why. "The impression she gave me," says Murphy, "was of a sleazy guy who had an appealing side, but that he became progressively more sleazy and abusive. However, the extent of the abuse, as it was described to me, was minimal. Certainly no torture or beatings."

After speaking to Stephens, the attorney contacted Caryn and explained the situation to her, emphasizing that Mike was securely locked up—again. "I realized she needed to cooperate," he says, "needed to get this guy off the streets forever. This was going to be difficult with her never-ending fear. And I also had to negotiate on other fronts. The Secret Service. The U.S. Attorney for immunity. Her family, and her psychiatrist. All of these people had to be in agreement before I could go ahead, get the immunity, then have her sit down and divulge the details."

Murphy debriefed Caryn, who amazed him with her descriptions of violent felonies dating back to her first year of marriage to DeBardeleben, offenses that she'd previously kept completely secret. Dennis Foos remembers noting plain astonishment in Murphy's voice on Tuesday, August 23, when he personally called on the lawyer at his Alexandria office to hear what Murphy might have learned.

Speaking from interview notes he'd written on a legal pad in green ink, Greg Murphy outlined for Foos six crimes that Caryn had been willing—and able—to discuss with her lawyer. The first occurred at 1:35 P.M. on Friday, April 30, 1971, no more than fourteen hours after Realtor Terry Macdonald was murdered in Barrington, Rhode Island.

According to Caryn, she and Mike DeBardeleben went to Springfield, Virginia, that day. While she waited at a pay phone, DeBardeleben drove to 7511 Elgar Street, the residence of Robert H. Campbell, Jr., a vice-president of the United Virginia Bank branch office in Springfield, and Campbell's wife, Gayle. Mrs. Campbell answered DeBardeleben's knock at her front door, and encountered a man she'd later describe to Fairfax County police investigator L. G. Smith as about six feet tall, wearing "a black stub small-brimmed Stetson-type hat, black business suit, white shirt, dark tie, and a small rectangular mustache, very black (possibly fake)." His prominent dark sideburns looked fake, too.

DeBardeleben introduced himself as a Secret Service agent and flashed a credential. He told Mrs. Campbell that he was investigating one of her former neighbors, a man named Aaron Salter, and that he'd like to show her some photos. Gayle Campbell invited DeBardeleben into her living room.

"At this time," wrote officer Smith,

he displayed a folder containing four photographs, asking Mrs. Campbell if she had seen Mr. Salter associate with any of the four subjects displayed. Mrs. Campbell then advised that she had not. At this time, the subject picked up a small zipper type attache case he was carrying and produced a pistol believed to be an automatic, calibre unknown. At this time, Mrs.

Campbell started to resist by screaming and fighting. The subject placed his hand over her mouth and told her to remain quiet, that he did not want to hurt her in any way. Mrs. Campbell was made to lie on the floor of the living room. . . . The subject placed handcuffs on the victim . . . The subject then proceeded to take adhesive tape, placing it over the victim's eyes and mouth. She was then advised to get up and walk into the dining room where she was made to lie on the floor. The subject then called the United Virginia Bank, asking for Mr. Campbell. When Mr. Campbell came to the phone, [the subject] acted as though it was a bad connection, and hung up. The subject then called an accomplice, advising the accomplice that he had three minutes to place the envelope on the side of Mr. Campbell's car. . . .

The Campbell extortion unfolded nearly exactly as had the earlier Smith case with Faye. After receiving her husband's call at the pay phone, Caryn taped the envelope to the side of Robert Campbell's car while Mike, still at the Campbell residence, called the bank vice-president again. DeBardeleben told him that his wife was being held in a motel, and that it would cost the United Virginia Bank $65,000 to ransom her. Instead of a library men's room, this time the money was to be driven to a shopping center and placed in a phone booth near a Grand Union grocery store. He allowed Campbell a few words on the telephone with Mrs. Campbell, then told him he had just seven minutes to save Gayle's life. After hanging up, DeBardeleben ripped the Campbell's home telephone from the wall, tied Mrs. Campbell's feet with a length of venetian-blind cord and departed.

At the bank, Mr. Campbell managed to find $32,500 in cash. As before, the note taped to his car told Campbell to ignore his previous instructions and to drive, instead, to a local real estate office where he was to park alongside a stockade fence, place the money (and the note) under his vehicle and walk away. Caryn retrieved the bag of money unnoticed.

DeBardeleben used some of the proceeds from the Campbell extortion to bankroll his first, and last, semilegitimate business, a nude photo-modelling service called the Naked Eye on the corner of 14th and I Streets in Washington, D.C.'s downtown red-light district. The shop opened Saturday, March 4, 1972, and welcomed among its very first visitors reporter Jerry Oppenheimer from *The Washington Daily News*. Under the headline, PICTURE THIS: RENT-A-NUDE, Oppenheimer painted a gritty, downtown Saturday morning street scene of "pornography hustlers," dirty bookstores' "groggy habitues" and topless joints whose open doors "exuded a bad breath of booze and butts from the night before. . . ."

> "It's opening day at 'The Naked Eye,' the district's first nude model studio. At 'The Naked Eye,' amateur photographers can rent amateur models and amateur cameras for up to an hour of what the proprietor bills as 'artist' picture-taking. "In the next year or so a half dozen places like this will be in the downtown area," predicts the affable, intense young man behind The Naked Eye, Mike DeBardeleben. "It'll be like the adult bookstores—it'll catch on like wildfire. I dropped out of college, gave up plans to become a lawyer because I see the tremendous possibilities."

The Naked Eye was a flop. The police raided the place and arrested DeBardeleben twice on gun charges before he closed the money-losing operation and went back to more familiar and (usually) remunerative criminal pursuits. On the afternoon of May 16, 1973, a Wednesday, Raymond Trythall, an officer of the Citizen's Bank in Rockville, Maryland, received a call from a phone booth informing him that his wife,

Carolyn, and the couple's two-year-old daughter, Kelly Lynn, were being held hostage. If he wanted to see his wife and child alive, Trythall was to take $75,000 of the bank's money, drive to a specified telephone booth, and there await a second call.

DeBardeleben, acting alone on this extortion, had forced his way into the Trythall residence and hand-cuffed Carolyn Trythall to her bed. After securing Mrs. Trythall, he tape-recorded her plea for help, gagged her with adhesive tape, and then left the house to telephone her husband, for whom DeBardeleben played the tape listing his demands.

Raymond Trythall selected just $200 in marked bills—the threshold take for grand theft—stuffed them in a canvas bag and headed for his car where he found DeBardeleben's signature second note. This time, it directed the banker to drive down an alley behind the bank, stop and to toss the money bag over a tall fence. Although Trythall was instructed to wait five more minutes before returning to the bank, he went back at once and telephoned the FBI. Mike DeBardeleben retrieved the bag himself and fled as bureau agents were dispatched to the Trythall house, where they found Carolyn Trythall gagged and bound to her bed, shaken but not physically harmed. Kelly Lynn lay bawling in her crib.

Greg Murphy continued reciting to Dennis Foos from his green-ink notes. He said DeBardeleben took Caryn to Fort Worth, where they lived on Spurgeon Street with his widowed mother, Mary Lou, until her death from cancer in September 1973. During this period, Caryn returned briefly to Washington for a surgical procedure, and was there recuperating one night when she received a telephone call from Texas.

It was Mike, who demanded that she get on a plane at once. There had been some sort of crisis that alleg-edly involved his dying mother—DeBardeleben wouldn't be any more specific than that—and he needed Caryn in Fort Worth that night.

Although barely out of surgery, Caryn dressed and headed for National Airport where she caught the next available flight. When she landed that night and did not find Mike waiting for her at the Dallas–Fort Worth Airport, she called the Spurgeon Street house. DeBardeleben answered the telephone and told her that he couldn't leave; she'd have to take the airport limousine.

Caryn arrived at Spurgeon Street to discover her husband had a young girl upstairs in the attic. She was a junkie he'd picked up hitchhiking and brought home, he explained. Before he'd raped her and tied up the victim, she'd smoked a lot of dope and thrown a lot of marijuana roaches around the attic. Now he was afraid he'd have to kill her or else she'd report the assault. He also worried that he wouldn't be able to find and dispose of all the discarded joints.

Greg Murphy explained to Foos that some of what transpired that night was lost in the fogs of Caryn's partially destroyed memory. His client wasn't sure if she actually saw the girl in the attic, or if it was later. She did remember that the victim was a blond, about Caryn's height, perhaps a few pounds lighter. Her age could have been anywhere from 17 to 30.

Caryn also had no clear idea why Mike wanted to involve her in the abduction. Once she grasped what was happening, however, she tried to talk DeBardeleben out of murdering the girl. Caryn argued that the victim probably wouldn't risk going to the police because of her own drug problems. Take her out somewhere, she suggested to her husband. Give her some money to make a phone call, and then let her go.

That, apparently, is what happened. Caryn told Murphy that she and Mike took the girl on a drive out into the countryside—Caryn couldn't remember how far or in what direction—and released her near what might have been a convenience store or a roadside honky-tonk. Again, Caryn was unclear.

DeBardeleben forced her to participate in at least two more unsuccessful extortion capers in the Dallas–Fort Worth area before they returned to Arlington, Virginia, and reoccupied the house at 1201 South Columbus, where DeBardeleben first began to consider becoming a counterfeiter as he prepared for his next known extortion attempt. This time, he consulted the newspaper classifieds to find a female in suburban Virginia with a used car for sale. While test driving her car, he made a wax impression of her ignition key, then returned overnight on Monday, April 8, 1974, to steal the vehicle. According to his custom, he also boosted a pair of license plates and affixed them to the stolen car.

At 7:50 the next morning, Marshall H. Groom of 2225 Carmichael Drive, Vienna, Virginia, walked out his front door and climbed into his new green Ford Maverick. Groom, CEO of the modest-sized Potomac Bank and Trust Company of neighboring Fairfax, had his mind on an 8:30 business meeting at the bank that morning. He hardly noticed any of the familiar landmarks as he steered the Maverick down Lawyers Road, right on Malcolm to Flint Hill, where he halted for a stop sign at the intersection with State Route 123.

As Caryn recalled the incident, she and Mike were waiting for Groom, whose habits and morning route to work DeBardeleben had studied in detail. Before Groom could start up again from his full stop, DeBardeleben rammed the banker with his stolen car from the rear, pushing Groom's vehicle about ten feet out into Route 123.

"I thought it was just a routine accident," Groom remembers. "I got out of the car and, as I recall, he said something like, 'Why don't you back up and we'll get this thing straight.' So I did, but when I got out the second time he said, 'Groom, turn around! We have a gun.' Then they slapped handcuffs on me and threw me right in the front seat of my car.''

Groom was outfitted with a pair of dark goggles and wedged between Mike and Caryn for the short drive in his car to a Holiday Inn; DeBardeleben had rented a ground-floor room in the back of the motel. On the way, Groom reports, his abductors talked of a $75,000 to $100,000 ransom. The banker warned them that there probably wasn't more than $20,000 in cash on hand at Potomac Bank and Trust, maybe $40,000 if they were willing to accept singles.

Their captive had no sense of the direction they drove, or for how long, before the car stopped and DeBardeleben hustled Groom into the room, a trenchcoat thrown over his shoulders. Caryn drove Groom's Maverick to the Mobil Station across the street from his bank, and left this note in the window:

ROLL (DRIVER SIDE) WINDOW DOWN—
LEAVE THE MONEY ON FRONT SEAT.
WALK UP WOODHAVEN DRIVE IN SAME
DIRECTION YOU WERE DRIVING.
DO NOT LOOK BACK—DO NOT TALK TO ANYONE
WALK 3 BLOCKS AND WAIT 3 MINUTES—
THEN RETURN TO BANK.
YOU WILL BE NOTIFIED OF MR. GROOM'S LOCATION.

It was about 8:30. DeBardeleben had turned on the motel room's bathroom shower, and switched the television set on high. He'd also hog-tied Groom with rope, removed the handcuffs, and blinded the banker with adhesive tape. Now it was time to call the bank. According to his instructions, Groom informed his chief teller, John Henning, to give the kidnappers whatever they wanted, and not to call the police. Then he was placed on a bed, gagged, and told to remain motionless for ten minutes. With a rope stretched around his neck, down through his crotch and secured at his ankles, plus tape restraints around his wrists, Marshall Groom did not have a lot of choice in the matter.

As it turned out, something Mr. Henning did, or didn't do, spooked DeBardeleben; the ransom money was found where he left it on the front seat of the Maverick. In the interim, Groom who had no idea where he was or if anyone was still with him, began rolling back and forth on the bed "just seeing if anyone was going to come tap me on the shoulder and say, 'Stay still,' or something." When no one did, he kept rolling until he fell onto the floor and hit his head on the frame of the opposite bed. Marshall Groom saw an orange sunburst for a moment. "I was a little woozy, and just sat there for a little while," he says. "When nobody said anything, I started moving around."

One foot came free as he knocked a lamp off a table. "Somehow or other," the banker continues, "I backed myself around the room so I could get up against a wall. My hands were still taped behind my back and the tape was still all over my head.

"I moved around the wall until I got hold of the drapes and tried to pull them down. I couldn't, but I'd moved around so much that everything started loosening up. The ropes started to give and I was finally able to pull the drapes. I remember I stood there for a minute in the front window, my head still taped up, but no one came. All of a sudden one of my hands then came loose. Of course, I ripped the tape off my face, walked to the door, and walked out of the room."

Groom told the first persons he encountered in the parking lot to please call the police. "These people," he recollects, "got into an automobile and drove away as if nothing had happened. I then walked into another room and found some maids working and asked them to call the police. They started to call the front desk, so I got hold of the phone and called the police myself and identified myself."

19

Caryn, Paula, And Melissa

The statute of limitations long since had run on the Groom kidnap and all the rest of the crimes Greg Murphy described from his notes to Dennis Foos that day, so Caryn (and, for that matter, her ex-husband) faced no legal jeopardy for the various abductions and extortions. No one but Caryn, however, knew what other secrets she harbored. Therefore, while her lawyer believed it best for Caryn ultimately to meet directly with the Secret Service to tell all that she could, Greg Murphy also wanted a deal for blanket immunity in place before he would advise Caryn to talk.

Yet as Murphy carefully worked out the details with the U.S. Attorney—and lined up the rest of his players—Stephens and Foos grew impatient. If Caryn had any more information about Mike DeBardeleben's crime career, the Secret Service wanted to hear it, now. "We decided we'd have to hunt her down," says Foos.

Early in the autumn of 1983, Mike Stephens obtained a subpoena for long-distance telephone calls billed to Caryn's parents' home number. Scrutiny of the toll calls revealed heavy traffic to an address in a middle-size community in another state. With the help of a local Secret Service agent there, Stephens determined that the number in fact belonged to Caryn. A short while later, he and Dennis Foos were on their way to interview her.

The nature of their work brings Secret Service agents into the company of the weird, the goofy, the merely troubled, and out-and-out psychotics on a routine basis. Each field office around the country maintains a list of people who have threatened—or tried—to kill the President, or some other protectee. These so-called "quarterlies" must be visited personally four times each year by an agent for a fresh evaluation of their potential threat.

When Dennis Foos did his first stint at WFO, he remembers, he was called to the northwest gate of the White House at least three times a week to interview and evaluate nut cases. The key always was to assess the threat while trying to defuse the moment. "We're quite sensitive to not pushing people over the edge," he says. "We're well experienced at calming down the situation."

Caryn would be another story.

Late on the afternoon of Tuesday, October 4, 1983, Foos, Stephens, and local agent Bob Cozart watched from Cozart's car as Caryn departed the computer store where she worked, along with a male coworker. Caryn and her friend got into their separate cars, then drove to the man's residence, a town house. The Secret Service team followed at a discreet distance. Upon arrival, as Caryn and her friend stepped from their cars in the parking lot, Foos and Stephens approached the young woman on foot.

"We were about fifty to seventy-five feet away when she turned around and looked at us," says Foos. "Other than the fact we were headed in her general direction, she had no obvious reason to believe that we were interested in her. But I'll never forget it. Her knees buckled! She started crying and moaning. It was bizarre. The first thing we thought was to identify ourselves, and calm her down. Well, we showed her our badges and that made it worse, if anything. She said something like, 'I've seen too many of those to trust them.'"

The agents had better luck communicating with

Caryn's friend. After identifying themselves and explaining they were on official business of a sensitive nature, he showed them into his house. There, Foos and Stephens tried to get Caryn focused, reminding her that she'd met Stephens seven years earlier in Greg Murphy's office. But the soothing words and reassuring manners had negligible effect. "Caryn," says Stephens, "thought DeBardeleben had sent us to kill her. She was hysterical, sobbing, shaking on the couch, her arms rigid at her sides."

After a half hour of patient ministrations, the stricken woman was sufficiently collected to accompany the agents downtown to the Secret Service office. Or at least she seemed to be. En route, seated on the passenger side of her car as Mike Stephens drove, Caryn began babbling, shifting in and out of voices and personalities, each of whom separately introduced herself to the agent.

First to emerge was the burr-voiced "Paula," who volunteered that she was a "protector." Caryn took over again for a while, then "Melissa," a little girl, introduced herself. This voice was familiar to Stephens, eerily like the one with which Caryn begged her husband for death on the "Caryn" tape.

"I have a lot of experience talking to mentally ill people," he says. "But this was the strangest episode I'd ever been through. It was a looney-tune twenty minutes. When we got to the office, I signaled Foos that we had someone here who's not quite right."

Caryn started shaking again in the elevator, wrenching her hands and sobbing. Although by this time she seemed reasonably convinced Foos and Stephens had not come to kill her, she was purely petrified at discussing _anything_ to do with Mike DeBardeleben, and refused to allow the interview to be taped.

Proceeding gingerly, Foos and Stephens elicited a few more details of the crimes Caryn already had divulged to her attorney; none of the new information was materially different from what Murphy had relayed to Foos. Failing to make useful progress in this area, the agents shifted the discussion to Caryn's life since her 1976 divorce. Their aim was to see if DeBardeleben might have acted out his handwritten plans to violently avenge himself on Caryn. What did she do for recreation? Had she made new friends? Gone back to school? Had any trouble? Had any trouble from *Mike*?

Caryn adamantly denied that DeBardeleben had bothered her in any way, although *someone* surely had. A stranger came through her window late one night, she said, and beat her up and raped her. She didn't know who it was, couldn't identify him and had not ever told the police of the incident. Caryn would persistently stick to this story, denying that her ex-husband actually had found her and assaulted her, even though Greg Mertz's cataloging of DeBardeleben's seized notes ultimately turned up her supposedly secret and safe address written in Mike's hand, as well as a description of her car and other jottings that suggested DeBardeleben had hired private investigators to find her for him.

Caryn talked with the agents for two to three hours that night. "She'd go on in a rational way for ten or fifteen minutes," recalls Stephens, "then take off into these other personalities. We got tidbits of information, but she was so excitable and so shook up that we couldn't focus her."

"She'd start in her normal voice," adds Dennis Foos. "Then sort of in midsentence would stop and then pick up again in this slow deep voice, considering her every word. Then she'd stop and go into another voice. When she'd get to a part that really seemed to trouble her, she would just simply stop. There obviously was more to follow, but she'd just stop and stare into space. Mike and I'd look at each other. We didn't know what to do, so we'd let her sit. Eventually, she would pick it up again."

Foos and Stephens were so concerned over Caryn's instability that they considered checking her into an emergency mental health facility. She assured them that despite her distraught aspect, an overnight commitment was not necessary. After consulting by telephone with Greg Murphy—who at first was furious at the agents for going around him to find Caryn—they drove her home that night, and returned to Washington.

Stephens spoke to the still-irate Greg Murphy by telephone the next day. "I said, 'Listen, we gave you every opportunity to come forward with her. I told you it was our intention to locate her and interview her, either with you, or without you.' Murphy then seemed to calm down."

Caryn had talked to her lawyer, too, telling him that although she certainly hadn't enjoyed her conversation with the government agents, they at least had treated her gently and with great care for her emotional well-being. On October 18, with her immunity all but negotiated, Greg Murphy visited WFO where agents Foos and Stephens graphically demonstrated to him why Caryn seemed such an important potential witness, and what they knew that had made them so impatient to interview her. They played for him the "Caryn" tape, or as much as he could take before he asked Foos and Stephens to turn off the machine.

"That tape was the most horrible thing I've ever heard in my life," says Murphy. "It had an incredible impact on me. It's hard to remember what I thought about DeBardeleben or the case before I heard it. I do remember the agents. I could see in their eyes that it was equally upsetting to them—although upsetting is not nearly strong enough a word. I think there may have been tears in our eyes. I remember remarking then on the irony that I was a strong opponent of the death penalty, yet if DeBardeleben had been in that room at that time I would have had no hesitancy to kill him. Without saying a word, they indicated back to me that I wasn't alone."

Three weeks later, Murphy at last had Caryn's immunity deal in place. On November 10, he brought her to WFO for a full, tape-recorded debriefing by Foos and Stephens. Caryn kept composed throughout most of the often-difficult session, breaking into sobs and silences from time to time, but remaining Caryn, not Paula or Melissa, as far as the agents and her lawyer could tell.

From a law-enforcement point of view, the interview was a disappointment; Caryn could offer little of substance beyond what she'd already revealed. To Dennis Foos, she seemed to be practicing selective amnesia to protect her fragile mental health.

Caryn, like Faye, was shown the photographs recovered in the three searches. And like Faye, she recognized a handful of the nude females; a number of them were veterans of The Naked Eye. Of the other women, some obviously in great distress and others looking drugged or possibly even dead, she professed to know nothing.

Caryn confirmed that DeBardeleben buried money; in her experience, the site was a derelict chicken coop somewhere in Pennsylvania. She knew of other hiding places, as well. DeBardeleben, she said, rented a number of safety-deposit boxes where she believed he stashed cash. Weapons were sometimes stored in the walls at 1201 South Columbus. Up in the attic, Mike would tie a length of cord around a handgun and ease the weapon down a few feet through the space between the inner and outer walls, then tie it off. He also sometimes wore what he called "bus" shoes, low cuts with hollow heels in which he claimed, to Caryn, that he could secrete money, drugs, a file, and even a Derringer.

Mike Stephens asked if DeBardeleben ever used disguises.

Mustaches, wigs, and hats, Caryn answered. He also wore his own mustache at several different lengths, and often dyed it, as well as his eyebrows. She remembered him experimenting with different sorts of clothing to mask his weight, too.

What did Caryn remember of Mike's mother? She'd only seen Moe drunk once, but that was enough. According to Caryn, Mrs. DeBardeleben underwent a violent personality alteration under the influence of liquor, changing from a reasonable-seeming adult female in her mid-sixties into a gutter-mouthed harpy with a vocabulary that'd make a teamster blush.

And what of Mike's relationship with Moe?

"It was just unreal," she told Foos and Stephens. "I've heard of love-hate relationships, but that was practically a textbook case. He was so *drawn* to her and so emotionally tied to her and *hated* her *so* much—and hated women because of her. He also feared men because of his father and hated men because of his father."

Did Caryn recall DeBardeleben using a lot of drugs?

"He was always in pain," she answered. "Always in pain with his stomach. He'd try to get pain pills from doctors, Darvon and codeine. When he had trouble, he started going down to the methadone clinic. He already was pretty hooked on Darvon and codeine, and then he got hooked on methadone. I think he later stopped doing that.

"When he smoked marijuana, he took on all the symptoms of an alcoholic drunk. He was out of control. He didn't drink, and he wouldn't allow me to drink. But I think he had the same pattern his mother did when she was on alcohol, as if the pattern somehow was in him. He got real crazy, real out of control."

As Foos and Stephens wound up their questions, Caryn asked, in tears, if henceforth the agents would please leave her be. "I've tried for a long time to build a life, to get over some of these things that happened to me," she said. "And it's very important to get out from under this again. As long as I have to keep coming back here and doing things like this, I can't even begin. I can't get out of this limbo."

With that, the interview drew to a close and Greg Murphy escorted his quietly weeping client from the room. Foos and Stephens thanked her for finding the courage to meet with them. They also tried, as best they could, to reassure Caryn that Mike DeBardeleben would spend the rest of his days behind bars. Then she was gone, returned to the tormented solitude from which the Secret Service would not again disturb her.

But they weren't yet through with Mike DeBardeleben's ex-wives.

In fact, the first wife the agents found in the 1983 investigation had been his last, Barbara Abbott: the fifth Mrs. James M. DeBardeleben II. Dennis Foos picked up her name on May 27 when he visited the Hileman Road neighborhood. On the same day, coincidentally, the Baltimore field office ran down an unexplained "conspiracy to commit grand theft" notation on DeBardeleben's FBI rap sheet. The entry noted a date, February of 1980; a location, Frederick, Maryland; and a disposition, "not prosecuted." The Baltimore field office's check with local authorities revealed that the case had been a failed bank examiner job. Besides DeBardeleben, there was one other suspect charged in the case: Barbara Abbott.

The Frederick police gave the Secret Service a Gaithersburg, Maryland, address for Abbott. Dennis Foos and agent Tom Doyle drove up to Gaithersburg on the afternoon of May 27, only to find that Barbara Abbott had since moved on. After the weekend searches of DeBardeleben's two storage facilities in Alexandria and Manassas, Greg Mertz telephoned Abbott's parents in Frederick and spoke to her father, explaining that the Secret Service was interested in talking to Barbara. On the afternoon of June 3, 1983, Mr. Abbott brought his daughter to WFO for the first of several interviews that would run through September.

Abbott was an articulate, generously proportioned young woman with thick eyeglasses. She told agents that her family was from New Jersey, her father a metallurgist, and that she'd graduated from college and was about to become an elementary schoolteacher in the summer of 1979 when she met Mike DeBardeleben in a Falls Church disco called Studio 50. As she later recalled, "He was very well groomed, intelligent, and soft-spoken. He used a lot of educated words and he seemed to know a lot. I had no experience with dating at that time. I was naive, into my books and school. I thought he was real strong and independent."

DeBardeleben put his usual hustle on Abbott that summer, paying her compliments, bringing her gifts, flattering the unworldly schoolteacher. He was vague about his background, and vaguer still when she asked why he was gone so much of the time. "He just said he had business," she recollects. "At the time, I didn't feel it was my place to say anything more."

Abbott's first inkling that her new boyfriend had a shady side came a few months into the relationship when he showed her a homemade driver's license. " 'What's going on here?' I said.

"He said, 'I have a good way of making IDs.' Then he showed me how he had IDs for all these different states. He was very honest about it. He said, 'I need these IDs to go around. I can get away with a lot of stuff.' I didn't really understand what he was talking about at the time.

"Several months later, he pulled a twenty-dollar bill out of his wallet. He said, 'Do you see this?'

"I said, 'It's a twenty-dollar bill, so what?'

"And he said, '*No*. It is *not* a twenty-dollar bill. This is *my* twenty-dollar bill. I *made* it.'

" 'What are you talking about?' I said.

" 'Isn't it great? Nobody can tell.'

"I handled it. It was very real."

Slowly, Abbott learned about the rest of Mike's world; the drugs, the guns, his hatred for the cops— and for his deceased mother.

"He said his father was pretty abusive, tyrannical," she remembers. "He sort of laughed about his father abusing his mother. He didn't think his father had a problem. He thought it was the right thing to do. He thought it was pretty funny. He'd say, 'My father abused my mother, and she just took it. She just sat there and didn't do anything about it.' "

Abbott, too, in time was victimized in ways that partially paralleled the sadism Mike practiced on her predecessors in the DeBardeleben nuptial couch. In her case, she says, most of Mike's brutality was psychological. One part of it was the guns. DeBardeleben was never without one, and pointedly claimed to Abbott that he'd once punished a former partner by shooting him in the kneecaps (a claim he'd also made to Caryn). To Barbara Abbott, the boast seemed credible.

"I remember one time we were in a car and someone accidentally cut him off. He put the car in park, got out, and just went chasing the guy on foot with a gun! He didn't do anything, but he threatened. Another time someone was tailgating him. He had this big flashlight that he always carried in the car. He turned around and used it to blind the guy who was tailgating him."

Although Abbott insists that DeBardeleben never physically assaulted her, he did force her to listen to his torture tapes, to pose nude for photos, and to submit to anal sex, often when both of them were under the influence of drugs. She, too, was forced to recite his scripts.

Her first criminal act with DeBardeleben, she says,

was the failed Frederick flimflam. At 12:50 P.M. on Thursday, February 21, 1980, according to a Frederick police report, Mrs. Ruth Flickinger of 105 West 14th Street in Frederick,

> received a call from a . . . male who identified himself as [a] Mr. Chapman. He told Mrs. Flickinger that someone from the bank had tampered with her account and had withdrawn over $700.00 . . . and that they "wanted to find out who was doing it."
>
> The caller told Mrs. Flickinger to go to the bank and withdraw $850.00 . . . He told her to make sure that she wore gloves because "we're trying to get fingerprints off the money." He also told Mrs. Flickinger not to tell anyone why she was withdrawing the money. . . . if she had to, she was to tell the bank personnel that it was for "personal reasons."
>
> The caller continued by telling Mrs. Flickinger that after she withdrew the money she was to return home. She was told that a police officer would be contacting her and that she was to give the money to the policeman. She was told, "Now you make sure you see his credentials." And without thinking, Mrs. Flickinger did exactly what the caller instructed her to do. . . ."

The flimflam began unraveling as soon as Ruth Flickinger arrived by taxi at the Farmers and Mechanics National Bank on North Market Street. Manager Rosie Thompson telephoned the Frederick police to report that she had an elderly depositor in her office, wishing to make an unusually large savings withdrawal for "personal" reasons. Thompson further reported

> that there was a female subject in the lobby who was very interested in what was going on in her office. . . . the female subject walked up to the teller's cage next to Mrs. Thompson's office, requesting change for a quarter. She then wanted pennies for a nickel, etc.,

staying in the area near the office. She then walked out into the lobby, stood there, wrote some things and fiddled around, moving back over near the office when she could see Mrs. Thompson talking on the telephone.

Office Robert A. Servacek responded to Rosie Thompson's call. Inside the bank, he observed both the nervous "female subject"—Barbara Abbott—and Mrs. Flickinger, who left Thompson's office about two minutes after Servacek's arrival, carrying an envelope containing $105 in marked bills. As he followed her out the door and into her waiting cab—which Servacek would tail back to Mrs. Flickinger's house—a sharpeyed teller named Cindy Brown watched Abbott bolt out of the bank herself and run for a powder-blue, fourdoor '79 Chevy Nova. DeBardeleben was at the wheel of the car. Brown noted the Nova's Maryland license plate number and provided it to the police. A DMV check showed that the car was registered to Abbott.

The next day, officer Servacek interviewed Barbara at her parents' house. She fully confessed her role in the Flickinger job and implicated DeBardeleben. Abbott told Servacek how they'd researched the caper at Frederick's C. Burr Artz Library three weeks before, and how Flickinger was one of perhaps a dozen elderly women they'd dialed from a local pay phone the previous morning, searching for a properly credulous mark.

The following Monday, however, when Barbara Abbott appeared with Mike DeBardeleben at the Frederick Police Department to be charged in the case, she approached Servacek with a new version of her story. "Officer Servacek," she said, "before you read those warrants I think there's something you should know. The other day I was confused and afraid. I didn't lie about what I did, but it wasn't Mike who was with me. I was threatened by a guy by the name of Joe Dalton."

DeBardeleben, says Abbott, had imparted some advice to her over that weekend.

"You better change your story," Abbott remembers him saying.

"What happens if I don't?" she asked.

"You don't want to know. Tell them anything. Tell them it was a friend of mine."

Even though Abbott's change of story was a transparent lie, there was no way to bring DeBardeleben to trial as long as she stuck to it. Three days later, he convinced Abbott that they should marry. "He said to do it to protect myself. He said, 'I think you'd be better off. That way you wouldn't have to testify if I get caught.' "

In fact, after spending some time in the Frederick city jail, DeBardeleben was released, and never was tried for lack of evidence. After their honeymoon—a counterfeit-passing tour down into the Florida Keys and back—his wife took her lawyer's advice and pled guilty. She'd been told to expect probation. Instead, the judge gave her thirty days for her part in the scheme. However, since she was a beginning schoolteacher needed in class during the week, he allowed Abbott to serve her jail time over fifteen consecutive weekends.

Saturdays and Sundays in the Frederick jail were in some way a relief for Abbott from life with Mike DeBardeleben. Inside the sealed bungalow on Hileman Road, he moderated his sexual demands on her, but at the same time heightened the psychological stress. He forced her to turn over her paychecks, and to make her daily work commute in his tired blue Thunderbird which, Abbott distinctly recalls, he'd outfitted with a siren. To turn on the headlights required connecting two wires under the dash. Opening the driver's side door turned the lights off.

DeBardeleben did most of his traveling in Abbott's blue Nova. He was out until dawn at least three nights a week, and drove the Nova on the four or five occasions that he took Abbott along to assist him passing his twenties. The great majority of his Mall Passer excursions, however, were taken alone. According to Abbott, DeBardeleben disappeared for up to two months at a time. He'd call once a week, never disclosing where he was. Sometimes, he mailed back cash for her to deposit in one of his bank accounts. By the end of 1980, he'd put sixty thousand miles on her car. Every time he returned, the vehicle reeked of dirty clothes, stale cigarette smoke, and rotted food. The Nova's trunk always was stuffed with cards and socks, umbrellas, paperbacks, toys and women's underpants, his counterfeit proceeds.

Intense, skeptical questioning from Mertz, Foos, Stephens, and even Jane Vezeris did not dislodge from Abbott any further incriminating testimony of substantive value. On the question of sex crimes she adamantly knew nothing.

Abbott did vividly recall her own personal deterioration in 1980, her enforced isolation from the world and a progressive loss of self-esteem. "I hardly ate anything, I was so out of it," she says. "I was very frail and emaciated, and I didn't care about my appearance."

DeBardeleben's diagnosis was mental illness. "He told me I was a paranoid schizophrenic, because I was so depressed and didn't know how to deal with my life. He said my parents made me that way." By late in the year, Abbott was sleeping on the floor, next to Mike's bed.

Then came her chance to break free. At Christmas 1980, Mike and Barbara visited Mike's sister Linda and her family in New York. Linda's two children were fond of their uncle, who always came with gifts for them, but it was apparent to Abbott that Linda's husband suffered his brother-in-law's occasional presence in his house only to keep peace. "I don't think he wanted Mike around," she says.

Over the 1980 holiday, Linda took her aside. "Whatever he's involved with," Abbott recalls her sister-in-law saying of Mike, "you better get out of it if you don't want him to hurt you."

"I said, 'You're his sister. Doesn't it bother you?'

"She said, 'Yeah, but he's my flesh and blood. There's nothing I can do.'"

A monster snowstorm swept the eastern seaboard that Christmas. Mike DeBardeleben had a flat tire in the midst of it and took a chill that quickly escalated into pneumonia. Back in Virginia, with his condition worsening, Abbott saw her chance to escape. "I should have just let him die," she says, "but I called the hospital in Arlington and then drove him over there and dropped him off. I might have taken a suitcase with me, but I don't think so. I just left. It was the last time I saw him and it felt wonderful. I immediately got my life back on track."

20

"Becky"

In all, Mike DeBardeleben would face six separate criminal prosecutions on charges stemming from his May 25, 1983, arrest in Tennessee, and the subsequent Secret Service searches. In the first proceeding, a federal bench trial in Knoxville held Monday, August 8, 1983, district judge Robert Taylor listened to several hours of testimony, principally from agent Pete Allison, before finding the defendant guilty as charged. Sentencing was set for September.

By this time, the task force had helped connect DeBardeleben to two homicides (Jean McPhaul in Bossier City, Louisiana, and Joe Rapini in Greece, New York), plus four bank kidnap-extortions, as well as the failed Flickinger flimflam with his fifth wife, Barbara Abbott. Greg Mertz even had found Marshall Groom's name in one of DeBardeleben's handwritten bank personnel rosters. Foos and Stephens interviewed the banker, who identified DeBardeleben's picture as that of the man who'd abducted him nine years before. DeBardeleben faced at least two more trials for counterfeiting, one in Nashville and another in Charlotte. Should anything go amiss with these prosecutions, Federal Prosecutor Justin Williams in Alexandria was prepared to indict, as well.

It had been a solid summer's work. Yet no one on the task force felt particularly satisfied with what they'd accomplished. Having accidentally snared a lethal shadow, a savagely warped predator who'd rampaged undetected for years, probably decades, Foos, Mertz, and Stephens had but a single, overriding objective.

"Our goal all along was to get him convicted of murder and then executed," says Mike Stephens bluntly. "Before we could do that, we had to get some prosecutor willing to indict him. There has been nothing in my life that has meant more to me, professionally, than to put him in the electric chair. I was obsessed with it. All three of us were. That was our focus."

Although the task force wasn't yet three months old, the stress of the investigation was barely manageable. "It began to wear on me," says Stephens. "What he'd done to his wives was just unbelievable. And we talked to so many police departments, and had so many cases sent to us, some of which DeBardeleben was involved in, some not. But whether he was or not, it began to open my eyes that violence against women, serial murder, and serial rape, is rampant. I became much more victim-oriented than ever before. I really felt his victims' pain."

The same realization forcefully struck Dennis Foos. "Before we even met any of the victims we had all this stuff coming in from various police departments," he says. "I mean, I saw pictures of things that I never knew were done to people. Once we started interviewing, my stomach just tied up in knots."

Greg Mertz's life was further complicated by an acrimonious divorce. "I was very upset about it," he explains. "But in a way the case allowed me to focus my attention in a creative, useful way instead of brooding or becoming worthless, so to speak. I had no social life, so I didn't mind working late into the night. I wanted to work hard and get him. But I was going to do it in an upright way. Of course, there were times when I was indifferent to my feelings, or didn't know how I felt."

All three men had daughters. "I became overprotective," admits Stephens. "I was almost paranoid about shopping centers and strangers. I wanted to share my knowledge of what went on with Linda and the children, but I just was never comfortable getting into those details. These were some of the things you try to protect your children from knowing about."

"My wife," reports Foos, "says I made my daughter's high school life miserable. I demanded to know where she was every minute she was gone."

The case consumed more and more of the agents' time and attention, and this created some tensions within the service. "We did receive animosity," Mertz recalls. "Some supervisors and other agents questioned what we were doing, and why. We got a couple lectures about being too autonomous, and some questions about why a punk agent like me was being given all these privileges, like speaking to police groups. Jane, however, did a great job of shielding us from most of that. She ran interference with the bureaucracy for us."

When Foos, Mertz, and Stephens were together, in or out of the office, they thought of, and discussed, little else but Mike DeBardeleben and his crimes. The experience forged deep and permanent bonds among them. "We grew very close," says Stephens. "We shared every emotion with each other. Frustration. Anger. And we communicated freely. No one person gave orders. And no one tried to advance his career at the expense of the other two."

Of the three, Stephens easily was the most impulsive. "We'd be talking and someone would say, 'Maybe we should try this,'" remembers Foos. "You'd then have to peel Mike off the door. He'd be on his way without further thought. There were times I'd rein him in as he was kicking me in the ass, saying, 'Let's go!'"

Greg Mertz recalls that when friction did occur, it usually was between him and Stephens, with Foos poised thoughtfully on the sidelines. "Mike and I would have an argument and Denny would say, 'Well. I can see Greg's side, and I can see Mike's side, too.' Stephens and I were the ones who butted heads."

"Bottom line," says Mike Stephens, "is that we were three very different personalities with different types of expertise, and we meshed together as one. We yelled at each other. We argued. We laughed a lot of the time. It worked."

In their search of DeBardeleben's seized belongings, the agents sorted out photos of at least forty still-unidentified females whose expressions and positions bespoke the sorts of horrors of which DeBardeleben clearly was capable. "Several of the girls were photographed in the same room, on the same bed," says Greg Mertz. "Girl Number Twenty-four was a really pretty one with a tattoo. She drove me crazy. In a couple photographs you can see ligature marks around her wrists. Then there was another young girl, kneeling on the bed. We had a whole series of pictures of her. In the first one, the bed is made and her hair is nice and clean and combed. She has a kind of sickly smile. Then we found further photographs in which her hair's dirty and the bed sheets are gone. It's obvious she's been there for a day or two, or longer. Her eyes were bruised.

"So we knew there were victims out there. It was frustrating, extremely frustrating, to know that you had victims, but you couldn't find them. We had no way to deal with these photographs. Do we publish them in a magazine and say, 'If you're a rape victim, call us'? What if a victim never reported the assault and now is married with four kids?"

The agents also found several more audiotapes. One, labeled "Becky," was every bit as harrowing as "Caryn." Who was Becky? And who were the other girls he had recorded during acts of apparently consenting sex? What of the "Goals" tape? Did DeBardeleben ever build his dream house-cum-torture-chamber-and-counterfeiting-shop? Weirdest of all was an unmarked cassette on which the amazed Secret Service agents heard DeBardeleben assume two roles; the torturer, played in his natural voice, and the victim, which he did in a piping falsetto. Excerpt:

> I want you to do it, do it do it! Bite it! Bite it! Bite it!
> Okay, here goes.
> You're bitin' it right now! Aw! You're bitin' it right now! Oh, the pain's sharp! I love the pain! Bite it harder! Suck it! Bite it! Make the nipple bleed! I hate myself! I hate myself! I hate myself! I'm a bitch! I'm a bitch! I'm a bitch! Bite! Bite! Bite! Make it bleed! Rip it off! Hurt me! Ahhh! *You did it!*

"This guy continuously surprised us," says Stephens. "It just got sicker and sicker and sicker. We kept shaking our heads in disbelief, because we knew there was still more to come."

Friday, September 2, Dennis Foos received a letter from Detective Sergeant Dennis Niere of the police department in Ballwin, Missouri (population: 27,000), twenty-two miles west of St. Louis. Quite by chance, Niere had seen and read Foos's earlier DeBardeleben advisory. As a rule, the detective explains, "it would have ended up buried on a clipboard, or just thrown away." Niere instantly recognized DeBardeleben's physical description in the Teletype, as well as the Secret Service synopsis of his police-stop M.O. Niere believed he had a candidate case.

On April 19, 1979, Niere informed Foos, 24 year-old Sheila Grant* was driving home from a local singles bar at about 1:00 A.M. when the young waitress, who was married, noticed flashing red lights in her rearview mirror. Believing the vehicle behind her to be an unmarked police car, Grant pulled over. The young woman, a buxom, blue-eyed blond, five-four and very attractive, according to Niere, produced her driver's license and was preparing to open her door when she looked up to see a pasty-faced white male in his late 30s to early 40s, five-ten, 150 pounds. He was pointing a small handgun at her. In a light southern drawl, he ordered her back into her driver's seat as he climbed in the back of her car.

According to his instructions, she drove on for a way, then stopped for him to get in front with her. He then took the wheel and drove around haphazardly, obviously unfamiliar with the area but also clearly looking for a specific location. While driving, he commanded Grant to disrobe, except for her blouse. "He also made numerous degrading comments," wrote Niere in his report,

> indicating that she had done this before and enjoyed it. He inserted his finger in her vagina and played with her for several minutes. He then had Ms. Grant insert her finger in her vagina. He asked several times how it felt and if she was ready to "cum." The subject then turned west on Clayton Road at which time he unzipped his pants and pulled his penis out. He ordered Ms. Grant to "go down on this and suck hard." A short time later the subject stated "I'm about to cum and I want you to swallow it."

Throughout the ordeal Sheila Grant begged the man not to harm her, pleading, which he seemed to enjoy. "His demeanor and tone," noted Niere, "demanded that she be humble and submit totally to him."

When he was through, he relied on her to guide them back to his car. After directing Grant to remove her blouse, he threw her keys in the back of her vehicle, climbed in his own car, which Grant described as a tan or light-bronze Chrysler, and drove away. Several days after that, Grant's trauma was compounded by personal tragedy when her husband, evidently unstrung by the assault on his wife, killed himself.

Four and a half years later, Dennis Foos sent Detective Sergeant Niere a packet of investigative information on Mike DeBardeleben, including fingerprints and photographs. Niere reported back that Sheila Grant had positively identified DeBardeleben as her attacker. Requiring corroborative evidence to secure an indictment, the Missouri detective then subpoenaed guest records from twenty-two motels in the vicinity and discovered that DeBardeleben, under one of his pseudonyms, had checked into a Scottish Inn at the St. Louis airport, Lambert Field, just prior to the assault.

In March of 1984, Niere telephoned WFO to report DeBardeleben had been charged with sodomy, robbery, and "armed criminal action" in the case and that a detainer had been issued, signaling Ballwin's intent to bring him to trial once the other pending charges against him were adjudicated.

Meantime, "Becky" surfaced.

The same week that Dennis Foos fielded the inquiry from Dennis Niere, he went before a gathering of local police investigators in Northern Virginia to discuss what the Secret Service knew about James Mitchell DeBardeleben, and to encourage the detectives to consult their own files for unsolved cases that DeBardeleben might have committed. These direct contacts with local law enforcement had begun the month before, and would continue on for at least two more years.

On hand for this particular gathering was FBI agent Chuck Flagg of the bureau's Wilmington, Delaware, office. Flagg well remembered both the Lucy Alexander and Laurie Jensen rape-abductions of 1978 and 1979. Listening to Foos describe DeBardeleben's photos and tape recordings and his police-stop M.O., the FBI agent strongly was put in mind of the two unsolved sex crimes. When he got back to his office, Flagg telephoned agent Cathy Kiser at the FBI office in Hyattsville, Maryland. He repeated what he'd just learned to Kiser, and then gave her Dennis Foos's telephone number. Kiser in turn called WFO and made an appointment to meet with the task force. In the meantime, she forwarded copies of the FBI's files on Alexander and Jensen.

Dennis Foos was first to read them. "I don't think I got past the first page before I was excited," Foos recalls. "Laurie Jensen was a fantastic witness. Her description of the car was consistent with DeBardeleben's blue T-bird. By then we knew about the root beer and the scripts. I read where she remembered being forced to call him Daddy, which we'd read in his writings and heard on the "Becky" tape." Foos also set aside in his desk drawer several sets of DeBardeleben's nude photographs.

September 14, a Wednesday, Cathy Kiser arrived at WFO with Joe McElhenny, FBI case agent for Alexander and Jensen. "When McElhenny started describing Laurie," says Foos, "I remember him mentioning her reddish hair and overbite. Immediately I *knew*! I reached in my desk and I pulled out a picture and said, 'How's this look?' "

"That's my girl," said McElhenny. "That's definitely her."

"All right!" Foos yelled.

Becky had been found.

"This was a rare moment in police work," Joe McElhenny recalls. "To see a piece of physical evidence that came out of this fellow's own little personal archive was the next best thing to coming upon the crime in progress. I knew we had him."

Cathy Kiser was as amazed as anyone. "Joe showed me the picture of a girl lying on her side on a bed. 'Cathy,' he said. 'Look at this one. Look at this.' I said, 'Oh my God, Joe!' "

"He said, 'Do you remember when we talked to her last year and she told us that she was heavier when this happened?' I said, 'Yes! Joe, that's Laurie! Her hair's shorter in the picture, but that's Laurie.'

"So with that, we're all standing around with our mouths hanging open. Then Dennis Foos says, 'Let me get you a tape that goes with this.' He puts it into the machine and we listen to this voice."

"Can you feel the pain?" Kiser heard DeBardeleben ask, the sound of bed springs squeaking in the background.

"Yes I can feel the pain," Laurie Jensen, unmistakably, replied in a mechanical, partially muffled voice that suggest she, like Caryn, somehow had moved her mind to another plane.

"Do you like the pain?"

"Yes, I like the pain."

"Do you love the pain?"

"Yes, I love the pain."

"How much do you love the pain?"

"I love it a lot."

"It was just unbelievable," says Kiser. "I cannot describe to you what it was like to have met and interviewed Laurie, then to hear this voice on the tape. Joe and I were just standing there in shock."

Agent Kiser then reached for a telephone. "I had Laurie's number with me," she remembers. "I wanted to call her *right then* because I wanted to hear her voice. She answered and it was just incredible! The same voice I'd just heard on the tape, Laurie's voice.

" 'What's going on?' she asked me.

" 'Oh, not a whole lot. But something's come up and I wonder if you could come and visit us for a day or so. We'll pay for everything. Do you think you could do that, Laurie? I think it's important. We may have stumbled on something.'

"She got real excited. 'Oh my God! Wouldn't that be great?' "

Laurie agreed to fly into Washington that Friday, the 16th, from Knoxville, Tennessee, where she'd fled from Maryland after her nightmare Memorial Day, 1979. "Becky," in fact, was living in Knoxville the day DeBardeleben was arrested there, and would be coming up from Knoxville on the same day Mike DeBardeleben was to be sentenced by Judge Robert Taylor.

Midmorning that Friday, Kiser and McElhenny met Laurie Jensen at National Airport, and drove her to 1800 G Street, where an office had been reserved for their use. "It was a nice big office," remembers agent Kiser. "Joe had the tape recorder. He sat at the desk with a big window behind him. Sunlight was streaming into the room. Laurie and I sat together on the leather couch, a few feet from Joe. When she was ready as she ever would be, he turned it on.

"Laurie gripped my hand as we listened to the tape together. And it was *awful!* She knew instantly that it was her voice *and she relived the whole thing!* It was horrible. It really was. She was shuddering and crying. Sobbed in my arms. I remember stroking her head and hair.

"We listened to the tape for no more than two minutes, hearing his voice and then hers, and then Joe left the room. She went on crying for another ten minutes and I just kept saying to her, 'We've found him. We've found him. We have found him, Laurie! He's never going to hurt you again. He's in jail and he's going to stay there. We have found that bad man.' "

Four hundred miles to the south in Knoxville, at the same hour, Assistant U.S. Attorney Charles Fels walked into court for DeBardeleben's sentencing. The prosecutor had with him several cassette tapes, which he placed on the counsel table before him. The recordings, including a copy of "Becky," had arrived from Washington just one day before. They so appalled the federal prosecutor that he had not been able to listen to more than a minute or two of any of them.

Defense attorney James A. H. Bell, standing with his

client opposite Fels, waiting for Judge Taylor to appear, saw the cassettes and assumed they were wiretap or electronic bug recordings.

"Looks like you're getting ready to try another dope case," he said to Fels.

"I want to talk to you about your client," Fels responded.

"Okay. We're here. What do you want?"

"He is a monster."

"What? For passing counterfeit money?"

"No," said Charles Fels. "Listen to these tapes."

"So he played them for us," remembers Bell. "They were extremely chilling."

Judge Taylor also listened to some of the recordings in chambers that morning. Pete Allison, who came to court to see DeBardeleben sentenced, says that Taylor emerged from chambers with a set look in his eye. Tersely, the judge pronounced DeBardeleben's as "one of the worst records that's ever been presented in this court," and then sentenced him to maximum time— twenty years.

As the sentence came down, Allison tried to make eye contact with DeBardeleben, who would not return the agent's gaze. "The man was extremely cool," says Allison. "Totally devoid of emotion during the whole process. When they talked about the tapes, he just shook his head. No outburst. Not even a scowl."

21

"There's A Cop!"

Except for the task force members, no Secret Service agent devoted more time and effort to the DeBardeleben investigation than did Jim Rich in Fort Worth. A former Marine and Vietnam vet who joined the Secret Service in 1971, Rich remembers being personally affronted by the ease with which the Mall Passer sailed in and out of his territory, passing his fake twenties, seemingly immune to capture.

"I really got caught up in it," says the agent. "To be honest, there aren't that many counterfeiting cases that capture your imagination. Over the years, I've seen such garbage put out and passed that sometimes I think the person who accepts those notes *deserves* the loss. So when a case like the Mall Passer comes along, you say, 'Hey! Well here's somebody I want to go after!' "

Jim Rich consequently was of two minds on the afternoon of May 25 when the Teletype brought word of the Mall Passer's capture in Knoxville by agent Pete Allison, a personal friend since 1975 when Allison and Rich worked together on Treasury Secretary William Simons's protective detail. "I was excited for Pete," says Rich. "I was glad it was he who caught the Mall Passer. But like Dennis Foos, I was a little dejected, too. Damn! I wanted to catch him."

The next phase of the investigation would prove to be an even greater, and more frustrating, challenge for agent Rich. He was able to confirm Caryn's sketchy recollections of attempted banker kidnap-extortions in

Texas and, working from Debardeleben's several lists of potential flimflam targets, Rich found three older women whom, as "Mr. Benson," DeBardeleben had victimized in the Dallas–Fort Worth area. However, the agent could not find a trace of the drug addict Caryn reported her husband had kidnapped in 1973. "Which means," he said, "that the incident in the attic never happened, or the victim didn't report it because she decided not to, or because she couldn't."

Rich estimates that he reviewed at least twenty unsolved local homicides going back as far as the early 1960s, hoping that somehow, somewhere, DeBardeleben had made a mistake, that a fingerprint, bloodstain or some other piece of physical evidence might tie him to a local murder. Some of the reviewed cases, he says, bore unmistakable similarities to DeBardeleben's known M.O., but in the end none of them yielded up the crucial evidence necessary to charge him.

A last, longshot possibility was to search the family house on Spurgeon Street, which in the decade since Mary Lou DeBardeleben's death from cancer had been a rental property. With the tenant's consent, Rich and a team of Fort Worth Police Department detectives carefully examined and extensively photographed the house's empty attic. They found an old Valentine's Day candy box, a pair of women's sunglasses, crushed, two adjustable initial rings bearing the letters *L* and *E* and, consistent with Caryn's description of the attic scene ten years before, a plastic cord laced through three eyebolts screwed into the attic's rafters. Having read DeBardeleben's notes on the subject, it was simple for Rich to imagine the full apparatus by which he might have trussed victims to the exposed beams.

They checked under the house as well. Greg Mertz had recovered from DeBardeleben's belongings a copy of crime writer Jack Olsen's *The Man with the Candy,* the story of south Texas serial killer Dean Corll. DeBardeleben had underlined Olsen's passages that dealt with how Corll poured lime on his victims and wrapped them in plastic before burying them. Could DeBardeleben have tried the same thing?

The searchers discovered a trapdoor that opened down into the crawl space beneath 3920 Spurgeon, a not unusual feature for houses in Texas. With flashlights, they explored the area, discerning a distinct pattern of depressions in the dirt, and what appeared to be an old bone off in the distance. Although these discoveries at first seemed promising, on further inquiry they fizzled. The hollows, Rich learned, occur commonly under houses; they are the result of natural settling. The bone was that of a pig, and probably had been dragged under the house by a dog or some other creature.

Rich reluctantly wound his inquiries to a close just as the Secret Service's DeBardeleben investigation took a sudden and unexpected turn 1,700 miles away in Connecticut where, in late August, the service's Hartford field office released DeBardeleben's physical description via the statewide police Teletype, together with a preliminary summary of his M.O. and known travels. In the neighboring Hartford suburb of Bloomfield, an alert police department secretary named Sue Brown saw the routine message—the sort that ordinarily stands little chance of catching anyone's attention—and took it to her boss, Detective Carl Dillenback. "She knew I was looking for a guy," says Dillenback, "and she saw that the description fit."

Dillenback, 41, and like Jim Rich a Vietnam vet, joined the Bloomfield Police Department in 1974. He had been looking since springtime for a white male in his 40s, brown-haired, balding, mustachioed, of medium height and weight. This Unsub had tried at least one police-stop abduction in Bloomfield, and may have been responsible for one, or both, of two other attempted abductions in the Hartford area. Dillenback's victim was 18-year-old Jane Trombley,* a University of Hartford sophomore from New Jersey.

Friday night, May 6, 1983, Trombley attended a party hosted by her boyfriend at his residence in Bloomfield. Shortly past midnight, the brown-haired, brown-eyed coed, a B-average business major, gave another partygoer a lift back to campus in her AMC Spirit. Then Trombley returned to her boyfriend's, hoping that while she was gone that the rest of the guests had left, too. "It was very late," she says. "I was ready to crash. Unfortunately, the party was still going full blast when I got back. So I got in my car and took another drive, thinking, 'Okay, I'll give him time to get everybody out of there.' "

Minutes later on the clear night, as she waited for a red light to change on Albany Avenue in Hartford, Trombley glanced to her left and noticed a fair-complected male she remembers as "an old, wimpy-looking guy, nothing you'd want to stop and stare at," seated behind the wheel of a "small, reddish-orange car, sort of a Chevette type," vintage mid-1970s.

She drove on, vaguely aware that the pale stranger had fallen in behind her, but unworried about him or his possible intentions. When Trombley passed the entrance to the University of Hartford on Bloomfield Avenue, she looked into her rearview mirror to see the man take a quick look toward the school, as if he had assumed Trombley would turn in. Still not concerned, she reasoned that he'd noticed the University of Hartford stickers on the back of her Spirit, and had been innocently surprised when she didn't turn. Nothing suspicious about that.

Jane Trombley remained untroubled until she'd crossed back over the Bloomfield city line and looked in her mirror again to see that the man now was flashing a white light from the dashboard of his vehicle. "Oh shit!" she thought. "There's a cop! Was I speeding?" Worried lest a traffic ticket would inflate her auto insurance premiums (and consequently upset her father, who paid them), Jane Trombley pulled over "and started wondering," she remembers, "how I might be able to wriggle out of this."

Ordinarily, her door would not have been locked and she would have automatically rolled down her window at least halfway to speak to the officer. However, "there had been recent assaults on women in New Jersey," she explains, "and my mom was on my back. 'There are nut cases out there! We've got all these things going on down here! Lock your doors! Don't roll down your window!'

"I went, 'Yeah. yeah, yeah.' But for some reason I did as she said that night. I kept the door locked and I only rolled down the window a bit."

Trombley didn't wait to be asked for her license and registration. She was reaching back for the papers in her purse on the Spirit's rear passenger-side floor when the man, clad in a brown and tan jacket, suddenly snaked an arm through her window, unlocked her door and tried to push his way into the car.

"We started struggling over the door," she says. "I was trying to pull it back, but I couldn't. So he got that open and put his body next to mine, pushing and trying to get the key out of the ignition.

"You could describe me as athletic; I'm pretty strong, or at least as strong as he was. I was cursing at him. I braced one foot on the brake and one hand on the steering wheel and the other on the horn. He couldn't move me because the gearshift was on the console between the front seats and it created a sort of barrier. And he couldn't get the key out of the ignition, because it was the kind where you had to push a button on the column to get the key out. All he did was bend it.

"I don't know how long we fought, maybe for five minutes. I know it bothered me that we were right in front of someone's home. I was blowing the horn and nobody turned on a light or came out to see what was happening."

As Trombley and her attacker continued their struggle for control of the car—the man did not produce a weapon and never actually grabbed Trombley, but rather kept trying to push her aside—a pair of passing car headlights suddenly raked the dark scene, frightening the stranger away. "All I saw were the headlights," Trombley says. "The car didn't stop or even slow down, but I guess it scared him."

She returned to her boyfriend's, called the Bloomfield police and gave them a statement that night. After several weeks without an arrest, Detective Dillenback was assigned the case. He, too, was at a loss to produce a suspect, but the detective did soon discover a nearly identical attempted kidnap, which had occurred at approximately the same hour on Friday, April 15, in Newington, Connecticut, about twenty miles south of Hartford. Alone in her car, as Trombley had been, Joan Phillips* also had seen a flashing light from the dash of a copper-colored Rabbit, or maybe a Pinto, as she recalled, and had stopped, "believing that the vehicle was a police car," as the subsequent police report read. Because Phillips's window was stuck shut, the young woman opened the door to hand out her driver's license and registration.

At this point, the suspect lurched into the driver's side of the vehicle, grabbed the complainant by the shoulders and attempted to get into the car. The complainant became confused and frightened, yelling to the suspect that he wasn't a police officer and beginning to struggle. The complainant stated that she kicked and thrashed at the subject, literally kicking him out of the car. Complainant then drove south . . . with the driver's side door still open and proceeded home. . . .

"Because of the type of vehicle the two victims described," says Detective Dillenback, "and their general descriptions of the subject and particularly the M.O.

involved, I felt that both women were talking about the same guy. But there's no way I'm going to pin this down. Phillips just was not certain enough about things. So I had two assaults by the same person, but I'm probably not going to be able to prove it."

In early June 1983, Jane Trombley helped a police artist produce a composite sketch of her assailant, which Dillenback provided to the *Hartford Courant*, along with a description of the crime and a request that "any persons having any information concerning the above, or who have suffered from a similar incident . . . contact Detective Carl R. Dillenback, Bloomfield Police Department. . . ."

Days later, Carl Dillenback received a visit from 25-year-old Betsy Goodwin* of neighboring Wilson, Connecticut. Goodwin informed him that she, too, had been accosted, by two assailants, and that one of them matched the composite drawing, as well as a written description, Goodwin had seen in the newspaper.

At a little past eleven on the night of October 29, 1981, she told Dillenback, Goodwin had pulled into a fast-food outlet in Hartford. The place was crowded, so she parked in the rear. As Goodwin walked from her car, she said, two men approached her from behind, identified themselves as police officers and handcuffed the young woman, telling her that she was under arrest for prostitution and drug possession. The younger of the two was a big man, beefy. The other, who Goodwin believed she recognized from the *Hartford Courant,* seemed middle-aged and was far less robust. The two suspects then took her to their car, a large, older Ford or similar vehicle that resembled a retired police cruiser.

After rifling her purse for $17, the Unsubs took Goodwin to her vehicle, which they searched as well. Finding nothing, they walked her back, still hand-cuffed, to their own vehicle. Just then, a blue-and-white Hartford police car pulled through the parking lot. As soon as the cruiser departed, Goodwin's kidnappers removed the handcuffs and released her before driving off together.

Detective Dillenback reports that Goodwin was "hot" that the Hartford police had put very little effort into solving her case, understandable irritation even though she'd given the local police very little to go on. Although the detective himself had no trouble believing her story—"I thought she was credible," he says. "I didn't think she was making this up at all"—there wasn't much he could do with her information, either.

His investigation stalled through the summer until Bloomfield police department secretary Sue Brown showed the Secret Service Teletype to Dillenback on August 25. After learning more about DeBardeleben from Jane Vezeris at WFO, Dillenback decided to take what he knew to the next meeting of the local Valley Detective Association, which Dillenback describes as a regularly scheduled "bullshit session" of local detectives. "We sit around and hammer things out," he explains. "We trade information."

At the September 1983, gathering, Dillenback presented his information and asked for ideas. After hearing his account of the Goodwin case, one of the other investigators offered that the younger of the two assailants reminded him of a well-known local thug, "a big ugly guy into everything and anybody," as Dillenback describes him, "someone who'd break your leg or, if the price was right, put you in the river." Following the meeting, Dillenback ordered up the suspect's rap sheet and a photograph.

He also reviewed Mike DeBardeleben's rap sheet and noticed that DeBardeleben's latest entry was his February 1980, arrest in Frederick, Maryland, with fifth wife Barbara Abbott for the attempted Flickinger flimflam. Dillenback dialed the Frederick Police Department, explained his situation, and asked if they could forward DeBardeleben's mug shot.

To Dillenback's pleased and deeply appreciative surprise, Private Beth A. Bohrer of the Frederick force not only found a mug shot, but put together a first-rate, seven-man photo lineup for Dillenback to show his witnesses. All seven looked a good deal alike, and each featured a Frederick P.D. identification plate around his neck. "Bohrer did a beautiful job," says Dillenback. "This was a photo lineup that would stand up in *any* court."

Jane Trombley unequivocally identified Mike DeBardeleben as her attacker. "It wasn't hard at all," she says. "For some reason his face just clicked. I had no doubt." In late October 1983, DeBardeleben was charged with first-degree kidnap in the Trombley case.

Betsy Goodwin also positively identified DeBardeleben, as well as Dillenback's second suspect, the "big ugly guy." Moreover, the Secret Service task force's computerized records reliably placed DeBardeleben in Albany, New York, no more than two and a half hours by car from Hartford, on October 29, 1981, the night of the Goodwin assault.

Despite this evidence, Hartford authorities never pursued a case against DeBardeleben, or his alleged accomplice. Nor could Joan Phillips of Newington ever positively identify the man who attacked her.

Dillenback believes he also has connected Mike DeBardeleben with murder. The detective recollects that he interviewed several witnesses who recognized DeBardeleben as a familiar figure (in company with the second Goodwin suspect) at a truck stop, infamous for its crowds of prostitutes, located on I-84 southwest of Hartford. A good friend of Betsy Goodwin's husband at the time was a trucker. As a result, Goodwin herself was acquainted with many members of the same truck stop crowd.

When Dillenback showed her the photos of still-unidentified women recovered from DeBardeleben's mini-storage caches, Goodwin indicated with firm conviction that photo number fourteen was that of a hooker she'd known only as "Hot Lips," and that number twenty-three also was a truck stop whore Goodwin remembered by the name of Donna, or "Little Hustler." Both women were missing at the time, and both, says Carl Dillenback, later were found dead in New York.

Could DeBardeleben have murdered them? Dillenback thinks so, even though Debardeleben's fourth wife, Caryn, told the Secret Service that she, too, recognized number twenty-three as a former employee at the ill-starred Naked Eye nude photo salon.

"I contended then, and I contend to this day," says the unpersuaded detective, "that my witness's identification was correct. It was fresh. Betsy Goodwin *knew* this girl, saw her on several recent occasions. As I recall, the Feds were much, much less certain of their identification. Interestingly enough, both these girls had the same pimp. They worked the same block. They knew each other. They both disappeared about the same time. And both of them wound up dead. There's just too much coincidence there."

22

"Hey, Man, I Gotcha!"

Although DeBardeleben's photos of Laurie Jensen and the "Becky" audiotape found in his possession left no plausible doubt that he was responsible for the Maryland teenager's 1979 abduction and rape (and likewise the nearly identical assault on Lucy Alexander in 1978), the prospects for a successful prosecution in the Jensen case were clouded by the fact that the victim hadn't gotten a good look at her attacker. Laurie Jensen could not identify Mike DeBardeleben as the man who grabbed her off the street in Ocean City. At trial, besides recounting her harrowing ordeal, Jensen only would be able to identify her likeness in the photos, and her tormented voice on the "Becky" tape.

Barbara Abbott was shown DeBardeleben's photos of Jensen. She told Mike Stephens and Joe McElhenny, the FBI case agent, that the pictures had been shot inside an upstairs bedroom at 1913 Hileman Road in Falls Church. Abbott, who had lived in the house for a year, recognized features of the room and some of the furnishings and mirrors in the photos.

The next step was to prove her ex-husband himself took them. When DeBardeleben printed the pictures from his original negatives, he had taken great care to crop portions of his own body from the photos. When the Secret Service printed its own set of images from his negatives, they discovered a number of them included parts of his anatomy—a leg, his stomach, a shoulder—exposed to the camera as he pushed Jensen into various poses, performing various acts. None showed his face. Some, however, were tightly focused enough to clearly reveal his moles and scars and other skin blemishes.

According to what the task force learned from Peter A. ("Pete") Smerick, a forensic photographic analyst at the FBI, if these unique, distinguishing marks and imperfections also appeared in known photographs of DeBardeleben, the match would establish a legally sustainable identification of the suspect as the person appearing in the pictures with Jensen. Smerick explained that the technique, officially referred to as Portrait Parlay and informally known among forensic analysts as "Freckle Analysis," had withstood all legal challenges. Smerick himself had presented Freckle Analyses in court fifty times.

The first priority was to secure the necessary comparison photographs and other forensic evidence as soon as possible. "We wanted to do it before DeBardeleben was given any heavy time anywhere," says Greg Mertz. "If he'd been convicted of kidnap, for example, and already was looking at a long sentence, he might not be too concerned over a contempt charge for refusing to submit."

In late October 1983, as he awaited his second counterfeiting trial in Nashville's Metro Criminal Justice Center, DeBardeleben was transported under court order to Baltimore (where the Jensen trial would be held) to submit to body photographs. The federal order also directed the suspect to provide voice and handwriting exemplars, as well as head and pubic hair specimens. Since there was no proposed serological evidence in the Jensen case, the judge who signed the order refused to allow blood samples to be taken.

Awaiting DeBardeleben on Thursday, October 27, in a back conference room on the eighth floor of the Garmatz Building, the U.S. courthouse in downtown Baltimore, were Dennis Foos and Mike Stephens, Paul

Rakowski from the Baltimore field office, several other Secret Service personnel, and Joe McElhenny from the FBI.

Mike Stephens, who'd last seen DeBardeleben seven and a half years before, in 1976, when he'd interviewed DeBardeleben at the Alexandria City Jail, didn't notice much difference in the suspect, except that he'd grown older. Stephens asked DeBardeleben if he remembered him. DeBardeleben said nothing. "So, we told him to take all his clothing off, except for his underwear," says Stephens. "He did. He was surprisingly docile, basically expressionless. He did what he was told to do. Not a whole lot of attitude."

DeBardeleben, stripped to his shorts in the cold room, spent forty minutes on the conference table, assuming position after position according to instructions that Pete Smerick had given Secret Service photographer Jim Winand. "When I looked at the photos of the victim in bed with her attacker," says Smerick, "I requested that they pose DeBardeleben in a similar posture. I also told the photographer to try to duplicate the camera angle from which these photos were taken, and the lighting conditions."

The process was an unambiguous humiliation for DeBardeleben. "We tried to keep it as professional as possible," says Mike Stephens. "We didn't harass him. Snide remarks? Yes. But no relentless questioning or anything like that.

"Just before the photography was finished," Stephens continues, "I grabbed Dennis and Rakowski. I said to them, 'Hey, we cannot let this opportunity go by. I'm going to get a trophy shot.'" The three agents slipped to the end of the table and stood together over the supine and unsuspecting DeBardeleben as Stephens nodded to Wineham to squeeze off one extra photograph.

After the photographs came collection of the head and pubic hair specimens. Dennis Foos and Joe

McElhenny then took handwriting exemplars. The voice recordings were the responsibility of technician Stephen Cain, the service's expert on voice identification, who had isolated seventy-eight words and phrases from the "Becky" tape, ranging from "Hurry up!" and "Start cooperating," to "Lower," "Suck it harder," and "Jaws real wide" for DeBardeleben to repeat six times each.

With the forensic work out of the way, Rakowski, Winand, Cain, and the rest left the conference room while DeBardeleben was allowed to dress. It was time to try a little conversation. "I think the reason he didn't give us any trouble during the photography was that he might have been frightened, intimidated," says Stephens. "When it came to interrogation, however, he knew his rights. He clearly hated our guts."

"I told him he was a prime suspect in two kidnaps [Jensen and Alexander] and what he was facing," recalls Joe McElhenny. "I also warned him of his rights and supplied him with a standard interrogation 'Advice of Rights' form. He wouldn't sign it.

"Then I asked him, 'Do you want to make any statements? Let's talk about it.'

" 'No comment,' was about all he said. His sentences were very short, and to the point. 'Scumbag. Railroad. Government. Frame.' Venom. I mean, it was coming from every pore of his being. He was not a happy camper. He made it clear that he didn't want to talk to any of us at anytime—ever."

A few days later—Halloween 1983—as DeBardeleben waited in the Baltimore City Jail for the U.S. marshals to escort him back to Nashville, an urgent message came down from the Baltimore field office to WFO. According to a jail snitch, DeBardeleben was boasting of having buried a million-dollar cache of counterfeit bills, the location of which he'd disclose if his fellow prisoner, scheduled for imminent release, would retrieve the hoard, pass the fake money, and split the proceeds with DeBardeleben's sister.

"We were really hot on this when we first heard about it," remembers Greg Mertz. "I had found references in his writings to buried counterfeit, and using it as a bargaining chip if he was ever caught. Also, two of his wives, Faye and Caryn, had told us about buried money. So this was consistent with past behavior and indicative of DeBardeleben's careful planning."

The snitch passed out a hand-drawn map, clearly done by DeBardeleben. It indicated that the money was buried beneath a Sunoco truck-stop parking lot in Romney, West Virginia. Since the area covered in the map was fully a quarter-acre or more, Stephens and Mertz sent word into the jail that much more precise information was necessary. Back came a second De-Bardeleben map, this one complete with a helpful X drawn near a bank of telephone booths at the truck stop.

Mertz and Stephens headed out with shovels the next morning, November 2nd, a brilliant autumn day in Romney, a rural community in the hills of the West Virginia panhandle. They found the truck stop as depicted on the map—an encouraging sign that DeBardeleben at least had been to the place and knew it well enough to draw a map of it—and went to work by the phone booths.

The hard-packed dirt did not give way easily. "I mean," says Mertz, "that ground was so damn hard it was unbelievable! We worked for two hours and didn't get anyplace."

Exasperated by the hard work and slow pace, Mike Stephens leaned on his shovel, surveyed the lot and noticed standing idle across the way a big yellow back hoe, an ideal machine for the job at hand. The agent dropped his shovel, stepped over to the telephones and dialed WFO, where he asked to speak to the boss, SAIC Al Buskirk.

"We've got a problem here," he said.

"Yeah?" Buskirk answered.

"A hand shovel isn't going to do this, boss."

"What do you mean?"

"I have to rent a back hoe."

"A back hoe!"

"Yeah."

Buskirk, though dubious, approved the request. Stephens hung up and immediately walked over to the back hoe operator. " 'Billy,' I said to him. 'Federal agent. I need you to dig a hole in this parking lot.'

"Everyone was standing around, looking at each other, thinking, 'What the hell?'

" 'Hey,' I said. 'I'm Secret Service. There's supposed to be something buried out there. So I am going to dig up this damn parking lot.'

" 'Well,' Billy says, 'How big a hole do you want?'

" 'Oh, about twenty by twenty would be reasonable.'

" 'I'll do it for sixty bucks.' "

Greg Mertz remembers the excavation well. "Hey, he just went to town. Dug halfway to China, and came up with a lot of dirt, which we then had to put back into the ground."

"And that was that," adds Stephens. "Maybe DeBardeleben really did bury money there. Or maybe he was just playing games with us. If so, he got us good. It's probably the only part of this story that he's going to enjoy."

Several weeks following his return to Nashville, DeBardeleben received a visit from Bossier City, Louisiana, police detectives Doug Payne and Scotty Henderson. Though Payne still realized his best hope of proving that DeBardeleben murdered real estate agent Jean McPhaul probably lay with his eyewitnesses, he nevertheless wanted at least one shot at teasing a confession from his suspect. The detective reasoned that a local cop, playing half smart and posing as DeBardeleben's sympathetic buddy, perhaps could exploit his pathological hatred for the Secret Service.

DeBardeleben, for his part, no doubt recognized that in the McPhaul matter he faced a possible first-degree murder charge in a death-penalty state, and that it behooved him to learn as much as possible about the prosecution's case. He therefore agreed to talk to the Louisiana lawmen, although he refused their request to tape record the session, which was conducted on plastic chairs in the hallway outside the jailer's office.

"He immediately jumped up and said that he didn't do it, that the Secret Service had tried to set him up," says Payne. "I kinda went along with him, saying, 'I guess that's possible. Maybe they're grasping at straws right now.'

"I knew that the two agents he hated most at that time were Mike Stephens and Dennis Foos. So I told him I knew them and that I thought they were assholes, too. I played dumb with him, dumb ol' country boy from little Bossier City. I kind of made him feel I was on his side, and maybe I could understand why he did what he did."

While at WFO the previous July, Payne had noted printed material about the serial killer Ted Bundy in DeBardeleben's possessions. "I thought he was probably studying Bundy," says the detective, "and using what he learned to aid him in his crime.

"I said, 'Well, Theodore Bundy seems like a pretty sharp guy to me, you know. From what I've read about him, you kinda gotta look up to the guy. I can appreciate somebody like that. He *really* put forth an effort.'

"Of course, that got DeBardeleben stirred up. He said, 'Yes he did. But he made a lot of mistakes. He wasn't as smart as some people think he is. *I'm* smarter than Theodore Bundy.' "

DeBardeleben was attentive and poised throughout the hallway interview; he wasn't going to be conned into confessing anything. Yet he did frankly admit to visiting Bossier City, as well as to stealing the Louisiana license plate found in his Chrysler with the other tags.

At one point, DeBardeleben even drew a map for the cops, indicating on it exactly where he'd taken the plate, 2704 Shed Road, the Chapparell Apartments, less than a mile north of the Sheraton where Jean McPhaul had gone to meet "Dr. Zack" the morning of her murder. He sketched in the hotel and a nearby singles bar, then known as "Cowboys," as well as part of Highway 3, which runs north from the Sheraton. Highway 3 is the route that Jean McPhaul and "Dr. Zack" would have taken to reach GreenAcres Place that morning.

However, DeBardeleben traced Highway 3 only partway north, says Payne. The focus of his map was twisty Preston Boulevard, a much less direct route north from the Sheraton, which the suspect accurately drew in detail, down to Preston's intersection with Shed Road where he'd pilfered the plate three months before McPhaul's murder. "He knew the area very well, and I knew he was stringing me along. He played these mind games. To me, it was his way of saying, 'Yes, I did the crime. But you're not smart enough to put it on me.' I mean, he all but confessed to me right there. At the same time, though, he would say, 'I've never killed anybody.' "

Payne and Henderson did not collect DeBardeleben's map at the end of their two-and-a-half-hour conversation.

Some weeks later, Mrs. DeMoss, the rooming-house keeper in Shreveport, was shown a photo lineup. She identified DeBardeleben as the "Dr. Zack" from Alabama who'd inquired about a room for himself and his family the day Jean McPhaul was killed. Then in January 1984 Payne took secretary Bernadette Willadson and Tom Kennedy, the contractor, to Nashville where, on Monday the 23rd, both witnesses picked DeBardeleben out of a lineup as the man they saw with Jean McPhaul at the GreenAcres Place office.

Four days later, a federal jury in Nashville convicted DeBardeleben of two more counterfeiting charges. Sentencing was set for March as U.S. marshals arrived to escort him on to his next court date, a third counterfeiting trial in Charlotte, North Carolina. With sodomy, robbery, and "armed criminal action" charges filed against DeBardeleben in Ballwin, Missouri; a kidnap warrant signed in Bloomfield, Connecticut; and a federal kidnap indictment pending in Baltimore, Doug Payne figured his depression-prone suspect might have lost a bit of his earlier cockiness. Perhaps he was now vulnerable to a sharp application of stress. Consequently, Payne and Scotty Henderson arranged to pay DeBardeleben a second visit in the Nashville jail.

This time, Payne says, there was trouble with a U.S. marshal who seemed jealous of his prerogatives. "He told Scotty and me that he was in charge and that we would go by what he said. We would talk to DeBardeleben when he said we could. As he was talkin' he pulled his gun out of his desk drawer and laid it out in front of us, I guess to get our attention.

"So finally he takes us upstairs and gets DeBardeleben out of his cell and tells him that he doesn't have to talk to us, that he doesn't have to do what he doesn't want to do! Then he tried his best to talk him out of it."

At DeBardeleben's request, Payne brought with him a sheaf of the latest McPhaul case news clips from the Bossier City and Shreveport papers. "Witness reportedly identifies murder suspect as man seen with McPhaul," read one headline.

"I asked him how he was doing," Payne recalls, "and he asked me, 'Did you bring the articles?' I said sure, and laid out some in front of him. As he was goin' over them I started easin' into him. He's gettin' *real* nervous this time. He starts movin' in his chair and givin' me all the body language signs that he's tryin' to block me out, you know.

"I stayed on him and he finally says, 'I'm not talking anymore. I want my attorney.' I say, 'Okay, you can have your attorney. I won't ask you any more questions.'

"About this time, the interview room door *flies* open, and the marshal is standing there sayin', 'C'mon, he doesn't want to talk to you!' I said, 'Hang on just a minute.'

"Well, Scotty got the marshal out of there and I started to talk. DeBardeleben freezes up on me again, says, 'Nah, I'm not talkin'.' The door flies open again and it's the same thing. The marshal tries to get him out. Scotty pulled the marshal out by the arm.

"And I started over *again*. He's really getting pissed. I say, 'Okay, don't talk to me. You just be quiet. Take a nap. Do whatever you wanna do. *I'm* gonna talk, and you don't have to say shit, okay?'

"So he nods, leans his head up against the wall and closes his eyes. I say, 'Okay, Mike. I think I gotcha.' I saw his head move, downward. His eyes were still closed.

" 'I've got somebody identifying you from a photo layout. I've got two people pickin' you out of a physical lineup.' Everything I say, he drops his head some more. Eyes shut. Won't look at me. Crosses his arms. 'I've got the license plate you stole. Hey, man, I gotcha!'

"He keeps droppin' his head down until his chin's on his chest. He will not look at me. I keep on and keep on and keep on. He says nothing, won't volunteer nuthin', and I didn't think he was going to. Of course, I'll never know because that's when the marshal came back in *again* and messed it up!"

Four months later, on Wednesday, June 6, 1984, a twelve-person Bossier City grand jury heard Doug

Payne recite the case against Mike DeBardeleben. The panel then deliberated approximately three minutes before handing up a first-degree murder indictment. Next day, at a press conference, District Attorney Henry Brown, flanked by detectives Payne and Henderson, announced the indictment.

"My office will be seeking the death penalty in this case," said Brown, who also told reporters that he expected DeBardeleben to be brought to Bossier City for trial sometime that autumn. "This was the most intense investigation conducted by this department," added Henderson, "the longest and the most expensive." One reporter inquired if the authorities were positive that they'd indicted the right man. "I am absolutely sure that DeBardeleben did kill Jean McPhaul," Doug Payne answered.

23

Another Indictment

The serendipity with which the Laurie Jensen and Jean McPhaul cases came to the task force's attention was easily exceeded for improbability by discovery of the Edna ("Terry") Macdonald murder case through Doug Payne in Louisiana. It had been thirteen years since Reverend Bernard Norman and Detective Robert Casale had found the Realtor's grotesquely trussed body in the basement of the empty house on Heritage Road in Barrington, Rhode Island. And while the case always had remained active, it seemed a homicide of the increasingly common sort that never gets solved. Once again, however, chance stepped in.

The Barrington police were aware of Bossier City's case within weeks of Jean McPhaul's killing. Not until the spring of 1984, however, and nearly a year after Mike DeBardeleben was captured and then implicated in the McPhaul homicide, did the Rhode Islanders begin looking at him as a suspect in the Macdonald case.

"When I first heard of Barrington's case I called up there and tried to get information," says Payne. "I told them, 'Look, I believe the same guy that killed our agent down here is gonna be the one that killed yours. Would you please check into it?'

"I gave 'em a few weeks and called back, askin', 'Did you do something with this?' I didn't hear anything more."

Barrington Detective Louis Gelfuso remembers events differently. "We asked for all their informa-

tion," he says, "and basically we didn't get any."
Whatever its cause, the inter-agency communications
lacuna was only the latest in a series of frustrations in
an investigation notable from the start for its almost
complete lack of progress, or even hopeful leads.

The first problem was the crime itself. As was true
in the McPhaul murder, Terry Macdonald's killer left
no fingerprints or any other useful physical evidence
behind. Even more important, the homicide unmistakably was the work of a deviant stranger who lacked
any rational motive. The police knew from the outset
that he likely would not turn out to be a friend, acquaintance, or relative of the victim, and he probably
was not a local resident.

Although there were strong sexual overtones to the
killing, Dr. Joseph A. Palumbo, of Providence, who
performed the autopsy, reported no evidence of oral,
anal, or vaginal penetration, or physical molestation of
any kind. This also was consistent with Jean Mc-
Phaul's killing.

There was a bruise on Terry Macdonald's head, and
several of her fingernails were broken, two facts which
would serve as starting points for the police theory of
what happened to the Realtor that night. "We believed," says Gelfuso, "that he got her into the basement on a pretext of measuring, either for furniture or
maybe to build a partition or something. That's why
she went home to get the flashlight and tape measure.
While she was reading the tape measure, he either hit
her on the head with his hand, or with the flashlight, to
render her unconscious. Dr. Palumbo speculated that
her fingernails were broken when she fell."

The blow to her head did not kill Terry Macdonald,
says Gelfuso, but it is uncertain whether she ever regained her senses. Marks on her wrists and mouth indicate she was bound and gagged with adhesive tape,
pieces of which were found near her body. The death
instrument was the right leg of Terry Macdonald's ny-

lon hose, torn from her body and tightly knotted around her neck, from behind. Cause of death was asphyxiation.

"But the really strange part," Gelfuso continues, "is that Dr. Palumbo was sure that she died on her stomach. Yet Casale found her lying on her back with her neck and head about eight inches from the floor, trussed to the pipe. So he did this to her after she was dead."

Barrington Police Chief Stanley Gontarsz, a retired New York City police detective lieutenant, perceived he was searching for an aberrant killer, and looked for help in the Macdonald case anywhere he could find it. One source to whom Gontarsz turned was Dr. James A. Brussel, a New York City psychiatrist and scholar of deviant criminality famous for his unerring profile of George Metesky, New York City's "Mad Bomber" of the 1940s and 1950s, and later for his insights into the Boston Strangler case. In the view of many modern practitioners, James Brussel is criminal personality profiling's founding father.

On the evening of May 3, 1971, the Monday following Terry Macdonald's murder, Stanley Gontarsz conducted the first of two telephone interviews with Dr. Brussel, whose first observation, according to Gontarsz's notes, was that the Unsub probably was a psychopath and possibly was schizophrenic, too. Brussel suggested that Gontarsz continue protective surveillance of the Macdonald family, and that the Barrington police contact regional facilities for the criminal insane, inquiring if there had been any recent escapes from maximum security sections. The psychiatrist further advised that plainclothes officers attend both a memorial service for Mrs. Macdonald, and her funeral on Tuesday.

A week later, Gontarsz and Brussel spoke again by telephone. This time, Gontarsz recorded in his notes, Brussel opined the Unsub was "aware of what he is doing and has probably left the immediate area." And in what would prove his single most important insight Brussel also shared his belief that, "this subject has had a problem, possibly with his mother, identifies [the victim] with his mother and has hostility for [the victim]."

This was as close as the Barrington police would get to identifying Terry Macdonald's killer until 1984, when the investigation was catalyzed by the Secret Service. "Bossier told us to contact the task force," says Louis Gelfuso. "We were told that they had the most information about this guy. They did. They became the source of ninety-five percent of what we knew about him."

At WFO that spring, Detectives Gelfuso and Gary Palumbo were provided a full DeBardeleben tutorial, as well as access to the recovered evidence. For Gelfuso, the investigation's defining moment arrived on this visit to the Secret Service when, as he was sifting through some photographs, Gelfuso first saw a picture of Mary Lou DeBardeleben. "When I saw that it was like, 'Wow!! This is it!' I could not believe the similarity. His mother and Terry Macdonald looked just alike! 'This is *why!*' I thought. He searched out someone so he could take out his hatred for his mother.' "

The Barrington policeman also had come in search of help from the Forensic Services Division. He told the Secret Service that in April 1971, when "Charles Murray" was making his rounds of Barrington-area realty offices, he visited one in North Scituate, Rhode Island. Mr. Murray was asked to fill out a brief questionnaire in a lined, eight-by-five spiral notebook; name, address, employer, and so on. Murray obliged, and the pages bearing his handwriting luckily had been preserved. Now that DeBardeleben was a suspect *and* the Secret Service had secured exemplars of his handwriting, would one of their questioned document experts examine the pages?

On May 4, 1984, Examiner Thomas V. McAlexander released his conclusions. At least three notations, "Charles Murray," "Sales Mgr." and "Re Manufacture Engines," were in DeBardeleben's hand. "Further," reported McAlexander, "the notation 'Boring' . . . was probably written by DeBardeleben."

With a strong suspect at last—Tom McAlexander was *very* confident of his findings—the two detectives gathered copies of DeBardeleben's fingerprint cards and a nine person photo lineup, then returned to Barrington in hopes of bolstering their case. The fingerprints were no help. According to Gelfuso, he and Palumbo spent fourteen weeks comparing them to latent prints lifted at the murder site. None matched.

They had much better success with their witnesses. Ms. Gladys Coleman, who had worked in the North Scituate realty office, identified DeBardeleben as the man she remembered as Charles Murray. Coleman earlier had also identified Murray as the suspect pictured in the composite sketch.

Hope Davidson, who worked with Terry Macdonald at Child's Realty, had met "Peter Morgan" there on his first visit, April 2, and then on April 27 took his call in which he asked that Mrs. Macdonald meet him at the Sheraton–Biltmore on the 29th. Davidson selected three of the nine photos, including that of DeBardeleben, as appearing "most like him, except he was better looking, more handsome, and a little heavier," according to Gelfuso's notes. "[She] was thanked for her cooperation, and, before leaving, she advised that the more she looked at the photo of the suspect the more she would say he was the man."

Ann Kroll, another agent who was visited by "Peter Fuller" on April 21, eight days before the Macdonald murder, identified DeBardeleben as Fuller, as did her associate, Madeline Neubauer. Finally, there was

Marlene Lawlor. At approximately 7:30 on the night Terry Macdonald was killed—a half hour or so before she stopped to pick up the flashlight and measuring tape at home—she and "Peter Morgan" called on Mrs. Lawlor, in whose house Macdonald thought Morgan might be interested. Marlene Lawlor got a good look at Terry Macdonald's companion that night. Thirteen years later, in late June of 1984, Gary Palumbo showed her the photo lineup. Lawlor unhesitatingly selected DeBardeleben's picture as that of Mr. Morgan.

Four months after that, on October 26, the Rhode Island state attorney general's office announced that "the Providence County Grand Jury today indicted James Mitchell DeBardeleben, 44, for murder in connection with the April 29, 1971, strangulation of Barrington real estate agent Mrs. Edna Macdonald.... Attorney General Dennis J. Roberts II said today he has begun extradition proceedings aimed at returning DeBardeleben to Rhode Island for arraignment...."

24

"That's The Sonuvabitch, Right There."

Wednesday, February 29, 1984, DeBardeleben was led in handcuffs and belly chain before U.S. District Court Judge John T. Nixon in Nashville to be sentenced for his second counterfeiting conviction. Upon entering the courthouse, he kicked Nashville *Tennessean* staff photographer Ricky Rogers in the knee. Inside, he encountered Mike Stephens again. Stonily silent at the defense table, DeBardeleben listened as the agent discussed the aggravating circumstances that the prosecution wished Judge Nixon to consider before he fixed DeBardeleben's sentence. Stephens described the torture tapes—Judge Nixon would not allow them to be played in open court—and summarized the rest of the incriminating evidence seized by the Secret Service. He also detailed the lengthening list of assault, kidnap, rape, and murder charges already filed or being prepared against the defendant.

When Stephens finished, DeBardeleben rose to excoriate the Secret Service and the prosecution. "They are using these allegations—all of which are patently false—to get me more time on the counterfeiting charges," he angrily asserted. "They are holding court behind closed doors. They have fabricated and created a theory that I am a mass murderer. They have formed a conspiracy designed to coerce me into a confession."

At the tirade's conclusion, Nixon gave DeBardeleben another fifteen years, bring his total assessed prison time to thirty-five years. Next stop: Charlotte, where Assistant U.S. Attorney Ken Andresen was preparing a surprise for the defendant. Come June, Andresen intended to prosecute DeBardeleben under the thirteen-year-old federal dangerous special offender statute. If convicted, he faced a far sterner sentence than the two so far meted out in Knoxville and Nashville.

In March, as he awaited his next court date in Charlotte's Mecklenberg County Jail, three more victims came forward to identify Mike DeBardeleben as their assailant.

The first was Lori Cobert of Manassas, Virginia, where the Secret Service had discovered DeBardeleben's second mini-storage locker. In the subfreezing early hours of February 5, 1981, Cobert, 19, a petite veterinarian's assistant, was driving home from a night of roller skating with a friend when a stranger, posing as a policeman, pulled her over. Cobert was forced to fellate the man in his car, before he masturbated to climax. He then let her go and drove off.

No suspects were developed in the case until 1983 when Don Cahill, a detective with the local Prince William County Police Department, learned from a fellow officer that the Secret Service had arrested a suspect whose M.O. closely matched that of the Unsub who'd assaulted Lori Cobert. Cahill visited WFO, collected DeBardeleben's picture, and included it in a photo lineup he showed Cobert on March 7, 1984.

"I gave her the lineup," Cahill remembers. "She looked at it, pointed at DeBardeleben and said, 'That's the sonuvabitch right there.'" Two weeks later, Prince William County issued a warrant for DeBardeleben's arrest.

On March 12, Greg Mertz took a telephone call at WFO from Sergeant James A. Updegraff of the Maryland State Police. Updegraff, in charge of the long-inactive investigation into the November 2, 1980, assault on Dianne Overton, the data-entry clerk from

Knoxville, Maryland, recently had learned of DeBardeleben's capture from FBI agent James E. Duffy of the bureau's Frederick, Maryland, office. Duffy had suggested Updegraff contact the Secret Service task force.

"This one was another layover," says Mertz. "Updegraff described the crime to me, and then sent me the reports. A late-night police stop, flashing lights, the handcuffs—it all sounded like DeBardeleben. Her description of him fit, too. Of course, her description of a blue Thunderbird also got our attention. We knew that DeBardeleben was driving that dark blue Thunderbird at the time the crime occurred. He'd purchased it in Virginia in 1978, the summer he was released from Danbury. And we knew the car's VIN from his records. So we put a track out on it."

On April 2, 1984, nearly three years after the investigation into her assault had been suspended for lack of progress, Dianne Overton, accompanied by her mother, came to the Frederick barracks of the Maryland State Police. After introductions to Greg Mertz and Agent Duffy of the FBI, Updegraff showed Overton a six-photo lineup. The three men looked on as Overton immediately fixed on number three, DeBardeleben. Staring at the picture, she began to shake. Fine beads of cold sweat broke out on her forehead. There was no doubt that Dianne Overton had made an identification. Without uttering a word, she forcefully communicated to the lawmen her absolute assurance that number three was the man who tried to kill her.

Greg Mertz brought with him several photos of DeBardeleben's Thunderbird, which by this time had been located in Massachusetts. He asked Overton to examine the pictures. The first photo was a three-quarter perspective of the Ford's right front grill and fender—Overton's view that night as she'd bounced up and off the onrushing vehicle, thereby saving her life.

"Just tell me what comes to mind," said Mertz.

"Fear," she answered.

In all, Mertz showed her six photos of DeBardeleben's blue Thunderbird. Overton felt that five of them resembled her assailant's car. The sixth shot, a view of the Thunderbird's floor-mounted transmission control, gave her pause. In Overton's memory, his gear shift had been on the steering column. In her wild fight, that was where she remembered kicking the car in and out of gear.

Despite this one inconsistency, Overton had made a strong positive identification. None of the lawmen doubted that DeBardeleben was her attacker. But there also were further bits of physical evidence. As he had tried to run over Dianne Overton, DeBardeleben had scraped the Thunderbird's paint on a nineteen-inch-high vertical drainpipe in front of Miller's general store in Knoxville. FBI analysts conclusively determined that the blue automobile paint found on the pipe was the same deep metallic blue that the Ford Motor Company applied to its Thunderbirds in 1977. When the bureau's technicians examined the car itself, they found that body putty had been used to repair a small dent along its side, nineteen inches high.

As the Maryland authorities contemplated the appropriate assault and attempted murder charges to file against DeBardeleben, yet another police detective with an unsolved sex-assault case contacted WFO. This time it was Donald Cramer of the Willingboro, New Jersey, police department. Cramer had doggedly sought the man who kidnapped and assaulted clothing-store clerk Maria Santini since November 12, 1980, exactly ten days after Dianne Overton nearly was killed. By coincidence, it also was ten days after James Updegraff first spoke to Greg Mertz about Overton that Cramer made his own first contact with the Secret Service.

After Maria Santini was released along the weedy fire road in the Pine Barrens, she had walked out of the woods onto the main road where a school bus driver discovered the young mother of two, frightened and disoriented, clutching the rope with which she had been bound. Don Cramer, who with fellow detective James Thompson was the first policeman to interview Santini that afternoon, says that he initially was incredulous at her fantastic-sounding tale of daylight, gunpoint robbery, kidnap, and then her abductor's patently sick but curiously passive sex games; bondage, fondling, photography, and finally the strange interlude during which he teetered around the room in his high heels and yellow mini-skirt. The detective grew even more doubtful when Santini refused to be examined or treated at the hospital. A police polygrapher termed Santini's reliability "inconclusive."

"I indicated it was my feeling that she should go to the hospital," says Cramer. "Her contention was, 'Hey! He never touched me. He never penetrated me. So there's no need for an exam.' I couldn't very well force her to go."

Cramer has never fully accepted Santini's story. "I think she was sodomized," he says. "I think that's why she didn't want to go to the hospital. You'd play hell convincing me that she wasn't."

In time, however, he came to accept the rest of what Santini told him. As for her attacker's peculiar sexual demands as Santini described them, "they're weird," says the detective. "Too weird for her to have made them up. And she told a consistent story, never changed the details. She just convinced me."

Cramer made several early assumptions about his Unsub. "I didn't think he was from around here, but I thought he knew the area. He did not, for instance, head out to the Pines with her accidentally. He had an idea of what he wanted to do. I also think that he was staying in the area, probably at the place he took her. I didn't believe the guy was nuts enough to take her to his own place. But I also couldn't imagine him driving up here and saying, 'Well, here I am,' without some advance planning."

Assumptions, unfortunately, were all that Cramer had. After years of tireless work he couldn't substantiate a single detail of his victim's story, much less produce a viable suspect. "I hit one dead end after the other," Cramer remembers. "But it was a case I was *not* going to let go. I told Maria, 'You've been through hell. But I promise you *somebody* is gonna lock this guy up. As long as I'm around I'm gonna keep working it. I'm *never* gonna stop!' "

Cramer assiduously vetted every sex-assault case flyer that came into the Willingboro Police Department, a monotonous self-assignment he undertook in the absolute faith that Santini's assailant one day would be tripped up. "I told myself, 'Somebody's going to arrest this guy and they're gonna be puttin' out flyers.' And that's exactly the way it went down.

"There was this one-page flyer. I don't even remember if it came from the Secret Service, or how it got to our department. It had to do with counterfeiting, but there was also something in there about bondage. On the bottom left was DeBardeleben's 1983 arrest picture. I looked at it and said, 'Aw, this guy is way out, you know. He looks like an old man. Maria said he was 30 to 35 years old. And Christ! He's six feet tall! I'm lookin' for a guy who's maybe five-seven. It can't be him.'

"But I would have felt guilty if I'd let it go by."

The detective called WFO, asked for the DeBardeleben task force and was connected to Dennis Foos. "I told him what I had," Cramer recalls. "He says, 'Well, we've got a whole bunch of stuff down here. Why don't you stop on down?' "

Easier suggested than accomplished in Willingboro.

"*Nobody* wanted to do anything about the case," says Cramer. "I'm talking about my department, the prosecutor's office—the whole friggin' route. You know, it was like, 'Hey, the guy's going away for a long time. What do you care? Don't worry about it. It's over.' "

Not for Don Cramer. "I kept calling back down to the Secret Service, asking what they had. And they told me they had a little handwritten note of his that said, 'Levittown' and 'Route 130.' Levittown is just across the river in Pennsylvania, and Route 130 runs through Willingboro Township. That's when I knew. 'This sonuvabitch was *here!*' "

Cramer and another detective eventually were allowed to visit WFO. "My department put us up in a dump," he says. "Bugs all over the place. Everything but bodies in the swimming pool. That's how bad it was."

Yet the trip was a success. The detective recovered a New Jersey state road map, copyrighted 1980, with various sites around Willingboro highlighted in ballpoint. One location was no more than a half mile from the store where Santini worked. Cramer also found notes and receipts indicating that DeBardeleben had contacted or hired mail drop-telephone answering services in Moorestown, Haddonfield, Cherry Hill, and Blackwood, New Jersey, all within twenty miles of Willingboro. Leafing through DeBardeleben's reading material, Cramer received an eerie jolt in the pages of one bondage magazine. "It was a photograph exactly like the Chinese Hog-Tie position Santini described," explains the detective. "If I hadn't seen the girl's face, I would have said, 'Hey, that's Maria.'

"Then I listened to the tapes, and I *knew.* It was a gut feeling."

Back home in New Jersey that April, Cramer played the "Goals" tape for Santini. She didn't recognize the voice. Then he played a short piece of the "Becky" tape for her. "All you had to do was look at her and you knew," he says. "I mean, her eyes starting filling up. I was kinda embarrassed, to tell you the truth. Then

I showed her a photo lineup. Like that, she says, 'That's him!' No hesitation, nothing.

"So then this clown assistant prosecutor tells me it was nice work, but that he won't give me all the subpoenas I need. I told him he was an asshole and I told him that whether he helped me or not, we were going to get this guy. Of course, I had the same trouble with my department. As soon as DeBardeleben became a suspect they started worrying that it was going to cost them some money. My chief came right up and asked me, 'Why are you going through with this?'

"I'll tell ya, I almost started crying. Then I went and talked to one of the female assistant prosecutors. I told her what was happening and that I was considering going to the state attorney general's office. If I didn't get her help, I was gone, whether I got fired or not."

On July 7, 1984, a grand jury was convened at the Burlington County Courthouse in Mount Holly. The panel heard Assistant Burlington County Prosecutor Beth A. Wright lead Maria Santini through her testimony, including her identification of DeBardeleben as her abductor. Later that day, the grand jurors voted an eight-count indictment against DeBardeleben: Two kidnapping charges, one for robbery, another for "aggravated sexual contact," a fifth and sixth for making "terroristic threats," and two gun charges.

25

The Mind Hunters

Professional law-enforcement interest in Mike DeBardeleben was not confined to the police and prosecutors. In the late winter of 1984, as officers from Virginia, Maryland, New Jersey, and several other states traveled to WFO in search of answers to their individual unsolved mysteries, a different sort of detective dropped by to visit the task force, too. He was FBI agent Robert R. ("Roy") Hazelwood, a criminal personality profiler at the bureau's Behavioral Science Unit at Quantico, who came to WFO that winter to begin his own psychological investigation of the suspect.

DeBardeleben fascinated Hazelwood both for the nature of his crimes, and because of the extensive records DeBardeleben had maintained. Hazelwood understood that no law-enforcement researcher ever had gained access to anything quite like DeBardeleben's personal archive.

The FBI already had twice profiled DeBardeleben as an Unsub, in the '78–'79 Alexander–Jensen cases, and also after Jean McPhaul's 1982 murder in Bossier City. Now Hazelwood—whose particular expertise lay in the explication of deviant sexual behavior from rape to autoerotic fatalities—was eager to begin sifting through this trove of primary source material. The DeBardeleben case promised to teach the FBI agent a great deal about his specialty.

At Hazelwood's suggestion, a selection of DeBardeleben's notes and other documents also was sent to Syracuse University for a so-called psycholinguistic analysis by Murray S. Miron, a psychology professor and authority on the delineation of psychological traits and disorders from an individual's writings and utterances. Miron, whose cases for the FBI later included a consultant analysis of Branch Davidian cult leader David Koresh, worked exclusively from DeBardeleben's writings. "It is my evaluation," wrote Miron in his two-page report,

> that the subject is a tormented, lonely individual, with a very low self-image and self-esteem. He is caught in a compulsive struggle to ward off depression which—if not overcome—may turn into self-destructive behavior. The subject sees himself as ugly, poor, fat, unlovable, unlikable, insignificant and worthless—all of which make him believe he is . . . deserving of punishment. He is a masochist who engages in compulsive sadistic fantasies which— without adequate intervention—may become dangerous. The target of his fantasies seems to be his ex-wife Caryn. Her rejection of him has become an obsession. . . .
>
> It is my evaluation that he identifies with his father and resents his mother. There are homosexual overtones in his sexual fantasies and his expression of distrust toward women ('broads.')
>
> All of the symbolic imagery of the subject's writings dwell upon the themes of anal intercourse. His nearly overt fantasy is to be the passive sexual partner of an anally intruding father. His imagery of hiding in a trailer (colon) buried in the ground (feces) with a moped cycle located in an escape tunnel (anus) with his victim (father surrogate) is richly Freudian in import.
>
> The subject shows a high level of intelligence, capability for self-analysis, insight (albeit distorted and

incomplete) and sensitivity. He has obviously tried to gain some measure of control over his self-destructive, unconsciously motivated drives. To such end, he has engaged in elaborate self analysis, extensive reading and self medication with drugs he has obtained from cooperative physicians. He identifies with and prefers to associate with professionals.

In an attempt to resolve his conflict between the feminine like traits of his artistic abilities and the role emulation of his military, machismo father, he has turned his talents to the pragmatic uses of forgery. His protective imitation of the police officer is more than just criminal; it is psychologically symbolic of his identification with the aggressor. With psychiatric intervention, he may be able to overcome his obsessions and compulsive behavior. Without it, he is certain to act in a self-destructive manner. He may do so either by committing a crime that would lead to severe punishment or, if he sinks into deep depression, by taking his own life. Certainly as it now stands, he matches many of the standard profile characteristics associated with the psychologically motivated multiple murderer.

Roy Hazelwood, in preparation for his much more extensive probe of DeBardeleben's psyche, received a full briefing from the task force. He questioned the Secret Service agents, as well. Then Hazelwood reviewed the seized materials and chose for his own analysis a broad sampling of the evidence, including tapes, photos, and DeBardeleben's handwritten notes. These items were then duplicated and delivered to his underground office at the FBI Academy. Joining Hazelwood in the review and analysis would be the noted forensic psychiatrist, Dr. Park Elliott Dietz, then on the faculty of the University of Virginia at Charlottesville. Dietz, who has examined aberrant offenders as diverse as John Hinckley and Jeffrey Dahmer, consults closely with the FBI profiling team, teaches at the academy, and periodically undertakes joint research projects with BSU staff agents.

In Hazelwood's subsequent, forty-page report, "An Analysis of Materials Seized from James Mitchell DeBardeleben," his major conclusion appears on page six, where the agent describes his subject as a sexual sadist, a term coined in the late nineteenth century by the German neurologist, Richard von Krafft-Ebing, in his *Psychopathia Sexualis,* after the infamously perverted Marquis de Sade. According to American Psychiatric Association criteria published in the APA's *Diagnostic and Statistical Manual of Mental Disorders* (DSM III), the modern sexual sadist, like the eponymous French nobleman and writer, inflicts "physical or psychological suffering on another person in order to achieve sexual excitement."

At first glance, the definition would seem to subsume many, if not all, sex offenders. It does not. Cruelty, including sexual abuse, can have many nonsexual motives, from revenge to creating pain as an end in itself. Hazelwood cites for example the late serial sex killer, Ted Bundy, who usually preferred intercourse with female victims who were unconscious or dead, and thus beyond pain. "Bundy exhibited sadistic personality disorder," says Hazelwood. "He enjoyed tormenting people and being cruel to his victims, but there is no evidence that he was sexually aroused by that cruelty. DeBardeleben definitely was."

How common is sexual sadism?

"Sexual sadism is not unusual behavior," says Hazelwood. "But it is unusual criminal activity. There's a continuum of sexual sadism, as there is a continuum of practically any other sexual deviation. It begins with fantasy, which is not a crime. Or, the sexual sadist may act out against symbolic objects; most commonly, photographs, dolls, or clothing. He may act out with prostitutes. In a lot of states, that is not a crime. Also, he may act out against a compliant victim, a woman he seduces much like a child molester seduces a victim. Unless that victim files a complaint, no crime has occurred. At the far end of this continuum the sexual sadist acts out against strangers in an overtly criminal act. DeBardeleben acted out in all these ways, with the possible exception of symbolic objects; we don't know if he acted out against symbols."

It was evident that DeBardeleben felt no guilt or remorse for his crimes, classic symptoms of psychopathy, a personality disorder common—but not universal—among criminals. There were signs, as well, of a third condition, narcissism, probably connected to the psychopathy. Narcissism is a personality disorder that psychiatric experts such as Park Dietz regard as an important emergent factor in the study and understanding of violent offenders. "I see narcissism in more and more criminals," says Dietz. "It is the second most important thing to understand about the criminal personality, after psychopathy."

In DeBardeleben's case, perhaps the plainest manifestation of narcissism was his obsession with his fourth wife, Caryn. "A narcissist with a fragile sense of self will react with rage at the slightest insult or criticism," Dietz explains. "When abandoned by a female, he may devote himself completely to venting his rage, trying to destroy her reputation, her career, her family relations, her friendships and, in some cases, her very life."

DeBardeleben's punctilious vanity as recollected by all his wives, particularly Charlotte Weber, is consistent with narcissistic personality disorder, too (and is another common trait among criminal sexual sadists, according to Hazelwood), as were his complaints and carping over the raw deal he'd gotten in life, the unfairness with which he'd been treated.

"The narcissist cannot admit to any weakness," says Dietz. "If something goes wrong, it must be someone else's fault."

Hazelwood, Dietz, and a third researcher, Dr. Janet Warren, a professor at the University of Virginia, have collaborated on a study of thirty sexual sadists. It is the largest survey of its kind conducted in the past one hundred years. Among the ongoing research's more powerful initial findings is the stunning amount of harm sexual sadists cause. "In my opinion," says Hazelwood, "they are the most intelligent of sex criminals, and the most dangerous. Perfectionism is very common among them. DeBardeleben fantasized his crimes for years and years and years, probably beginning in his teens. He perfected his fantasies and reinforced that perfection through masturbation. In this way, his desires become *very specific*. If you listen to those tapes, it's all the same. He has a script that has to be followed. It's got to be done just so."

The sexual sadists' intelligence (DeBardeleben's IQ was measured at 127 while he was at Danbury), together with their obsessive planning and rehearsals of crimes, make them among the most difficult criminals to detect, and enables the more successful ones like Mike DeBardeleben to remain at large for many years. Says Hazelwood, "I always tell my classes at the academy, 'When you investigate the first crime attributed to one of these guys, you're going to say, "I'm dealing with someone who's been doing this for years!"'" That may not be the case. It may be the first time out of the box for him. The reason it's so well carried out is that he's rehearsed it over and over and over. He is not at all spontaneous in anything he does.

"And he inflicts incredible trauma," Hazelwood goes on. "For example, the FBI serial killer study conducted by our unit covered twenty-six serial killers with 127 victims. We have thirty sexual sadists, twenty-two of whom were murderers, and they killed at least 187 people. Seventeen of those twenty-two that we studied were serial killers in addition to being sexual sadists."

The psychic wellsprings of sexual sadism are unknown, although it certainly must be significant that the overwhelming majority of subjects in the Hazelwood–Dietz–Warren study are males who violently despise women. "There is deep-seated hatred," says Hazelwood. "I don't mean just angry. They *hate* women. To the heterosexual sexual sadist, *all* women are bitches, whores, and sluts. This means *all* women; his mother, his sister, his wife, his Sunday school teacher, Mother Theresa.

"He believes that if he pushes the right buttons he'll find this to be true of all women. And to prove this is true, he takes a nice, middle-class woman and tears her down. He tries to create a slut, or a prostitutelike personality. This proves his theory. Then he punishes her for being like that."

It is tempting to posit a connection between Mike DeBardeleben's towering hatred for his mother and the real estate-agent murders, especially that of Terry Macdonald who, as Detective Louis Gelfuso and others have noted, bore a general physical similarity to Mary Lou DeBardeleben. Lots of aberrant offenders do have serious emotional problems with their moms; it's one of their hallmarks. And many of these men also dream of owning secluded, specially equipped places to sequester—and ultimately dispose of—their victims. In fact, if there's any ambition that all serial killers seem to share it is to some day own a very high-temperature incinerator.

Roy Hazelwood doesn't discount the possibility that somehow DeBardeleben expressed his despite for his mother by murdering surrogates, but the agent emphasizes other aspects of the crimes. "The real estate women are available, accessible," he says. "To me, it's the most dangerous legitimate profession in America. They go with total strangers to isolated areas on weekends, nights, and holidays. And I think that's the reason DeBardeleben chose them as victims. He could get them away. Generally, no one was suspicious if they were gone a considerable period of time."

Hazelwood agrees that female Realtors' poise and self-confidence also might have played a role. "Absolutely," he says. "They meet his criteria. They're professional. They're very articulate. They're neatly groomed. They're white collar and, for him, they are unattainable while, at the same time, available and vulnerable."

What would Dr. Freud have made of this pattern?

"It is the raw material for which psychoanalysts became famous," says Dietz, whose personal views in the case coincide closely with Hazelwood's. "The traditional dream interpretation of house is mother. It is the secure, womblike, open, accepting, nurturing object. The sex offender who enters a house symbolically is entering his mother.

"If Mrs. Macdonald did in fact resemble his mother, then you'd want to ask if there was a period in DeBardeleben's life when his father was unavailable, which there was. Did Mother bring home a succession of 'uncles' to share her drunken bed? Was DeBardeleben exposed to his mother as a slut, and develop this notion that's been called the whore-madonna complex? 'Sluts like mother must die.' You look for that in prostitute killers."

Equally difficult for the experts to explain is why some victims were murdered, and others, particularly Lucy Alexander and Laurie Jensen, were not. "I've thought about that at length," says Hazelwood. "These guys seem to have some type of subconscious criteria for people they decide to kill. They unexplainedly release victims. They'll kill five or six in a row, then release two or three."

Alexander and Jensen hardly resisted him. Dianne Overton fought back, and he tried to kill her.

"I once wrote an article on the dangers of providing confrontational advice to women who are faced with rape," Hazelwood answers. "No one knows for sure what to do. This type of individual, however, *loves* for the victim to do things that she doesn't want to do. That's part of her degradation and humiliation. Fighting indicates to him that she is prepared to go to any length to keep from doing what he wants her to do. That's a turn on. Conversely, however, we see in other cases completely compliant victims who nevertheless were killed."

Some of DeBardeleben's other aberrations are a bit more easily understood. Of the thirty cases Hazelwood and the others have studied, six men besides DeBardeleben were reported to have cross-dressed. Hazelwood and Dietz point out that sexual offenders sometimes experiment with deviant acts outside their repertoire. DeBardeleben therefore possibly was experimenting that day he pulled on the yellow mini-skirt in front of Maria Santini. "If he was just exploring," says Dietz, "it would be like Jeffrey Dahmer tasting one of his victims. He's checking to see if he'll get a rush from it. When you have a person with multiple deviations and above-average IQ, he's likely to be aware of the whole gamut of sexual deviations. He'll have read about them, even if it is in something he's found in a porn shop. Then he'll try them. He'll try a bunch of them. Those that do nothing for him eventually are abandoned."

Likewise for the homoerotic magazines Linda Johnson said she discovered in DeBardeleben's Landmark Mini-Storage locker. Thirteen of the study's thirty sexual sadists engaged in consenting adult homosexual acts. "The erotic images that a man collects usually indicate his sexual preference," observes Dietz.

Then what of DeBardeleben's partiality to anal sex and fellatio? These also appear to be traits consistent among sexual sadists. Twenty-two of the thirty anally raped their victims, as opposed to seventeen who committed vaginal rapes. Twenty-one of the subjects forced victims to fellate them.

"Logic tells me that homosexuality, or latent homosexuality, plays an important role here," says Hazelwood. "We do not have scientific data to back that up. It is simply a gut feeling, based on my experience."

Anal sex is also more painful and degrading to the victim, a factor of paramount importance to the sexual sadist. Yet even when he'd created what for him seemed to be perfect situations, Mike DeBardeleben apparently had frequent trouble with retarded ejaculation. "That's consistent with sexual sadism," explains Hazelwood. "He's using sex as a weapon to dominate. Also, until he gets to the extreme torture you hear on the tapes, he's not really aroused sexually, so he's having difficulty ejaculating."

By contrast, some of the victims DeBardeleben forced to masturbate or fellate him in his car reported that he ejaculated rather quickly. "In some cases," offers Dietz, "danger and the threat of apprehension heighten sexual excitement, speeding ejaculation."

Whatever his sexual orientation, or orientations, Mike DeBardeleben is extremely rare, in Roy Hazelwood's experience, for exhibiting so may characteristics associated with sexual sadism. "Normally," he says, "we find an individual with four or five of the twenty to twenty-five characteristics we find in various offenders. DeBardeleben fit almost all of them."

Reasoning from what he knows of sexual sadists in general, and Mike DeBardeleben in specific, Hazelwood guesses that he may have murdered twenty victims, possibly more. "How many more? I have no idea. But this guy did not start and stop and start again. He continued killing."

Is that, in the end, what makes him so different, so unusual?

"No," answers the agent. "He's different because Mike DeBardeleben is the best-documented sexual sadist since the Marquis de Sade. He's the one I use as a standard for all others."

PART
FOUR

26

"I'm Sure Glad We Convicted Him."

A few weeks prior to DeBardeleben's third counterfeiting trial, scheduled for June 1984, in Charlotte,
Elizabeth Mason received a call from her brother,
named Zack, who lived in Tennessee. It had been five
years since the man calling himself Al had assaulted
Mason in the empty house in Fayetteville; time enough
for her to have healed, physically, from her ordeal, and
to have pulled her life back together. Mason and her
husband had moved to another state, and she once
again was selling residential real estate. The memory
of the attack, however, was fresh as ever. She still
lived in emotional pain and deep anger for what had
been done to her.

Her brother Zack had been reading a Tennessee
newspaper, and noted in it a story about Mike
DeBardeleben. The piece described DeBardeleben as a
suspect in the Macdonald and McPhaul murders, which
immediately raised a question in Zack's mind. His sister was a Realtor, too, and she also had been attacked
in an empty house by a man posing as a would-be
buyer. Could DeBardeleben be the same man who tried
to kill Elizabeth? Mason herself strongly doubted such
an extraordinary happenstance, but nevertheless telephoned the Fayetteville police to see what she could
learn. They put her in touch with Mike Stephens at
WFO.

Days later, Mason and Fayetteville Police Detective
Jimmy Cook met with Mike Stephens in the task

force's seventh-floor office, where Stephens was to show her a photo lineup.

"I was very nervous," Mason recalls. "I really did not know if I would be able to identify him from a picture." But she did, with complete certainty, as Mike Stephens and Jimmy Cook looked on. Mason was ecstatic. "I mean," she recalls, "I left there and *flew* home. I was so excited. I couldn't believe it. I mean, *major elation.*"

Which didn't last for long.

Jimmy Cook returned to Fayetteville to learn, he says, that identification or not, there would be no prosecution. "The DA," explains Cook, who has since left the Fayetteville police, "felt that her brother may have shown her a picture of DeBardeleben. We didn't have any fingerprints or any other physical evidence. The next door neighbor was not a good witness, either. The DA told me that he wouldn't go to court unless he could win it, and he just felt like it was a weak case."

"I wanted to prosecute," says Mason, "but they didn't want to. I was told that we were so far down the line behind other cases that they didn't want to spend the money. And I was told that all they had was my identification. Well, that seems *inconceivable* to me. What about all the blood in that house? There *must* have been some fingerprints. And my *car!* He *drove* my *car!* I cannot figure out why he wasn't tried."

"We dealt with lots of local law-enforcement people," adds Mike Stephens. "Some were extremely professional, hard-working police departments, and tough prosecutors willing to take chances in order to do the right thing. Unfortunately, too many didn't care enough about victims, what victims have to live with for the rest of their lives and the psychological importance to victims of seeing their attackers held accountable in court for their crimes. People like Elizabeth Mason."

Justice would be pursued much more aggressively across the state in Charlotte, where U.S. District Judge Robert D. Potter convened DeBardeleben's third counterfeiting trial on Monday, June 11. The scowling defendant came into Potter's somber, wood-paneled court that morning in a dark, three-piece suit, light-colored shirt, burgundy tie, and wire-rimmed glasses. What with the spiky black whiskers DeBardeleben had sprouted that spring in the Mecklenberg County Jail, his aspect at the defense table was eerily Mephistophelean.

The charges against him grew out of his April 28, 1983, visit to the Eastridge Mall in Gastonia. Specifically, Assistant U.S. Attorney Ken Andresen alleged that DeBardeleben possessed and passed four bogus twenty-dollar bills at the mall that night, a pared-down, eight-count, no-frills indictment designed to ensure that the trial phase of the prosecution was a walk-over. "It was simply a preliminary to our real goal, the sentencing hearing," says Andresen, a native of upstate New York and a onetime rock musician who took his law degree at Wake Forest. "Putting on the evidence to make sure we convicted him was a necessary first step. We didn't want to drop the ball. The biggest fear I had was that we'd somehow stumble at this really basic, preliminary stage. It would have been exceedingly embarrassing, and very unfortunate."

After extensive testimony on the Mall Passer case from agent Robert Turner, Andresen led the Eastridge Mall witnesses through their recollections, from B. Dalton manager Dean Huey's story of his initial confrontation with DeBardeleben (a copy of the paperback, *Singles,* that Huey sold him later was found in DeBardeleben's storage lockers) to security woman Achwha Dean's retelling of her nervous moments spent shadowing the suspect across the Matthews–Belk sales floor and out into the mall parking lot. All the witnesses positively identified DeBardeleben as the man they encountered that night.

On the second day of the trial, agent Pete Allison from Knoxville described for the court the incriminating contents of DeBardeleben's 1971 Chrysler as he and T. J. Bondurant and the rest of the Secret Service agents discovered them in their search of the vehicle the day after Allison arrested DeBardeleben at the Foothills Mall. Tuesday's final witness was Barbara Abbott, who took the stand, as she had in Nashville, to relate her experiences as her husband's assistant counterfeiter. She described his printing operation, and also told of joining DeBardeleben on bill-passing expeditions. All of Abbott's testimony strictly was limited to her knowledge of counterfeiting.

The day and a half of testimony was routine and colorless, just as the prosecution planned it. "There wasn't much there to get the jury riled up," says Andresen. "As far as they were concerned, he was just another guy who had been caught passing bad money."

Next morning, Andresen sought to introduce one further bit of evidence, DeBardeleben's three prior counterfeiting convictions. Defense counsel Keith Stroud objected, arguing that introduction of his client's past record would unreasonably prejudice the jury against DeBardeleben, who in any event stood scarce chance of acquittal. "Judge," said Stroud, "as a practical matter the evidence in this case is overwhelming. You know that."

Potter agreed, and also agreed with the defense lawyer that Andresen should not tell the jury of the defendant's record. This was about the only courtroom skirmish in which Stroud prevailed. The jury went out at 11:02 on Wednesday morning, and came back forty-eight minutes later with their verdict: Guilty on all counts. Sentencing was set for July.

In order for DeBardeleben to be sentenced as a dangerous special offender, Andresen first needed to show that the defendant was *both*—dangerous *and* special. Establishing specialness required that the prosecution demonstrate three factors. One, that DeBardeleben's visit to the Eastridge Mall was part of a larger pattern of criminal conduct; two, that counterfeiting produced a substantial portion of DeBardeleben's income; and three, that DeBardeleben evinced special skill and expertise as a counterfeiter.

His dangerousness was a simpler matter to address. Here, all that was necessary was for Andresen to show that an "enhanced" (i.e.—longer) sentence would afford the public added protection from further criminal acts by DeBardeleben. Not a tall order.

Judge Potter, one of Ronald Reagan's earliest appointees to the federal bench, was a stern jurist who in 1989 would whack televangelist Jim Bakker with forty-five years for the TV preacher's fraud conviction. Never before or after Mike DeBardeleben, however, had Potter occasion to sentence anyone under dangerous special offender statute. He gaveled the sentencing hearing to order at 9:40 A.M., Thursday, July 26. Aware of the explicit material that the federal prosecutor intended to present, Potter cleared his packed courtroom of all children before nodding to Andresen to begin.

Andresen's first witness, Secret Service Document Analyst Larry Stewart, told the court that DeBarqdeleben had passed a total of $165,000 in counterfeit money in sixty-five cities across the U.S. in a little less than four years. Plainly, forgery was a major source of income for him, and plainly his appearance at the Eastridge Mall was not an isolated criminal act. Stewart also testified that in his expert opinion DeBardeleben's bills were of "very high quality," the work of a talented craftsman. Judge Potter, who's tried many counterfeit cases, agreed. "As I recall," says the judge, "he produced a pretty fair bill. I've had 'em who've tried to pass Xeroxes."

The defendant's specialness firmly established, Andresen then called on the three task force members to help him address the issue of public danger. It was to be the first full public disclosure of what the Secret Service had learned about DeBardeleben, as well as a graphic presentation of what the agents had discovered, including the audiotapes. For the balance of the day, the crowded courtroom would be held breathless. "The silence," remembers Ken Andresen. "You could have heard a pin drop."

First up was Dennis Foos, who itemized DeBardeleben's counterfeiting paraphernalia as the Secret Service had discovered and seized it.

"Now," asked Andresen, "what other types of material did you find at the storage lockers?"

"A large amount of police-type equipment," Foos answered matter-of-factly, "including handcuffs, police emergency lights, a police-type siren. . . . There was a large amount of pornography discovered in these units, tape recordings, news articles, which largely appeared to relate to crimes against people, specifically crimes against women, as well as robberies, bank robberies, and such things."

Foos continued on with his list of seized materials. Ropes, chains, tape, license plates, a dildo, fake IDs, badges, drugs, handwritten notes, jewelry, approximately three hundred pairs of women's underwear, mostly new, some not so new, guns, ammunition, and road maps. Before stepping down at midmorning, he also summarized for Andresen DeBardeleben's dozens of second selves—James R. Jones, Roger Blanchard, Maurice Paquette, and the rest—and the meticulous documentation the defendant had established for each, especially Jones; birth certificates, medical records, bank accounts, driver's licenses, car registrations, and business cards.

Foos was excused pending afternoon recall. Greg Mertz then was sworn in to present a portfolio of photos and documents. Some of the pictures were taken during the searches. They depicted the evidence as it was discovered in DeBardeleben's Chrysler and his two mini-storage sheds. "Photograph number twenty," said Mertz, pointing out a representative shot, "we have a reel-to-reel tape recorder in the background, three tubes of K-Y Jelly, some type of mask, a lock mechanism with blank, uncut keys, female jewelry, male jewelry. On the right side in the background is a manila envelope with white adhesive tape. This adhesive tape contains human hair. Obviously, at some point this adhesive tape had to be on a person and then removed."

Later in his testimony, Mertz reached picture numbers thirty-one and thirty-two, close-up photos of a printed page from a psychiatric handbook. "This chapter," Mertz explained,

is entitled "Abnormal Sex Offenses." This particular underlined portion reads:

"There are two varieties of rapists who may be called rapists in every sense of the word. One is the man who is loaded with hatred of women and acts out his hatred by an assault on a woman, of which actual sexual intercourse is only one part. The second type is the sadistic rapist. He is a person who finds greatest satisfaction when he can inflict pain. It excites him to strike, to injure, or perhaps to murder his victim, and there are some who have been known to have eaten the flesh of those whom they murdered."

Mertz read aloud some titles of magazines recovered from the storage lockers: *Anal Lovers, Girls Who Love It from Behind, Famous Anus* and a pamphlet, *Stuff It up My Ass*. He also noted that DeBardeleben had bought Jack Henry Abbott's prison reflections, *In the Belly of the Beast*.

"Photograph number thirty-eight," the agent went on, "[is] more reading material. *You're Under Surveillance*. Other books, *The Complete Book of Locks, Keys, Burglar and Smoke Alarms and Other Security Devices, Crime Pays!, The Big Con, Killer Joey*. . . .

"Photographs forty-two and forty-three are various types of pornographic photographs that were seized in the storage lockers. There are several pages of these types of photographs of fifty to sixty different females. . . . [Including] photographs and negatives there are eight-hundred to a thousand pictures."

Mertz explained about The Naked Eye and discussed one older photograph that pictured a nude and apparently drugged, or drunk, young woman being sodomized with a Dr Pepper bottle. DeBardeleben's third wife, Faye, had recognized the couch on which the girl was splayed, and indicated it dated to the early days of her marriage to Mike.

DeBardeleben's 1977 letter from Danbury ("I feel that I have been unjustly tormented, degraded, and shit upon by society. . . .") was read aloud, as were a number of his coded notations—KRK, SMB, FHITA—which Mertz decoded for the court. He also read into the record the "Mr. Benson" bank scam script.

After lunch, Dennis Foos returned to gloss for Andresen all the crimes DeBardeleben was known or suspected of committing, or for which he awaited trial. These included the four bank extortion-kidnaps, his three previous counterfeiting convictions, the rest of the information on his rap sheet, the pending two murder indictments, and various kidnap and rape charges in Missouri, Virginia, Maryland, New Jersey, and Connecticut. The ghastly McPhaul case crimes-scene photos also were entered into evidence.

The final witness was Mike Stephens, whom Andresen used to introduce four of the audiocassettes; DeBardeleben's "Goals" tape ("Also of prime importance—top priority—would be an incinerator . . ."), the torture session with Caryn, "Becky," and the so-called Falsetto Tape, in which DeBardeleben himself plays the victim's role.

Stephens remembers that the courtroom was filled to capacity and utterly hushed as Andresen at the prosecution table played the first cassette, "Goals," in its four-minute entirety. The agent made eye contact with DeBardeleben, who fixed him with a fierce, cold-blooded stare. Judge Potter allowed but two minutes each of the "Caryn" and "Becky" tapes, long enough to hear the women's agonies and to clearly make out DeBardeleben's lifeless voice as he went about torturing them. Stephens noticed that several women dashed from the courtroom as the tapes were being played.

At 3:15 that afternoon, the testimony concluded and Judge Potter called a recess. "I noticed that DeBardeleben's jurors had come to the sentencing," remembers Dennis Foos. "At the break, several of the women on the jury came out of the courtroom, crying. One of them said, 'You know, I thought there was something more to that guy than just counterfeiting. I'm sure glad we convicted him.'"

"After the testimony," says Greg Mertz, "I went back to the judge's chambers, with the permission of the prosecutor, to apologize, not so much to him but to his clerk and stenographer. In the courtroom I'd said things like 'fuck her in the ass' and 'eat shit and die,' and I wanted to apologize.

"So I went back and said, 'Your honor, I want you and your court to know I apologize for reading those lines in front of you.'

"He said, 'Oh, that's okay, agent. I understand that you were just doing your job. I have a pretty good idea what I'm going to do with this ol' boy.'"

A week later, on Thursday, August 2, Judge Potter reconvened his court to pass sentence. Fully persuaded that DeBardeleben was both special and dangerous under any reading of the statute, Potter merged the eight counts into four, and gave the defendant twenty-five consecutive years in federal prison for each one. "It appears to this court that the defendant is a sado-masochist," understated the judge, "a man without morals."

DeBardeleben's total assessed jail time to date: 135 years.

27

Close Call

Prosecutor Henry Brown's published intentions not-withstanding, Mike DeBardeleben's next trial would not be in Louisiana on capital charges for Jean McPhaul's murder. Nor did Brown indicate to the Secret Service when he expected to get underway. Thus, with no other trials yet scheduled, the legal focus shifted to the Laurie Jensen case, in which federal kidnap charges were pending in Baltimore.

As preparations for this complicated proceeding got underway in late summer of 1984, agents Foos, Mertz and Stephens heard from yet another law-enforcement agency, a surprise communication from the U.S. Park Police, the law-enforcement arm of the Interior Department's National Park Service.

It was a one-page wanted circular. Under a composite drawing that closely resembled Mike DeBardeleben, the Park Police described a July 13, 1982, incident in the 100 block of Riggs Road NE in Washington, D.C., where, at about 11:00 P.M., a 15-year-old black girl was abducted while she waited for a bus.

The victim described her white male assailant as approximately 40 years old, and six-four or six-five. He was clean-shaven with medium-length black hair, and drove a big black or dark blue car, with a fancy interior, a floor-mounted transmission, CB radio, and sunroof.

The man drove her to Washington's Rock Creek Park where he ordered the girl out of his vehicle at knifepoint. Then, as the flyer described it, he "began to fondle her and stuck his finger inside of her vagina against her will. [She] broke away and ran into the woods. The subject attempted to find her, but was unsuccessful."

On August 1, 1984, the Park Police showed the victim a photo lineup from which she positively identified Mike DeBardeleben as her attacker. There was no physical evidence to support the identification, and the Secret Service had nothing substantive to offer, either. Greg Mertz's computerized records showed that DeBardeleben as J. R. Jones had been in Springfield, Virginia, on July 8 of that year, and that he reappeared as Maurice Paquette at a Charlotte medical clinic on July 15. The time between these dates was a void. As for whether the crime fit DeBardeleben's M.O.—it did, partly, and partly it did not. All that the task force members could tell the Park Police was what their psychological experts, Roy Hazelwood and Dr. Dietz, had told them about DeBardeleben and most other criminal sexual sadists: "No sexual offense was necessarily out of character for them." When the victim refused to press charges against DeBardeleben, the Park Police closed their case, unadjudicated.

DeBardeleben was arraigned in Baltimore three weeks later. Until this time he'd said little in court, only occasionally punctuating the silence of his ceaseless scowl with outbursts of anger. Now, however, the defendant suddenly started demanding a much greater share of everyone's time, and attention. His health, long a preoccupation, became a favored courtroom topic. On September 10, at a pretrial hearing, clad as before in his funereal dark suit and still sporting the sparse, sinister-looking beard, DeBardeleben complained theatrically to U.S. District Judge Walter E. Black, Jr., that "I have several serious medical problems. I have an ulcer. I have colitis. I have arthritis. I have a spot on my right lung, which is not eliminated to be cancer. They don't know."

According to DeBardeleben, he was getting no sympathy or treatment for his multiple maladies in the Baltimore City Jail. "The denial of this medication causes me to be ill daily, your honor. I'm talking about diarrhea, loss of weight, passing blood. Every day this goes on. It's wasting me away." Judge Black did order that DeBardeleben receive medical care, going so far at one point to see that he was taken to a downtown hospital for treatment.

For their part, Federal Prosecutors Juliet Eurich and Max Lauten suspected DeBardeleben was malingering, a belief consistent with their overall low opinion of the defendant. "It was visceral disgust," explains Lauten. "I felt like spitting in his face, frankly. He really disgusted me. I sort of looked at him as evil personified. The mere color and texture of his skin put me off. Very pale. Very sickly looking."

DeBardeleben also contended at the September 10 hearing that a conspiracy existed to prevent him from exercising his constitutional rights. He told Judge Black that he wished to fire his court-appointed attorney (the third one provided for him by Black) and to proceed *pro se*, as his own lawyer, in large part because of the conspiracy.

"I have been prosecuted in three counties," DeBardeleben protested, "and in each case court-appointed attorneys have [tried] trickery, fraud, deceit, and deception ... to get me away from my fourth-amendment rights. They consistently worked against me. I have caught them numerous times in this sort of tactic."

His central contention was that his fourth-amendment protection against unreasonable search and seizure had been traduced, disgracefully, by the Secret Service. DeBardeleben complained that his belongings had been hauled away indiscriminately in a "wholesale" confiscation. What was more, Greg Mertz and the others had compounded their offense by listening to his private audiotapes without first securing another court order allowing them to do so.

The federal prosecutors took DeBardeleben's legal points very seriously. If the defendant were able to sway Judge Black with this argument—that the seizures were, in fact, illegal, and therefore the evidence gathered at the storage lockers could not be used against him—he effectively would gut the government's case, and seriously imperil any subsequent prosecutions, of which at least eight more still were contemplated.

"The search warrants," explains Max Lauten, "were specifically directed toward counterfeiting. There wasn't a lot of leeway for other things. You could really ask yourself, 'What could tapes possibly have to do with counterfeiting?' And you could also say, 'If these tapes are so important, why can't the agents go back and get another warrant for permission to listen to them?'

"Now, to the average citizen that may sound ridiculous, and I guess that in the eyes of the law it perhaps should seem somewhat ridiculous to have an additional warrant requirement. But there have been cases decided involving tapes in closed containers. When they are encountered in a search, there has been a lot of scrutiny as to whether or not agents can go ahead and examine the contents of those containers without further judicial approval.

"On the other hand, you have to look at the good faith of the agents. They got a warrant and, in my mind, they conducted their searches in a very reasonable way. God bless them for taking pictures all the way, too. It would have been impossible to demonstrate how enormous their task was without being able to show the judge pictures of all the stuff they encountered."

DeBardeleben may have shrewdly perceived that the fourth amendment offered his main chance of beating the Jensen kidnap charge (rape is not a federal offense), and Judge Black later would commend him in court on the quality of his presentation. But while he put together exhaustively researched and fully competent pleadings, he also exhibited a goofy paranoia about his fourth-amendment rights. Even after Black conceded DeBardeleben legal control of his defense, for several months the defendant refused to personally examine seized material that the prosecution considered using against him at trial. He explained that to do so might be construed as a waiver of his rights.

"He had some kind of blind spot," remembers Judge Black. "I never followed his point. Of course, the lawyers I appointed couldn't understand him at all. There was something about him not being able to talk to them because he'd be waiving his fourth-amendment rights in some way. Other than that, his points usually were solidly grounded in the law, and made a lot of sense. At least you understood what the issues were."

Which does not mean that Judge Black welcomed DeBardeleben's *pro se* appearance before him. "It put a major burden on me," he explains. "You've got to protect the interests of the person who doesn't have a lawyer. I've got to be sure that he's given all his rights and performs all the functions that a litigant performs in a trial. I have to advise him. 'Now's the time to do this, or that.' That kind of thing."

Judge Black, a 1982 Reagan appointee, is a onetime U.S. Attorney whose legal career until he was named to the federal judiciary had been spent mostly in a private civil law practice, trusts and estates. In his brief tenure as a federal district judge in Baltimore, he hadn't yet presided over a case involving serious sexual violence, and that worried prosecutor Max Lauten. "I think," says Lauten, "we probably would have preferred one of the tougher, no-nonsense judges who was more experienced. But in retrospective, I'm *very* glad that we had Judge Black."

Lauten, 33 in early 1985, had been an Assistant U.S. Attorney for nearly fours years, and before that did civil tax litigation for the Justice Department. He had very little experience himself with violent offenders. About the worst criminal defendants Lauten had taken to court were bank robbers and dealers in illegal firearms. He'd never prosecuted a kidnapping case.

He was brought into the DeBardeleben case by the lead prosecutor, Juliet Eurich, who came to the Baltimore U.S. Attorney's office from private practice in May of 1982. "I also wasn't really experienced at something like this, kidnapping and rape," says Eurich, who at least had done one murder case, the killing of a federal witness.

This collective lack of violent criminal case experience hardly proved a critical inadequacy, however. By the time Eurich and Lauten rested their case, there would be no question where justice lay. But before they reached trial, the young prosecutors faced trench warfare on the suppression issues, where their chances of prevailing were far less certain. "Those suppression hearings were the whole ball game, really," says Lauten. "And I'd say DeBardeleben's was one of the tougher motions I'd ever been involved with. We had some real concerns about the audiotapes, particularly."

The hearings opened Wednesday morning, February 27, 1985, with Greg Mertz called as the first government witness. Under Max Lauten's questioning, Mertz described the Landmark Mini-Storage search of twenty-one months before, emphasizing the surprise discovery of police equipment and other gear that soon persuaded the Secret Service agents Mike DeBardeleben was no ordinary counterfeiter. "We hadn't been there maybe thirty minutes at most," Mertz testified, "and we were thinking, 'You know, what do we have here?' It was a little bit puzzling."

"How did you make a decision as to what you were going to take and what you were going to leave behind?" asked Lauten.

Mertz answered that there were a lot of pieces of paper stuffed into various containers, which obviously were going to require "more thorough examination at the Washington field office."

"Had you found his plant?"

"No, we had not."

"And did that cause you concern?"

"Yes, it did. We found approximately fifty-thousand dollars in counterfeit currency, which was much less than we originally anticipated [because] of the nature and length of the investigation, and the amount of counterfeit money that had been passed.

"We did not find any plates, negatives, or the printing press. We knew that again we were going to have to pursue various investigative leads in an attempt to locate the plant, the same as when we searched the Oakwood apartment."

"Why did you not consider it possible to totally complete the search on the premises?"

"The hour was growing very late. The business establishment wanted to close ... [Mrs. Johnson] could not lock up the business until we left, and we could not do a proper inventory, and examination, with all the stuff that was commingled with the counterfeit, the handwritten notes, et cetera."

Further on in his direct examination, Lauten turned to the "Caryn" tape and asked Mertz what the agent expected to hear when he played the audiocassette that night alone in his office at WFO. "I had assumed," answered Mertz, "that there was something of a criminal nature [on it]. I was pretty well convinced of that, in light of the information we knew about Caryn and in light of all the notes we read. I didn't know if it would be criminal in relationship to the kidnappings, or just strictly counterfeiting. My main motive in looking through all of the notes was to pursue further investigative leads toward finding the plant."

"At any point in time did you consider whether or not you should get an additional search warrant before listening to the tape?"

"No, not at all."

"That thought never crossed your mind?"

"It never crossed my mind."

In a rancorous cross-examination, DeBardeleben at first focused on his handwritten notes, audaciously endeavoring to show that Mertz needn't have inferred criminality from them. To argue his point, the defendant asked the agent to read various of his notes aloud.

"Reading from the top," Mertz obliged him, "Item one, 'Surveillance, sufficient to determine schedule. Not in permanent car but in "travel" car—second car.' Number two, 'bogey car/ tg'—which I interpret as 'tag'—'or both on day of ht.' Number three, 'tested method to handle—ether, carb starting fluid. What is procedure if unpredictable? i.e.—run, shout. Chloroform. Taser. Careful, can be good leap.

" 'Push. Nudge hard, stab action. WG'—I don't know what that stands for. 'Mace. Cuff immediately, before in car. Uniformed pig. Might work, esp. with hat, sunglasses, mustache, etc. quick egress.

" 'In X's car? In van?' "

When Mertz finished reading the page to the court, DeBardeleben asked whether it gave the agent "some indication of kidnapping and rape."

"Kidnapping," answered Mertz.

"Any specific thing triggered it?"

" 'Cuff immediately, before in car.' 'Uniformed pig. Might work esp. with hat, sunglasses, mustache, etc. quick egress.' "

DeBardeleben directed the agent's attention to another page, once again asking that Mertz read it aloud.

" 'Straight jacket, neck/collar leash, leg leash, many and sufficient restraint, suicide prevention, make beg, crawl, do biggie to own AH, be aware and have procedure if terminated.' "

"Couldn't it be a procedure for a mental hospital patient," DeBardeleben interjected, "or for something of that nature?"

Mertz was incredulous. "Make beg or crawl? I don't know. I wouldn't think so."

"Something in there about sex you see?"

"AH."

"And you knew when you read this," DeBardeleben asked, "what AH stood for, correct?"

Mertz looked directly at DeBardeleben. "I thought it stood for asshole," he answered evenly, his intent obvious.

The room fell silent.

"Juliet and Max both had huge smiles on their faces," Mertz recalls. "I was biting my lip. I had to turn away before Judge Black caught on to what I'd done and slam-dunked me."

Black proved an indulgent judge, tolerant of both sides. Even as the suppression hearings dragged on into March—mainly due to DeBardeleben's sometimes balmy line of questioning—the judge remained patient and charitable, often overruling the prosecutors' objections in order to give the defendant every reasonable chance to make his case.

On occasion, however, the proceedings turned *too* strange, even for Judge Black. Tuesday afternoon, March 5, with Mike Stephens on the stand, DeBardeleben tried to draw invidious comparison between the 1983 storage-shed searches and the 1976 search of his house on South Columbus Street. After discussing a whip and some nude photographs that had been left undisturbed in the 1976 search, DeBardeleben handed Stephens an inventory of materials that were confiscated, and asked, "Does it not appear that the vast majority of the items listed indeed relate to counterfeiting activity?"

"It does."

"In other words, when you went there you seized what you were supposed to seize and nothing else, wouldn't you say?"

Stephens wasn't biting. "I don't have any recollection," he replied.

"I'm just asking you to draw on your experience, Agent Stephens, as a senior agent. With your knowledge of searches and what limitations of a warrant imply, you felt that was a pretty correct search. . . ."

"Objection." said Juliet Eurich from the prosecution table. "That's pure argument."

"I feel like I'm in Never Never Land," the judge answered her. "Mr. DeBardeleben is proving that the government made a good search and you are trying to stop him from doing so. It *is* argumentative and I will sustain the objection. But it's crazy."

Altogether, DeBardeleben kept Greg Mertz testifying for a total of nine hours over three days, Stephens for part of one afternoon, and Dennis Foos for eight hours. On March 18, the eve of the defendant's forty-fifth birthday, Judge Black heard oral arguments.

Black remembers that he found DeBardeleben's discussion of the law that day both cogent and persuasive, even if the defendant veered into odiously surreal bombast, describing the content of his "Caryn" tape as "of a most private nature concerning the sexual relationship of husband and wife in the privacy of their bedroom in the sanctity of marriage."

"He was so knowledgeable," remembers Black. "He knew his case better than anyone in the world. He was ready, and he hit the points. He was in a way, a brilliant litigator."

Nevertheless, on March 28, 1985, in a seventy-two page opinion, Judge Black found for the prosecution. He admits it wasn't easy. "They were tough and serious issues," he says. "And they required a lot of time and trouble to address."

"Judge Black," offers Max Lauten, "obviously did a lot of soul-searching over the suppression issues. I wasn't sure he was going to give us the tapes, even though we were prepared to go ahead without them. And I think we would have won without them, too. But once we won that suppression hearing—and especially with DeBardeleben representing himself at trial—we *knew* we were going to get a conviction. The only question was: How is Laurie gonna hold up?"

28

Daddy

The trial opened Monday, April 29, at 10:00 A.M. in courtroom 5D of the Garmatz Building. From behind his laminated wood rampart, Walter Black looked out over a low-ceilinged, windowless expanse of tan carpet, recessed lights, and more laminated wood court furniture. At his right would sit the jury. To their right was the prosecution table, with the defense table opposite, at Black's left. The witness stand, a raised chair enclosed by a low railing, was directly adjacent to where DeBardeleben would be seated.

The first day was spent picking his seven-man, five-woman jury. Ten members of the panel were parents, six fathers and four mothers. Among them they had ten daughters, ranging in age from eleven to forty-five years. It was a good jury for the prosecution, although as Max Lauten points out, "In this case, it would have been hard to get a bad jury."

Juliet Eurich first had met with Laurie Jensen after the close of the suppression hearings. "We knew that she had to testify," says Eurich. "There was no way around that. So the important thing for us was how to do that while causing her the least amount of pain."

Eurich's indispensable partner in this delicate business was Virginia ("Ginny") Mahoney, the U.S. Attorney's newly hired coordinator of so-called victim-witness services. Under a 1982 federal law, victim-witness programs afford individuals such as Laurie Jensen advice and assistance as they contend with the vagaries and frequent illogic of the U.S. criminal justice system. In Jensen's case, Mahoney's job was to help the young woman cope, as best she could, in her looming reconfrontation with Mike DeBardeleben.

Unsurprisingly, simple human warmth is one of the successful victim-witness coordinator's major assets. Juliet Eurich recalls the first time that she and Mahoney played the "Becky" tape for Jensen. "I kept my Dictaphone on my credenza in those days," says Eurich. "I reached back and put the tape in. She listened to it and her eyes rolled back in her head."

"We thought she was having some kind of seizure," remembers Mahoney.

Eurich walked around her desk and held the sobbing Jensen. Ginny Mahoney embraced her as well. "Of course," Mahoney adds, "the problem was that she was going to have to get through that. We *had* to do it again. It wasn't like we could just hug her and say we were sorry."

Since it was imperative that Laurie testify, Eurich and Lauten decided to make her their first witness. "Chronologically it made sense to first talk about the crime," says Lauten. "But also our feelings were that we should try to get her testimony out of the way early, so we'd know what we had to deal with. If she couldn't handle it, perhaps the judge would allow us to recall her later on."

Ginny Mahoney familiarized Laurie with the courtroom, and advised Jensen to keep her eyes fixed on the prosecution table whenever possible. Mahoney herself sat in the front row of seats, between the prosecution and defense tables, so that if Jensen's attention did wander to the left from Eurich and Lauten toward DeBardeleben, she'd first encounter Mahoney in the audience. Seated behind the defense table, also in the front row, were members of Jensen's family, an older brother and sister, and Laurie's mother, who had come to court despite the prosecutors' suggestion that their presence might make it even tougher for Laurie to tell her story.

After Max Lauten's opening statement—the defendant declined to deliver one—Juliet Eurich herself brought in the trembling victim, dressed in a pastel blouse and skirt. When she first saw DeBardeleben at the defense table, not ten feet from the witness stand, Jensen went limp. "Literally," recalls Eurich, "I almost had to carry her to the witness stand. She collapsed, despite all the good preparation."

Juliet Eurich managed to stabilize her witness and navigated Jensen to the stand. After the clerk administered the oath, Eurich positioned herself at the corner of the jury box to pull Laurie's attention as far away as possible from DeBardeleben.

Then the prosecutor slowly began taking a general personal history. "We were trying to keep her calm," says Mahoney. "We had told her that Juliet would start with just the basic stuff, and then move on."

Shaking with fear and shredding wads of Kleenex as she answered Eurich, Jensen kept herself in control through the preliminaries, until the prosecutor mentioned Ocean City, Maryland, and asked, "Can you remember the evening of June 1, 1979?" The question undid Jensen, forcing Eurich to ask for a recess.

During the break, Eurich, Lauten, and Mahoney gathered with Laurie in the hallway just off the courtroom, where they held her, soothing the frightened woman and wondering how she possibly was going to get through her testimony. Just then, Ginny Mahoney came up with an idea. If Judge Black okayed it, she said, why couldn't Mahoney sit with Jensen on the stand to help steady the witness? The prosecutors relayed the request to Black, via his clerk, and were delighted to receive his approval, which might easily have been withheld.

"Judge Black was absolutely tremendous in helping

Laurie through her testimony." says Lauten. "I'd never seen a judge allow something like that."

Jensen resumed her testimony at 11:06, with Ginny Mahoney seated to her left, just outside the witness stand enclosure. The two women held hands. "I was in unknown territory," Mahoney recalls. "I wanted to say something to her, tell her that everything was going to be okay, but I didn't want to screw up the case."

The victim didn't falter again until 11:45, when Eurich asked her to begin recounting what happened once her abductor had taken her to his bedroom. Judge Black called another recess for Laurie to collect herself, before Eurich's questioning resumed.

"Did he take off all your clothes?" asked Eurich.

"Yes," Jensen answered in her soft country twang.

"Did he also take off the handcuffs?"

"He had to, because they were behind my back and I had a T-shirt on."

"What did he do next?"

"Then he got undressed and laid on the bed and made me lay down beside him."

"What did he make you do?"

"He made me kiss him," Jensen said reluctantly. "And then he told me what he wanted me to do."

"What did he want you to do?" asked Eurich.

Jensen again was having difficulty.

"He wanted me to have oral sex with him."

"And did you?" Eurich insisted.

"Yes."

"While this was going on, did he give you instructions?"

"Yes. He told me how to do it."

"Do you know whether he was tape recording it?"

DeBardleben objected to the question as leading.

"Overruled," answered the judge. "Under the circumstances, I see no alternative."

Jensen testified that she had seen a tape recorder on the bed.

"Did he tell you to talk into it?"

"Yes."

"Did there come a time when you got sick?"

"Yes. He made me have oral sex and he ejaculated and I got sick and spit up."

"After he ejaculated and you got sick, did he also make you have anal intercourse with him?"

"Yes," Jensen said quickly. "Yes."

"And did he tape record that as well?"

"Yes, and he made me say stuff."

"Can you tell us what he made you say?"

"It's bad words. Is it okay? Can I say the bad words?"

"Yes," answered the prosecutor.

"Go ahead," Judge Black reassured the victim. "Say whatever was said."

"He made me call him Daddy, and he wanted me to say, 'Fuck me in the ass.' "

"And you repeated the phrases and called him Daddy?"

"Yes."

Eurich played two portions of the "Becky" tape to a transfixed courtroom. Even the prosecutors, who'd heard the tapes over and over were stunned anew by DeBardeleben's cruelty and ferocious deviance. After listening along with everyone else, Laurie Jensen identified her voice and her assailant's voice on the recording. She also identified herself as the nude female depicted in six of DeBardeleben's photos that Eurich showed to her, the judge, and the jury. In the first two photos, Jensen was seen kneeling on a bed. In the third picture, she held a dildo in her right hand. The fourth shot depicted anal intercourse. In pictures five and six she performed fellatio.

Sensing that Laurie was once again about to break from the pain, shame, and terror—compounded by her family's presence just behind the defense table—Mahoney leaned over to Jensen. "I began saying,

'They're just pieces of paper. They have nothing to do with you. They're just pieces of paper.' I didn't know what else to say. I just knew that we had to get through it."

Jensen completed her testimony shortly past noon, and then braced for DeBardeleben's cross-examination. Her fear of him was palpable. Even though he remained in his chair at the defense table as instructed by Judge Black, Jensen visibly shrank each time DeBardeleben spoke. She could not look at him.

"I think he was enjoying the part," says Joe McElhenny, who as the FBI's case agent was permitted to sit at the prosecution table. Max Lauten, seated next to McElhenny, similarly was sure the DeBardeleben savored the experience. "I saw some smirks," he says.

The cross-examination was brief, though hardly merciful.

"Miss Jensen," said DeBardeleben, "were you reluctant to testify in this case?"

"No," she answered, eyes averted.

"No? Did the government threaten or intimidate you in any way to testify here?"

"No."

"Did the government make you feel as if your well-being was in danger because of this case?"

"No, no, they . . ."

"Has the government made you feel that your testimony here is necessary?"

"Yes."

"Are you aware that the maximum sentence for kidnapping—"

"—Objection, your honor," said Eurich.

"—is life imprisonment?"

"Stop right there!" Judge Black ordered. "This is not a matter for discussion or consideration at this trial."

"Miss Jensen," DeBardeleben pressed on, "are you aware that the defendant has been given a prison sentence of over one hundred years?"

"Objection!" Eurich interjected again.

"Mr. DeBardeleben, stop," said the judge, who called a bench conference in which he sternly directed the defendant to abjure this line of questioning. "[You] cannot get into this business of penalties and your present criminal status."

"Okay," answered DeBardeleben, who in any event had but a single further question to pose his victim.

"Miss Jensen," he asked, "do you feel that in the interest of protecting society your presence is necessary here today?"

"Yes," Laurie Jensen answered.

"No further questions," said DeBardeleben.

Her agony on the witness stand was ended.

Although DeBardeleben's jurors seemed curiously impassive during Laurie Jensen's harrowing testimony, consensus opinion on the prosecution team was that Jensen had made a very good witness, despite her inability to point at Mike DeBardeleben and directly identify him as her kidnapper. As for the tape and the photographs, no one in the courtroom—with the possible exception of the defendant—was unmoved by their horror.

The balance of trial was spent with the introduction of physical and forensic evidence that tied DeBardeleben to the crime. Secret Service Technician Steven Cain, the voice identification expert, testified as to how he took voice exemplars from the defendant in October of 1983, and then scientifically compared them to the male voice on the "Becky" tape, of which he played several portions. Cain's professional opinion: "I would say it was highly unlikely that anyone other than Mr. DeBardeleben could have uttered each of the questioned phrases."

Greg Mertz testified that the negatives from which the six photos of Laurie were printed had been recovered in one of the defendant's lockers.

Barbara Abbott told the jury that she recognized the

room in the photos as a bedroom in the house on Hileman Road she shared with DeBardeleben as his wife. Abbott also told of being forced by her husband to call herself "Daddy's little bitch" during sex.

Thus having shown that the nude photos of Jensen were found in the defendant's possession, and had been taken on DeBardeleben's bed in his bedroom, the prosecution than called Pete Smerick, the FBI's forensic photographic examiner, who'd complete the picture, placing DeBardeleben in the bed with his victim.

"Every one of us is different," Smerick testified. "Even identical twins will have differences, and the differences I am referring to are scars, marks, moles, age spots, freckles, wrinkles—things that we as human beings have no control over. They appear at their own will on our bodies."

In order to do a photo comparison for identification purposes, Smerick continued, it is essential that the pictures be well lit and well focused and that the negatives be correctly developed. The images had to be precise and clear, which was no problem with negatives taken from Mike DeBardeleben's storage units. "I found," said Smerick, "that the negatives had been processed properly. There were no indications of chemical imbalance. The negatives were washed properly. The focusing was also quite accurate and the exposure for these negatives was quite accurate. They were excellent negatives."

As a result, Smerick could be very sure of his results. He showed the jurors one of the questioned photos. Jensen's body had been cropped out of it, leaving in the foreground a supine, seminude male figure on the bed, seen from above his right shoulder. A white towel was draped over his head. In his right hand he held a cable release for remote control of his camera. Next to this picture, Smerick placed a nearly identical view of Mike DeBardeleben, taken according to

Smerick's instructions by Secret Service photographer Jim Wineand.

Smerick then explained how he'd compared the two, finding dozens of corresponding marks and spots, which he indicated on his exhibit with tight clusters of arrows. His conclusion: DeBardeleben and the figure on the bed with Jensen were one and the same person—"identical," as Smerick put it.

Eurich and Lauten also entered into the record a selection of inculpatory notes, including the one that began, *"JUST BECAUSE I FELT FEAR (GUILT, IN REALITY) WHEN I HAD LAURIE, LUCY, ETC. . . ."* They rested the prosecution's case late on Wednesday afternoon, May 1.

DeBardeleben said very little, and questioned few of the witnesses after Laurie Jensen's testimony. Thursday morning, he rose and read a brief closing statement. "Ladies and gentlemen," he said, "I must tell you that we are here today only because of a violation of my constitutional rights. Had I been granted my rights under the constitution, there would be no trial. But I was not, and this trial is a further exploitation of this constitutional violation.

"I am innocent of this charge, and maintain that in a legitmate trial I would be able to convince you of this, to successfully defend myself with an aggressive defense by presenting my own evidence, calling defense witnesses, and testifying myself. . . . However, at this trial I cannot do so."

The peculiar plea seems not to have had much effect on the jury's deliberations. Judge Black sent the panel out at 12:02, and heard from the foreman at 2:12 that they'd reached a verdict: Guilty.

Peter Ruehl, a news reporter in the courtroom for the *Baltimore Evening Sun,* watched Laurie Jensen, seated with her family in the front row, right behind DeBardeleben, as the verdict was read. Under the head VICTIM SEES TORMENTOR CONVICTED, Ruehl described how Jensen "raised her clenched fists slightly, shook them briefly and then began to nod her head quickly. Relatives on either side threw their arms around her shoulders. She seemed to glare at the back of DeBardeleben's head."

In the pro forma jury poll that followed, Judge Black's clerk, Mrs. Didomenico, asked each member of the panel, "Having delivered the verdict of the jury, is that your verdict also?"

Most jurors replied, "It is." Juror Elizabeth Lookingland, however, was even more emphatic: "It most *certainly* is," the mother of four answered the clerk.

May 22, DeBardeleben's sentencing day, came up sunny and hot in Baltimore. Judge Black had pondered the defendant for three weeks, and remembers how impenetrable DeBardeleben seemed to him. "He was a complex man that I really didn't understand," says the judge. "I had never run into anyone like him. And this worked on two levels. On the substantive level, there was that horrible crime. At the same time, I had great respect for his legal ability and knowledge of the law and, particularly, his grasp of the case's legal ramifications."

His puzzlement aside, Judge Black had a firm notion of the sort of sentence he wanted to give DeBardeleben, but feared that he could not. "Because of parole board guidelines," he explains, "if I gave him life, he would be eligible for parole in ten years. Somewhere between 120 months and 148 months, he was going to get out."

Juliet Eurich captured Judge Black's dilemma in her brief remarks that morning. "Society," said Eurich, "should not tolerate someone like Mr. DeBardeleben being at liberty." She added, "There is no punishment that is available to compensate the victim or to really send a message to the defendant. He has shown no remorse. He has not admitted guilt. He read a statement to the jury that indicated he felt that the trial was a sham."

And he still did.

When Eurich was through, DeBardeleben rose to denounce his adversaries. "I am the victim of a personal vendetta," he alleged, "a vendetta carried out by painting a false label on me, a label designed to generate such prejudice and bias toward me that those in authority would have ample justification in denying me my constitutional rights and fundamental fairness."

DeBardeleben mentioned no one by name, but clearly the conspirators he had in mind were Foos, Mertz, and Stephens—his inexorable Furies—all of whom testified against him in the Baltimore suppression hearings and trial, as they had in Charlotte. A fourth member of this vividly imagined cabal was his fourth wife, the pitiable, psychologically fractured Caryn. DeBardeleben viciously maligned Caryn as "not only prone to exaggeration, embellishment, and fabrication [but also] a pathological liar, an emotionally disturbed and hysterical person who hides [her] neurosis well, and has the integrity and morals of an alley cat.

"These agents have utilized three tools to accomplish their objectives," he ranted. "The first tool, a hidden accuser, and hidden accusations. The second tool, their own perjury and false accusations. The third tool, certain information, most of a general or nonspecific nature."

Judge Black, who just minutes before coming to court that morning had learned of a solution to his sentencing quandary, listened in his characteristic outward calm as DeBardeleben's rage sputtered into silence.

Then Black dropped the hammer.

"Your offense," said the judge indignantly, "is the most outrageous, cruel and inhuman crime imaginable, and clearly calls for the maximum possible sentence. It is hard to imagine any crime that could be worse under the statue we're dealing with."

Black spoke of the need to keep DeBardeleben off the streets forever. "Release of this defendant, at any time, will threaten every woman in this country," he said. "In addition, the damage it would do [the victim], if she ever knew that this defendant was once more free in this country . . . would be incalculable."

That morning, Judge Black's law clerk had brought to him a Colorado case, *U.S. v. O'Driscoll,* recently affirmed in U.S. Circuit Court, upon which Black determined he could rest his authority for insuring that DeBardeleben, in fact, would spend the rest of his life in prison. *O'Driscoll* permitted Black to specify a minimum term.

"Accordingly," said Black, "Mr. DeBardeleben, I sentence you to . . . a term of 180 years. I specifically order that this sentence shall run consecutive to, and not concurrent with, the sentences heretofore imposed [in the counterfeiting trials]. Further, I specifically order that you shall become eligible for parole only on completion of serving fifty-nine years."

Total assessed prison time: 315 years.

29

"This Man Is Beyond The Pale."

The heavy time meted out by federal judges Potter and Black inevitably convinced various local authorities to save effort and money by suspending their own plans for prosecuting Mike DeBardeleben. Some state attorneys questioned the utility of piling up more prison years, while others lost enthusiasm for cases that might not come to trial for years, possibly long after they had moved on to new career opportunities. Also in the back of everyone's mind were the two murder indictments, especially the Bossier City case, where DeBardeleben's jeopardy was the electric chair.

In the Lucy Alexander case, Delaware State Police Detective Buddy Griffith reports that the victim easily spotted DeBardeleben in a photo lineup he showed her in March of 1984. On the strength of the identification, plus the "LAURIE LUCY" note and other, ancillary evidence recovered from DeBardeleben's lockers, a Delaware grand jury indicted him on eleven counts of rape and abduction in April 1984.

But after DeBardeleben took the 180-year hit from Judge Black, the local deputy attorney general wanted to drop the Alexander case. "So I called Lucy and talked to her about it," says Griffith. "She said that if he was going to go to jail for the rest of his life, she'd rather not go through a trial." According to Griffith, the case consequently was noll prose'd *(nolle prosequi)* officially discontinued.

In Maryland, where DeBardeleben was charged with

attempted murder, victim Dianne Overton was approached by local authorities not long after the indictment. "They told me that I probably wouldn't have to testify," she remembers. "They wouldn't need to bring him into court here, because he had enough other charges against him." Overton adds that if DeBardeleben were ever prosecuted for trying to kill her, she'd testify against him, although she'd rather not.

Similar sentiments prevailed in Bloomfield, Connecticut. Jane Trombley recalls being told that a southern jurisdiction "wanted him and wanted to put him away, so would I consider not pushing my case? At that time I said, 'Fine, no problem.' I didn't think that what happened to me was, by comparison, that significant. If someone else really wanted to put him away, let 'em have him."

Interestingly, Judge Black's innovative sentencing had just the opposite impact in Burlington County, New Jersey. There, Prosecutor Jim Ronca was persuaded that duty dictated he press ahead to trial in the Santini case. "Juliet Eurich told me there was a chance DeBardeleben could exploit a weak point in the law Judge Black used that would allow him to be paroled in ten years," says Ronca. "So we *had* to convict in our case. We had to. Of course, only a short exposure to DeBardeleben is all it takes to convince somebody in my position that he should never *ever* be let out."

With still no trial date in Bossier City, on December 18, 1985, DeBardeleben was shipped from the Federal Penitentiary at Lewisburg, Pennsylvania, for arraignment in Mount Holly, New Jersey, before Superior Court Judge Paul R. Kramer. Judge Kramer, tall, bald, jug-eared and prepossessing—"a John Wayne in judicial robes," as Jim Ronca describes him—would prove a far less patient jurist than his colleague on the federal bench in Baltimore. He regarded DeBardeleben as a security risk in the courtroom, and repeatedly told his three bailiffs that whenever DeBardeleben rose to his feet, they were to do so as well. Kramer seemed reassured to learn that Case Agent Dennis Foos, who would sit through the trial at the prosecution table, was armed.

Kramer brooked no antics, and no sass. Perched at his high bench along one wall of a circular courtroom vaguely evocative of Captain Jim Kirk's bridge on the starship *Enterprise,* Kramer clashed again and again with DeBardeleben, beginning at the arraignment when the defendant asked for a continuance and for special access to the county law library in order to adequately prepare his *pro se* case. Judge Black in Baltimore had handled a similar request by permitting DeBardeleben extensive use of Garmatz Building's ninth-floor law library.

"I'll tell you right now," barked Judge Kramer, "I'm not granting any continuances because you're *pro se.* Now, you better understand that." As for the law library, "We are not going to escort you over to the county law library and take up the time of a guard," said Kramer. "And we are not going to be carting wheelbarrow loads of books over to the jail."

At a February 5, 1986, pretrial hearing, DeBardeleben labored through a loopy discussion of why he believed he was being selectively and vindictively prosecuted. Kramer impatiently interrupted him. "Sir," said the judge, looking down through his half frames, "will you talk about the facts of the case? I don't think anyone knows what you are talking about.

"Let's get back to basics. You were indicted for kidnapping a young woman out of a store, driving her to a house or a dwelling, stripping her naked, tying her up, photographing her and humiliating and degrading her with a running commentary. Now those are the facts giving rise to the indictment."

"It seems," answered DeBardeleben, "that you accept the prosecution's position."

"Where do you come on saying, 'No, that's not

true?' " the judge snapped. "That's not why you were indicted? You were indicted because Mr. Ronca there is a vindictive man? Where do you get that? What facts are you basing this on?"

"Your honor keeps interrupting me."

"I am going to interrupt you until you start making some sense. Will you answer some questions and give me some facts?"

"With all due respect," snarled the defendant, "I think your honor should have an examination for senility."

"All right, sir," answered Kramer. "I will cite you for contempt of court for that!"

Ronca, 33, had his share of testy exchanges with the judge, as well, especially when Kramer ruled that DeBardeleben's jury would hear no part of the "Becky" tape. "I was very concerned about that," says the prosecutor. "We felt we needed something substantial to corroborate Maria Santini's voice identification. Basically, what we had was a woman making a photographic identification four years after she'd seen the man, and then waiting two more years before coming to trial. We had a lot of trepidation. She had to testify and she had to do well. We weren't going anywhere if her testimony wasn't strong."

A jury, on the other hand, was easy to pick. Ronca's standard operating procedure was to weed out those who knew anything about the law ("I don't like to be second-guessed"); journalists ("because they're cynical about authority"); and clergy ("because they forgive—as a prosecutor, that's the last thing I'm interested in").

In sex offense cases, Ronca says that he also ordinarily avoids older female jurors, "because consent frequently is an issue. Middle-aged women tend to think that younger women have too much freedom, and are asking for half the trouble they get into. In this case, I had no fear of any women of any age. All I really worried about were people who struck me as loners, people who didn't have families. I didn't want anyone who could relate in any way to Mike DeBardeleben."

The mostly white, eight-woman, four-man jury was impaneled on Wednesday morning, March 12, 1986, and took their places in two rows of gray upholstered swivel chairs, a quarter way around the room's perimeter arc to Judge Kramer's right. The witness stand was between judge and jury, and the court reporter sat just in front of it. Across the courtroom's straw-colored carpet, framed from Kramer's perspective by the maroon-walled public seating area, was DeBardeleben alone at the defense table opposite Jim Ronca, with the armed Dennis Foos, at the prosecution table.

At 1:45 the prosecution's make-or-break witness, the victim, was sworn in. Ronca had done his best to prepare Santini, but had reason to worry whether the young mother would be strong enough to endure. "She was very timid," he recalls. "I could sense there was a lot of trouble inside her. She's suffered for years, wondering, 'Who was this guy? Why me? Is he out there? Will he hurt me again? Would he harm my children?' She told me she could hardly stand to have her kids leave the house.

"I saw a lot of rage inside her, too. I don't think she ever got over the feeling of being terribly violated."

Santini, to Ronca's relief, handled herself well. In two hours of questioning, she evenly recounted her dreadful and strange encounter. Over DeBardeleben's objections, the witness also identified several bondage photos from his smut collection as identical to the poses she was forced to assume, including the painful Chinese Hog-Tie. At the close of her testimony, Santini identified DeBardeleben at the defense table as the man who'd abducted and assaulted her.

DeBardeleben began his cross-examination at 3:45 by going directly to the one major inconsistency in Santini's story. At the time of the incident, she described her kidnapper as no more than five-seven, while the defendant, whom she'd just identified as one and the same person, clearly was six feet tall.

Her explanation: The store cash register was installed on a raised platform in the middle of the selling area, so that a customer stood six inches lower than the clerk. Santini had gauged her kidnapper's height based on her first look at him, when he asked about speaking to the manager of the store, and so automatically had subtracted five or six inches from his true height.

Attack as he might, DeBardeleben could not shake Santini from this explanation, although he did intimidate her into using the third-person "he" to describe her attacker, rather than the more emphatic second-person "you," Ronca had told her to use. At four o'clock, when Judge Kramer announced he was gaveling the day's proceedings to a close, DeBardeleben argued for just a little more time to complete his questioning.

"He must have sensed he was winning," Ronca believes. "He was getting what he wanted. He'd maneuvered her into making simple yes and no answers, and when she referred to him in the third person it was as if she was admitting the possibility that someone other than he could have attacked her."

Next morning, however, Santini had regained her composure.

"Do you want to see the man who did this crime to you punished?" asked DeBardeleben.

"I would like to see you in prison, yes," she answered.

"So that you believe the defendant is this man?"

"I am sure—"

"Okay—"

"—that the person who did this to me is you."

"Can you honestly say this is because of your recollection? Or is it because the police persuaded you it's true?"

"The police had nothing to do with it."

Santini survived, and the rest of the trial for Jim Ronca was a straight schuss to the finish line, in which the livelier moments do not appear on the transcript. "During breaks," recalls Ronca, "Mike Stephens would walk up to DeBardeleben at the counsel table and stand as close as possible to him, just to unnerve him. At another point DeBardeleben started yelling about Foos being a Nazi. He asked one of the sheriff's officers to protect him from the Nazi Foos."

Greg Mertz testified, too, even though the agent candidly questioned DeBardeleben's guilt in the case. Off the witness stand and off the record, Mertz had bluntly laid out to Ronca his strong misgivings, based in great degree upon Santini's transvestitism testimony. "If DeBardeleben cross-dressed," insists Mertz, "I think we would have found something in all the stuff we seized." Mertz also wonders at Santini's ability to pick out her assailant in a photo spread after so many years.

Mike Stephens, for one, sharply disagreed with Mertz. He thought the right man was sitting in the defendant's chair. Dennis Foos, of course, saw merit in both his friends' arguments.

Evidently there were no such divisions on DeBardeleben's jury. At 10:43 A.M. on Monday, March 17, after two hours and fifteen minutes of deliberation, the twelve returned guilty verdicts on all counts.

At the sentencing hearing in May, the "Goals" tape was played in its four-minute entirety, and some of DeBardeleben's musings were entered into the record, including his chilling treatise on sadism ("... *The central impulse to have complete mastery over another person, to make him/her a helpless object of our will, to become the absolute ruler over her, to become her god, to do with her as one pleases, to humiliate her, to enslave her are means to this end....*").

Jim Ronca, arguing for the harshest punishment possible, informed Judge Kramer of the chance DeBardeleben's federal time might collapse to ten years. He described the defendant as "so far beyond rehabilitation . . . the only way for society to further its own legitimate interest in self-protection is to make sure that the only way he ever leaves prison is feet first."

DeBardeleben's oratory was far purpler. "I feel not the slightest twinge of guilt," he declaimed. "I am innocent of this crime. I didn't do it. Yet I was framed, framed in a sinister, evil, and insidious machination, a *conspiracy,* if you will. . . .

"A foul odor of corruption emanates from this courtroom. Corruption so pervasive, arrogant, and reprehensible that it is repugnant to any civilized notion of fundamental fairness or human dignity."

Jim Ronca, said DeBardeleben, was "a young, mentally ill, power-drunk sociopath," while Judge Kramer was "a sinister, vindictive, sadistic, depraved alcoholic who cares [nothing] for the law or constitution or fair play."

Interestingly, DeBardeleben said nothing of the Secret Service plot against him, or of Caryn's complicity in it. "I am now ready for sentencing by this kangaroo court," he concluded.

Judge Kramer than pronounced punishment.

"Someone might say, 'Well, for a man already serving 315 years in prison, why spend the money to try him again?' " observed the judge. "Of course, the prosecutor's purely logical answer to this [is that] these crimes deserve a prosecution as aggressive as if there was no other conviction. The very fabric of society is torn so terribly by these crimes that . . . even if he's serving a thousand years in prison it is not an idle thing to consider consecutive sentences in such a case. I quite agree with the prosecutor. This man is beyond the pale. He's beyond rehabilitation."

Further along, Judge Kramer termed DeBardeleben "a psychopath in the true sense of the word; a degenerate, a sadist who, according to his own words, has decided never to comply with society, but to take his revenge against society by these terrible things."

Kramer's sentence: sixty years, with no parole eligibility for thirty and a half years, to be served consecutively to DeBardeleben's federal sentences. "In effect," said the judge, "the man is now serving 345½ years." He dropped the contempt citation against DeBardeleben. "I don't want the matter to have the slightest flavor that either the prosecutor or I or the police were emotionally involved in this thing," he explained. "Indeed, the fact that we sat here ... through these tireless, abusive tirades that he calls his rights of allocution I hope bears that out." Judge Kramer did not, however, forget to levy fines against DeBardeleben under New Jersey's Violent Crimes Compensation Law. His bill: $150, the maximum allowable, payable to the Victim Compensation Board.

30

Real Scared

DeBardeleben's next—and, as it turned out, last—criminal trial was held in Manassas, Virginia.

In November 1986, two and a half years after Officer Don Cahill had shown Lori Cobert the photo lineup from which the Manassas teenager identified Mike DeBardeleben as the man who assaulted her February 5, 1981, Cahill and investigator James E. Guzdowski, also of the Prince William County Police Department, flew to Los Angeles and then drove north to the Federal Penitentiary at Lompoc where they read DeBardeleben his Miranda rights and arrested him for abduction "with intent to defile" Cobert, as well as for sodomizing the exceptionally pretty young woman.

The Cobert case would be the most tenuous prosecution yet, hinging almost exclusively upon the victim's testimony, many years after the fact. The sole bit of corroborating physical evidence, Cobert's semen-stained blue jeans, inexpicably had been lost, leaving Prosecutor Leroy ("Lee") Millette, Jr. (now a Virginia Commonwealth judge) with one eyewitness and "a little filler," as Millette puts it. "It was not the strongest case," he concedes.

The incident occurred around 1:00 A.M. on a clear, chilly February 5 as the five feet tall Cobert, a sandy blond with expressive green eyes, was driving north on State Route 28 through Manassas, not far from the veterinary hospital where she worked. She and a girlfriend had gone roller skating in Manassas that evening, and the two planned to sleep over at the other girl's house. At the skating rink, however, Cobert's friend decided that before heading home for the night she'd first like to visit a young man of her acquaintance. So Lori drove on alone in her friend's blue Oldsmobile Cutlass.

As she passed through a green light on Route 28, Cobert noticed a four-door sedan, dark burgundy, idling at the intersection, waiting for the signal to turn. Cobert, who had friends on the Manassas police force, thought that the sedan looked like an unmarked police car, but she thought nothing more of it until a few moments later when she looked in her rearview mirror to see the big sedan right behind her, a pair of red lights flashing from its grille. There was no sound of a siren.

She pulled over onto the shoulder near the entrance to the local IBM installation, and watched in her side mirror as the man she assumed was a cop approached. He was a white male, six-one, approximately 165 pounds, about twenty-five to thirty years of age, with brown curly hair and a mustache. Cobert noted that he was neatly groomed and attired in a beige overcoat of the sort an undercover officer might wear.

At his request, she produced her driver's license, at the same time explaining that the Cutlass wasn't her car, so she really didn't know where the registration might be. Saying nothing, the putative policeman returned to his car where, as Cobert watched in her mirror, he appeared to be radioing. Minutes later, he returned to her window and asked her to get out.

Cobert complied, still believing the man to be a police officer—although she did not ask him his name or for any identification—and allowed him to guide her by her elbow back to the front passenger-side seat of his car. Only when he shut the door and she looked around the sedan's interior did it dawn on Lori Cobert what was happening. "The inside was real plush," she remembers. "Like velour. And there wasn't any radio or scanner. All of the sudden I got real scared."

The stranger quickly was beside her on her left, and briskly explained himself. Lori wouldn't get hurt, he said, if she did as he directed. She instantly intuited that to save her life she better do as she was told, and she did. "Basically," she says, "the only thing that went through my mind is that I was going to survive. I was going to do whatever it took to survive. I didn't care what it was. I was going to come out alive."

The man grabbed Cobert's left hand, placed it over his exposed, flaccid penis, and began to masturbate, his right hand clasped over her left. As he did so, Cobert saw his left hand reach under the dashboard where she heard a click, as if perhaps the hammer on a handgun was being uncocked.

Cobert continued to offer no resistance. "I knew I was in trouble," she explains, "and I thought to myself, 'I've *got* to remember something here. There's something I've got to remember.' So I just stared at him. There was no life in his eyes. I mean *nothing*. No sparkle. No nothing. They were just dead. I mean, that was weird. I looked and looked at his eyes and I looked at his face as long and as hard as I could."

Failing to reach orgasm, the man groped under Cobert's blouse to roughly fondle one of her breasts, then pushed her mouth down over his now-erect penis. She noticed as had Laurie Jensen, that the organ was quite small. After a minute, according to her later testimony, Cobert pulled her mouth away. The man then grabbed her hand again and used it to masturbate to climax.

As she wiped his semen from her hand onto her jeans, he pushed open her door with his left hand, then shoved her across the bench seat and out the door with his right. He walked her back between their cars to her front door, calmly warned her, "Don't look back," and then let Cobert go.

She climbed into the Cutlass—the engine still was running—dropped the car into Drive and hit the gas, but not before glancing back once to see him standing in the narrow space between the cars. Cobert had hoped to get a license tag number. A few moments later and out on the highway, she suddenly considered what might instead have happened had she dropped the Olds into reverse gear at that moment. "I can't believe I didn't do it," she says.

Nearly six years later, on Thursday, December 11, 1986, Lori Cobert-Hubbard recounted the incident at a probable cause hearing before Judge William R. Murphy in Manassas. Since married and by then a mother, too, she also identified DeBardeleben in court as the man who abducted and sodomized her. "I was frightened to death," she recalls. "When I first say him that day I could have fallen through the floor."

With the semen-stained jeans missing, her account of the crime and identification were crucial. Cobert-Hubbard then gamely withstood cross-examination from DeBardeleben, who again was acting as his own attorney. On the strength of her testimony, Judge Murphy sent the case to the county grand jury, which indicted DeBardeleben in January 1987. Commonwealth Attorney Lee Millette was assigned to lead the prosecution before Circuit Judge Frank A. Hoss, Jr., who presided at DeBardeleben's preliminary hearing on July 1, 1987.

Since the photo of DeBardeleben that the victim identified in 1984 was part of the material seized by the Secret Service, Judge Hoss, like Federal Judge Black before him, was faced with potentially thorny fourth-amendment issues at the hearing. However, the U.S. Fourth Circuit Court of Appeals, sitting in Richmond, Virginia, felicitously relieved Hoss of his decision-making burden when, just days before the hearing, the federal judges affirmed DeBardeleben's Jensen case conviction and sentencing, including the legality of the Secret Service searches. As Lee Millette tells the story, Virginia state police officers relayed a hard copy of the Circuit Court's decision to Manassas in time for the hearing. Citing the Circuit Court as his authority, Hoss denied DeBardeleben's suppression motions.

At the hearing, DeBardeleben alleged generally that he was being framed, and specifically that the police deliberately had lost Lori Cobert's jeans. Why? Because, he argued, the semen stains secretly had been subjected to serological tests that unequivocally showed DeBardeleben was innocent of the crime. Lee Millette denied the accusation, and pointed out in his argument to Judge Hoss that DeBardeleben had offered no evidence to support his charge. Hoss then ruled that though the jeans' disappearance was egregious, he would not accordingly dismiss the case as DeBardeleben had moved.

The defense also challenged the photo lineup as prejudicial; only the defendant's hair, said the defendant, appeared curly in the manner Lori Cobert had described her assailant's. Judge Hoss disagreed.

On the afternoon of July 1, DeBardeleben questioned Cobert-Hubbard as a witness for the second time, hoping to impeach her strong identification of him.

"Going back to the time of the crime," he said, "you pulled over, I understand. Is that correct?"

"When you first stopped me, yes," she answered.

"And then [he] came back to your car and asked you to step out and enter his car. Is that true?"

"That's what you asked me to do. Yes, sir." Cobert-Hubbard was not going to be intimidated.

"I understand you got into the passenger side and the man got into the driver's side. Is that true?"

"Yes. You put me in the passenger's side."

"Now, after the incident, as I understand, he pushed you out of the passenger side of the car?"

"Yes, you did."

Lee Millette, who knew as well as Jim Ronca had that his case was history without a strong showing from the victim, savored Lori Cobert's testimony. "She was emotionally ready for him," says Millette, "and a terrific witness, the key to the case. Always real consistent. She conveyed this tremendous anger, distaste, and fear of him."

Late that afternoon, having denied the rest of the defense's motions, including one to recuse himself, Judge Hoss gaveled the hearing to a close, indicating that he hoped the case would go to trial soon. It would be another four and a half months before it did so.

Meanwhile, as DeBardeleben prepared his defense in the Prince William–Manassas Adult Detention Center, he received two surprise visitors from Beaumont, Texas. Detective Sergeant Frank C. Coffin, Jr., of the Beaumont Police Department, and Coffin's partner, Robert L. Hobbs, an investigator with the Jefferson County district attorney's office, had traveled from Texas to Virginia to question DeBardeleben about a murder.

Their case dated back to Wednesday night, April 27, 1983, and a local topless joint known as The Foxy Lady where dancer Rhoda Piazza, 22, last was seen around 11:30 with a tall white male whom no one at The Foxy Lady seemed able to describe with any detail, or much certainty. Two days later, the black-haired, brown-eyed Piazza, five-eight, 130–140 pounds, was discovered nude, horribly beaten, dead and dumped alongside a country road, not far from east-west Interstate 10. Adhesive residue on Piazza's wrists indicated that she had been bound with tape. "There literally was not a square inch of her body that wasn't marked in some fashion," says Hobbs, who worked the homicide as a team with Frank Coffin.

The two detectives report that apart from the paucity of reliable witnesses, one of the more irritating obstacles to solving Rhoda Piazza's murder was the ineptness of her autopsy. "It was absolutely horrendous," explains Hobbs, who says the pathologist's incompetence extended even to chemically cleansing the partially decomposed corpse's orifices without first examining them for injury, or taking the proper tissue specimens. As a result, it was impossible to establish scientifically whether and how Rhoda Piazza was sexually assaulted, though she surely was. Nor was it possible to collect the serological evidence (semen, sweat, saliva, and blood) that might help establish her attacker's identity. The pathologist may even have gotten Piazza's cause of death wrong. He concluded the dancer had died from the beating she'd received. However, according to Coffin and Hobbs, in a later reautopsy, Houston's noted medical examiner, Joe Jachimczsk, concluded that Piazza had been asphyxiated.

Largely because of these problems, says Coffin, "the investigation went nowhere until we received an intelligence bulletin published in June of 1984 by the Texas Department of Public Safety. Basically, the bulletin talked about DeBardeleben's M.O., but it also listed about twenty different license plates that had been found in his possession. One of them was from Beaumont. And that license plate was stolen shortly before Rhoda Piazza disappeared."

The license plate, stolen not far from where the murdered dancer later was found, was the first of many bits of circumstantial evidence and inference that soon made Mike DeBardeleben the lead suspect in Rhoda Piazza's death. Most obvious was the fact that he'd selected and assaulted a similar victim—Philippa Voliner—at least once before.

Another broadly curious aspect of the homicide was its date. A review of Mike DeBardeleben's known and suspected crimes reveals a consistent propensity to commit them in late April and early May, dating back at least as far as the April 25, 1969, Smith abduction-extortion caper with his third wife, Faye. "We noticed the pattern almost from the start of our investigation," recalls Greg Mertz. "There's something that really pushes his button every April," adds Detective Coffin.

Roy Hazelwood of the FBI explains that date-specific criminality is a well-known phenomenon among aberrant offenders. "It's called Anniversary Reaction," says Hazelwood, "and it is triggered by a traumatic event. If, for example, his mother kicks one of these guys out of the house, a year later he might begin killing women."

Terry Macdonald was murdered in Barrington, Rhode Island, on April 29, 1971. The Trythall case occurred in Maryland on May 13, 1973. Marshall Groom was abducted on April 9, 1974. And DeBardeleben assaulted Philippa Voliner in Memphis on May 5, 1975. From March 1976 to May 1978, DeBardeleben was locked up. On April 19, 1979, Sheila Grant was kidnapped and assaulted in Ballwin, Missouri. On April 27, 1982, Jean McPhaul was murdered in Bossier City, Louisiana.

Then, in 1983, DeBardeleben plunged into what appears to have been his most active spring ever, a spasm of crime after crime commonly observed among serial sex offenders in the days and weeks just before their final arrests. Some of these men—Ted Bundy was a good example—seem no longer capable of managing their deviant impulses. Others may deliberately take added risks to enhance the thrill of the crimes. Still others may simply get sloppy, as Debardeleben did at the Eastridge Mall one month before Agent Pete Allison arrested him in Tennessee. At times, the recklessness may also betray a killer's subliminal desire to be caught, although that seems unlikely in DeBardeleben's case.

Whatever the reason, Mike DeBardeleben unquestionably was a far less cautious Mall Passer in the spring of 1983, and a much busier criminal over all. Joe Rapini was murdered in Greece, New York, on April 13. Two days later, Joan Phillips was attacked in Newington, Connecticut. On May 7, Jane Trombley was stopped in Bloomfield. Sandwiched between Phillips and Trombley was the April 27 Rhoda Piazza case in Beaumont.

Only Mike DeBardeleben knows if, and possibly why, these were instances of Anniversary Reaction, although it is clear that he earlier had endured at least two emotionally charged springtimes; once, when he was released from the Texas State Prison at Huntsville in early May of 1963, and again when he attacked his mother with a razor and was committed by his parents to Western State Hospital in Virginia in April of 1964. Certainly either event might have had lasting psychological consequences.

A second singular detail of the case dovetailed with another of DeBardeleben's observed quirks. Fewer than twenty-four hours after Rhoda Piazza's disappearance, he was hundreds of miles away, passing twenties in Charlotte, North Carolina, malls, where Aschwha Dean identified him and he nearly was captured. This had been his pattern for at least a dozen years—ever since the Macdonald murder. DeBardeleben would commit a major felony, then jump in his car to drive (there are also hints that he sometimes flew) hundreds of miles to commit a second crime only hours later. The first offense may have left him on an adrenaline high, a psychic spur to commit the second one. Or maybe these were attempts to distance himself from the first, more serious, crime, with a second, alibi offense. Thus, the Gail Campbell abduction-extortion caper in Virginia occurred fewer than twelve hours after Terry Macdonald's estimated time of death in Rhode Island. Hours after Lori Cobert was assaulted in Manassas, DeBardeleben as the Mall Passer hit the Richland Mall in Johnstown, Pennsylvania. The day after Jean McPhaul's homicide in Bossier City, Louisiana, he was passing twenties in Charlotte, North Carolina, as he would be a year later after Rhoda Piazza's killing.

The Secret Service task force in Washington provided Detectives Coffin and Hobbs several more provocative—though far from conclusive—hints that DeBardeleben could have been Rhoda Piazza's killer. The computer record showed that the Mall Passer repeatedly had visited Beaumont, a major Gulf Coast petrochemical processing center on Interstate 10, east of Houston. He owned a detailed road map of the area. And one of his handwritten itineraries included the entry "Beau 3 = 2 to Hou," translatable from DeBardeleben's shorthand as "Beaumont, $300 in counterfeit will yield $200 in cash proceeds, to Houston."

"And," says Robert Hobbs, "the Secret Service gave us one of his handmade calendars which showed he was on his way to Houston on a Wednesday, April the 27th. We checked and found that April 27th fell on a Wednesday in 1977, when DeBardeleben was in prison, and not again until 1983 when Rhoda was killed."

Frank Coffin adds, "The whip marks on her body appeared to have been made by a western belt. You could make out the pattern of stitching and tooling, as well as marks that must have been made by a big buckle. DeBardeleben owned a western belt. The body had started to decompose, so the marks were difficult to measure and we couldn't match DeBardeleben's belt. Nor could we eliminate it.

"Remember," he continues, "where he writes about a 'ceiling harness' and an 'A.H. harness' and suspending victims by their shoulders—the 34½? Our girl had heavy bruising across the upper part of her chest to her left shoulder. These marks appear to be consistent with her being suspended. They're completely different from the whip marks. Also, DeBardeleben writes about torturing girls with cigars and cigarettes. Our victim appears to have a cigarette or cigar burn right on her back, consistent with where she'd be burned while being anally raped. We felt that was significant."

Suggestive as all these indications were, they did not add up to a prosecutable case against DeBardeleben. Nor did any of the witnesses from The Foxy Lady positively recognize him from his photograph. "We weren't close to having enough to charge him," says Robert Hobbs. "Our first hope was to find something in his property that would unequivocally link him to Rhoda. The only other possibility was a confession. That was a long shot at best, but it was one we had to try."

Coffin and Hobbs consulted a forensic psychiatrist for help in designing an interview strategy. Among their expert's recommendations was to dress well (it might help gain DeBardeleben's respect) and to continually shift the focus of the conversation "to keep him a little off balance without alienating him," as Hobbs explains it. The two detectives even devised a set of hand signals to help them guide the interview. "We got all this worked out," says Hobbs, "and then came what probably is the single most frustrating incident of my career. We were waiting for him in an interview room at the Manassas Jail. He walked in. We identified ourselves. And he excused himself. He said, 'I'm not gonna talk,' and walked out.

"They just let him go back to his cell! I pitched a fit. I said to the authorities there, 'Look, if you'd come all the way from Virginia to Texas to interview somebody and done all this work just to get ready for it, he *would not be able to get up and walk out on you!* He might remain silent. Stick his fingers in his ears and hum real loud. But if you'd come from Virginia to Texas, I *assure* you that he'd hear what you had to say, if you get my drift.' Well, they didn't go for that."

31

Intent To Kill

With investigators Coffin and Hobbs rebuffed, DeBardeleben resumed preparations for the Cobert trial, a one-day affair, which opened before the Honorable Frank A. Hoss, Jr., at 10:00 A.M. Monday morning, November 16, 1987, in Courtroom No. 2 of the Prince William County Courthouse in Manassas. As usual, the defendant wanted a continuance. This time, said DeBardeleben, he had not been accorded sufficient opportunity to subpoena personnel from the hospital in Fairfax, Virginia, doctors and nurses who could testify he was a patient there, sick with pneumonia, beginning February 7, 1981, or just two days after the attack on Cobert. Hoss denied the defense motion for extra time, explaining for the record that DeBardeleben had had plenty of chances to see to his subpoenas, and seemed only to be stalling for time, again. Hoss also again refused to recuse himself.

Jury selection required less than an hour, and by noon the victim already had told her story and identified her attacker in court. DeBardeleben's forty-five-minute cross-examination did nothing to shake Cobert's story, either. By an inadvertence, however, he may have done himself serious damage.

Sex offenders employ numerous strategies to help them relive and relish their crimes in memory. Some take souvenirs. Others revisit the scene of the crime, or even try to contact their victims if they survive. Dianne

Overton and Elizabeth Mason both report harassing telephone calls after they were attacked. Both believe the caller was DeBardeleben. Naturally, an even more vivid and forceful way to reexperience such an assault is to do it face-to-face with the victim.

According to those who watched him in Baltimore, Mike DeBardeleben had seemed to enjoy Laurie Jensen's painful courtroom reencounter with her ordeal. So it was that Lee Millette sensed excitement in DeBardeleben as he led Lori Cobert back through the details of her abduction and assault. "I felt he was really getting into it," remembers Millette.

"Now," asked DeBardeleben, "during the incident inside this man's car, it was dark all the time, wasn't it?"

"I could see," Cobert answered.

"The interior lights were not on, were they?"

"No."

"And there were no overhead interior lights, were there?"

"No."

"The only car lights they had there was [*sic*] these little small ones next to the door at the bottom of the door, right?"

"Correct."

At this juncture, Lee Millette at the prosecutor's table began to scribble. Lori Cobert had mentioned door lights twice before under oath, but she'd never described the lights as to their size or location or relative brightness.

"And those," DeBardeleben plunged on, "were only on when you open the door and shut the door, correct?"

"Correct."

"So they really don't show you any light by themselves, do they?"

"No."

The balance of Millette's case—his "filler"—

required less than three hours to present. Investigator Guzdowski testified to a conversation he had with DeBardeleben on the way back from California.

"Mr. DeBardeleben," said the cop, "inquired of us, so to speak, 'By the way, how is the construction around Manassas right now? Have they finished the construction on Route 28?'

"[I asked] him, 'Oh, you're familiar with the area?' And he stated he had been in the area. He was familiar with it."

On cross-examination DeBardeleben asked, "Officer Guzdowski, did I also tell you that two days after this crime I had pneumonia and was in the hospital?"

"No, sir," replied Guzdowski, "I don't recall that."

The next witness, Pete Allison, told the court that the Secret Service's May 1983, search of DeBardeleben's Chrysler in Knoxville turned up two so-called lens covers, both red, which were useful for changing the color of spotlights (Lori Cobert had reported seeing red lights on the grille of her attacker's sedan). Allison also explained how he'd discovered beneath the Chrysler's dashboard a toggle switch connected by a wire through the car's fire wall and over its left front wheel well to a set of lights recessed behind the Chrysler's grille.

Dennis Foos followed. He testified to searching the Manassas storage locker DeBardeleben had rented, and identified a sheet of the defendant's notes taken in that search. "Be rested," it read in part. "Alone. Edge of town. Cop. Police officer. 'Can I see some ID.' 'Turn off on side street.' *Stop.* (Night and Saturday.)"

In his closing, Millette artfully stitched these elements together, arguing that the circumstantial evidence strongly suggested DeBardeleben's known behavior was exactly consistent with the events of February 5, 1981. He outfitted at least one car with grille lights, for example, and controlled them via a dashboard toggle switch. Could it have been the click of a similar toggle Lori Cobert heard that night?

And what of those door lights?

"Ladies and gentlemen," said Millette, "remember when he was asking questions about the small light in the door? Now, your memory is what counts here, but it sounded to me like he was recalling things from memory, not from what she said. Just a small thing, but think about that when you go back."

At 6:22 the jury retired to consider its verdict. At 7:00 they were back. Guilty on each charge, they told the judge, and then recommended maximum sentences, life in prison, on both counts. In early January 1988, Judge Hoss reconvened the court to confirm the sentences and to allow Mike DeBardeleben a parting comment.

"He called us all a bunch of communists," recollects Lee Millette.

The Cobert case again divided the Secret Service task force. Mike Stephens thought the verdict correct. Dennis Foos agreed with Lee Millette that stronger cases have been made. Greg Mertz sided with DeBardeleben.

"I think he was framed," says Mertz. "All the victims told us and we could tell from the tapes that DeBardeleben has retarded ejaculation. This guy came right away. And what about those blue jeans? I know that the Prince William County Police are a professional force. They're not sloppy."

Stranger screw-ups, of course, have occurred. President John Kennedy's brain, for example, somehow was mislaid. And in Seattle, the King County Police actually lost a whole victim from an evidence locker, the skeletal remains of one of Ted Bundy's victims. In the end, Mertz and Stephens agreed to disagree about the Santini and Cobert cases. "Basically," says Mertz, "Mike's point was, 'Goddamnit, you're not the judge and jury.' And he was right."

Mertz, Stephens, and Foos also agreed that their string of six convictions, while gratifying, were but prelude to the main events, DeBardeleben's long delayed murder trials, particularly his capital case in Louisiana. While they'd heard very little from Bossier City since DeBardeleben's grand jury indictment there in June of 1984, Mike Stephens recalls that at no time had any of the agents doubted prosecutor Henry Brown's word, or his resolve.

Karen Bodden, victim Jean McPhaul's daughter, herself always believed that in time Henry Brown would put Mike DeBardeleben on trial for her mother's murder. And since Brown had built a strong record of securing death sentences in capital cases—he'd sent five men to Louisiana's electric chair since 1980—Bodden expected that DeBardeleben well might pay for her mother's life with his.

She says that after Brown called his June 1984, press conference to announce that he'd ask for the death penalty, local media interest in the case gradually faded. "On television," says Bodden, "the main scene they got the day they found Mom was of the front door of that house with her being wheeled out on a gurney. I can't tell you how many times I saw that on television. Every time there was a story about the case they'd show her being taken from that house."

One day—Bodden cannot remember the date—she came home from work and almost automatically started channel surfing, looking for something to watch. "All of a sudden," she says, "there was that scene again! So I flicked backed to that channel in time to hear them say they weren't going to bring this guy back to trial! I was *hot!* I was *so hot!* If I hadn't been flicking through the channels, maybe no one ever would have told me."

Henry Brown, according to Bodden, not only neglected to tell her he'd dropped the prosecution, but hadn't informed her father, either. She says she registered her anger and amazement in a local television interview. "They told me they were going to do everything they could," Bodden recalls telling the television reporter. "Blah! Blah! Blah! The *next* thing I heard was that they're not going to do *anything!* I feel like DeBardeleben got away with it. I really do. I don't care how many years he got elsewhere. *He got away with my mother's murder!*"

Henry Brown, a former Green Beret and Bossier-area prosecutor for eighteen years before being elected a Louisiana state appellate judge in 1990, says that several factors influenced his decision not to prosecute Mike DeBardeleben. "One of our biggest problems," Brown claims, "was just getting him down here. By the time we got in line where it looked like we could see some light at the end of the tunnel he had an ungodly amount of time, and I was assured that he'd never be released from jail. So at that time we sat down and evaluated the possibilities and practicalities of bringing him back down here."

One problem, according to Brown, was meeting Louisiana's Murder One criteria. Besides showing that the accused is guilty, and had the specific intent to kill, in Louisiana a prosecutor must also prove that the homicide occurred during the commission of certain specified felonies, such as robbery or kidnapping. In the McPhaul case, says Brown, "We didn't have any real proof that robbery occurred." He asserts that if the Realtor's purse, or any other piece of her property, had been found in DeBardeleben's possession, he would have been much more confident of a successful capital prosecution. Absent a death sentence, Brown argues, what would have been the point of another conviction? "Getting a life sentence in that case would not have been a success."

The former prosecutor recollects he also was concerned about Mrs. DeMoss, the rooming-house keeper, whose health and eyesight were failing. She would have been an important witness and her loss a heavy blow to the prosecution.

Then there was the question of cost. "I think he could have gotten a change of venue," opines Brown. "The publicity was overwhelming. That would have meant not only would we have to transport witnesses from Washington, D.C., and other places to Bossier for trial, but we'd have to transport ourselves to another jurisdiction, which would have been in south Louisiana. The cost would have been tremendous."

Sensible as all this sounds, the explanations did not go down well with the Secret Service task force. "We never were told there were problems getting DeBardeleben down there to try him," says Mike Stephens. "If there had been, I would have gone and got him and dragged DeBardeleben to Bossier City myself. We knew that the case had gotten old. But we also felt we'd held up our end of the bargain, and that we, along with the McPhaul family, were treated quite shabbily.

"I remember I called and called and called down there. Finally, I got Detective Payne on the phone and he admitted that they probably weren't going to go ahead. I told him that without a doubt we were owed an official explanation, which we never received. I believe that I questioned Mr. Brown's backbone at some point in the call. And I know I told Payne that sometimes you do something, not because you know you'll succeed, but because it happens to be the right thing to do, damnit!"

Greg Mertz was equally indignant. "That was a real, real bitter disappointment for us," he says. "We were pissed. We knew that as long as he wasn't facing some ultimatum, such as execution, there'd be no reason for him to finally talk. But beyond that, murder is the ultimate crime and you have to prosecute it. De-

Bardeleben is a killer, and he should be a convicted killer."

With Brown's decision not to try Mike DeBardeleben, only two of the eight state-level cases against him remained to be adjudicated; the Sheila Grant sodomy, robbery, and gun charges in Ballwin, Missouri, and the Terry Macdonald murder indictment in Rhode Island. In the summer of 1991, incarcerated once again at Lompoc, DeBardeleben invoked his speedy trial rights and formally defied these two jurisdictions—as well as any others who still had detainers out, even though they had no plans to prosecute—to try him or to drop their charges.

All, including Rhode Island, declined to proceed to trial. In the Macdonald case, once again no one thought to consult the victim's survivors about the decision. "We all assumed that one day he'd be tried in Rhode Island for murder," says Terry's daughter, Lynn. "In fact, we were told that it might be right after the Maryland trial because he'd do anything to avoid going to Louisiana, where they have the death penalty.

"So you could say I was a little shocked and disappointed when they called me to say that there wasn't going to be a trial. Then I talked to my husband about it. At one point he asked, 'Well, what more do you want out of it?' I thought about that and then I thought about a conversation that I once had with my sister, Susan. We decided that we'd like to sit and watch DeBardeleben be gassed for killing our mother."

The Secret Service task force, which along with Agent Pete Allison was personally cited by Treasury Secretary James Baker for their roles in DeBardeleben's arrest and imprisonment, ceased to exist a few months after he was sentenced in the Cobert case, and no further prosecutions seemed imminent. Two years later, on March 8, 1990, the Secret Service's investigation was declared officially closed.

Dennis Foos by then had transferred back to the Seattle field office. Greg Mertz left WFO, too, for the White House detail. From there he moved again to the Omaha field office. Mike Stephens retired from the Secret Service in 1991. Stephens now is an investigator with the Federal Resolution Trust Corporation. Their boss, Jane Vezeris, who at the time of the DeBardeleben investigation was the highest-ranking woman in the Secret Service, still is. In the autumn of 1993, Vezeris was named SAIC of the Intelligence Division.

Mike DeBardeleben remains a prime—or sole—suspect in at least four murders, and is suspected in several more. Eleven years after his arrest in Tennessee, however, the prospects for indictments, or for any new and explosive disclosures in the case, seemed dim.

Now in his early 50s, he is first eligible to be considered for parole in 2059. If DeBardeleben somehow were to survive that long and be granted release, the clock would then start in New Jersey, where his minimum sentence would expire about 2090. Mike DeBardeleben is never going to leave prison a free man.

A former fellow prisoner describes DeBardeleben as a savvy con who at first mixed with a circle of elite felons, mostly organized crime figures, until a pulp detective magazine detailed portions of his career in an article that received wide attention among other convicts. The piece disclosed DeBardeleben's sex-crime career in sufficient detail to alter his prison profile. "The mob guys knew DeBardeleben was smart," says this convict, "and a stand-up con. But when the weird stuff got known, they couldn't afford to keep him around."

Since those early days, DeBardeleben has been moved from penitentiary to penitentiary throughout the federal prison system, trailing behind him dozens of boxes of legal papers and filings as he continues his career as a jail-house lawyer, writing perpetual appeals and motions, none of which have been successful. All his convictions and sentences have been affirmed.

Fearful now of other prisoners, and of the guards, as well, DeBardeleben keeps to himself, spending as much as eighteen hours each day handwritting his endless lawsuits in triplicate and seeing to his intermittent correspondence. Only once in while, says his former acquaintance, does DeBardeleben—who likes to be known as "Professor"—pause for his peculiar forms of diversion.

There was a time at Leavenworth when he came into possession of a human prosthesis catalogue. DeBardeleben sat and peered at the pictures of plastic body parts, as if mesmerized, for hours. Sometimes, late at night, he and another convicted sex offender would sit up laughing and cackling together as they fantasized various ways of torturing their judges.

For sexual stimulation DeBardeleben has access to the standard skin magazines that circulate in prisons everywhere, and he sometimes receives what convicts call freak letters, salacious hand-penned fantasies sent in for the prisoners' entertainment by female correspondents.

Plus, DeBardeleben has found a private form of excitation. His old acquaintance reports that Mike searches his law books for the most graphic sex-abuse and assault cases, especially those involving young girls, and then reads them over and over and over.

"But you know, a lot of guys in prison are strange," cautions this inmate. "What makes Mike seem so different is his detachment, I guess you'd call it. I remember that every once in a while he'd take out his folder of magazine cutouts, pictures of various parts of women's bodies. Then he'd sit on his bunk and play with the cutouts, moving them around and staring at them in a kind of trance.

"He'd always told me that all his cases were frames, that the Feds had set him up, and that all he'd ever done was a little counterfeiting. But I'll tell you, when he gets those pictures out and starts looking at them, you can just feel what Mike's all about. He's a scary dude. I sensed he was capable of anything. Anything. It's a damned good thing he's locked up."

Epilogue

D r. Theresa Keaney* always wondered who she really was.

"It wasn't constant," says the young pediatrician, adopted at birth in December of 1961. "But at certain times such as holidays and on my birthday, I thought about my biological parents, what they were like and who they might be."

Five-three, blue-eyed, lightly freckled and very fair complected, Keaney was raised in Fort Worth by a God-fearing couple whom she regards as her true mother and father. The doctor's amused today to recall how some people mistook her and her adoptive sister for twins. "We looked a lot alike, superficially. But my sister and parents wanted *no* attention and I wanted *everyone's* attention. And I was mischievous. Not big trouble, but I was the one who talked back. When my mother would say, 'You can't do that,' my sister would say, 'Okay fine.' I'd argue, 'Why not?'

"The most important thing, however, was that I loved my family and they loved me. It was great. Everything was easy for me."

Bethene Jones, one year Terry's senior, has no such idyllic girlhood memories. "I had a horrible childhood," she says. "My mother was abusive, both physically and with words. She drank. And I was blamed for her unhappiness. Maybe I ruined her life. One time she told me that she should have listened to her father and given me up. I said that I wished she had, because then I could have had a mom and dad that loved me, too."

Terry Keaney always was a good student, her high school valedictorian. She went on to college and medical school and a pediatric practice in which she focuses her professional attention on the needs of poor children. "For some reason," she says, "I find them easier to treat than people who have a lot of money. You feel like they need you and they aren't as demanding."

Bethene Jones did well in class, too. "I enjoyed school because it was a chance to be away from home," she recalls. "I didn't want to go home, so I'd go to school and stay at school and work there."

After high school, Bethene won a full scholarship to a church-affiliated university and graduated with a business degree. Today, she is a computer systems specialist and the mother of two. Her husband is an architect.

Theresa Keaney's occasional curiosity about her origins notwithstanding, she never actively considered tracing her birth parents, especially since she knew the idea would upset her adoptive mother; her "real" mother as far as Terry was concerned. Then, at age 27, and in her final year of pediatric residency, Keaney and her husband, a mechanical engineer, decided they were ready to start a family. "Suddenly," she says, "I just had to find out."

In February of 1989, Dr. Keaney traveled back to Fort Worth, to search for her biologic self. By appointment, she went to the chambers of a civil courts judge. The judge, fresh from court and still dressed in his black robes, had placed her file, in a manila envelope, on his desk between them. He asked her a few questions, then leafed through the folder, closed it and ushered Dr. Keaney to a room where she could examine the documents undisturbed.

She'd conditioned herself against unreasonable expectations, never guessing the sorts of surprises that awaited her. "I didn't think I'd find information I could use right away," says the doctor. "And I knew that whoever my birth parents were, there had to have been problems. You don't give a baby up for adoption without there being some problem in the family."

The prospective mother-to-be opened the file and confronted, in utter bewilderment, the name Bethene Jones listed as her full sister. Bethene! Her old school chum! Dark-haired Bethene, with whom Terry Keaney had eaten lunch each day in the cafeteria. Bethene, an alto in the school choir, who liked all the same teachers that Terry did. Bethene, her friend, despite the competitive rift when Bethene joined the Girl Scouts, and Terry became a Campfire Girl ("Bluebirds eat Brownies," Terry and the other Campfire Girls used to say). Bethene, shy and reserved, so unlike her rambunctious and oft-married mama, Charlotte Weber, about whom there was plenty of talk among the teachers at school. Even Theresa's mother knew about Charlotte (although she'd never met her) and discouraged Terry from visiting Bethene at home.

Terry then glanced at her father's name: James Mitchell DeBardeleben II. He was totally unfamiliar to her, apparently just another guy named Mike. Of course, that was about all that an abandoned daughter expected after nearly thirty years.

As the shock of her discovery subsided, Terry perceived a problem in how to proceed. "Of course, my sister and mother's names were in the file," she says, "but the information was 28 years old. I had no idea what names they would be going by now."

Then a thought came to her. Keaney remembered that Bethene had a maternal grandmother, known as Nanny, with whom Bethene had lived for a time during one of her frequent estrangements from Charlotte. "So I picked up the telephone book and looked for her name. Sure enough, there she was."

Dr. Keaney decided to tell her adoptive mother of her discovery before telephoning Nanny, a decision she soon regretted. "My mother freaked. She said, 'You don't know who these people are! You might be opening a can of worms! I don't want you to be hurt.' She cried and cried and cried. She was pretty upset with me. So I said, 'Okay, I won't contact them.' "

Terry kept her word to her mother through the birth of her own first child, a boy, in March of 1990. But by her twenty-ninth birthday that December she'd resolved, pledge or no pledge, to contact Charlotte Weber via Nanny. What if the older woman suddenly were to die? Unless she acted at once, Dr. Keaney feared, she might never be able to find her biological sister or mother or father.

She chose an anonym, Suzie, and used a friend's residence in North Carolina as her return address. Terry Keaney then sat down, on her birthday, to compose in her careful longhand a psychologically fraught message to the woman who'd borne her into the world.

"Every year on my birthday," she wrote, "I think about how happy my life has been. I'm thankful you've allowed all of this to happen. Of course, I have no idea if you want to hear from me, or if you're curious about what's happened in my life. I'm writing you this one letter. If I don't hear from you, I promise I'll never bother you again." Dr. Keaney concluded, "consider this a thank you for providing the best for your baby. With love and appreciation from your biological daughter, 'Suzie.' P.S.: Tell me about you and my 'Birth Father.' "

The note was a shock, but not a surprise, to Charlotte Weber, who received it at her residence in South Carolina. "I'd expected it all my life," she says. "I had a gut feeling that my second daughter one day would show up."

The essential question was not if, but how, to respond to Terry—especially how much to tell her about

Mike. The whole story simply was too horrible to tell; not yet, anyway, and certainly not to his second daughter, the mother of his grandson.

So, in her return letter, written in a hand uncannily similar to Theresa's, Charlotte Weber only alluded to "unpleasant" truths about her ex-husband, and added, cryptically—as if to affirm for the uncomprehending Dr. Keaney that she, at least, was safe from the unspoken evil—"there's nothing personally harmful. I've been assured it's contained."

In the end, it would be Bethene, not Charlotte, who enlightened sister "Suzie." Jones, who though darkhaired like her mother physically favors her paternal grandmother, Mary Lou Edwards, especially in the shape and set of her sparkling blue eyes, has a single recollection of her father from age six.

"He came over to our house in Fort Worth with his wife, Faye," she recalls. "She was introduced to me as Faye and he was introduced to me as Mike. I called him Mike. During his visit, a motorcycle appeared and he took me for a ride on it. I was excited because it was my first time on a motorcycle and I told my mother and stepfather how exciting it was, hearing the noises of the engine and the gears changing. I mimicked Mike and he looked down at me in these big round dark glasses, smiling and nodding his head.

"I knew he was my daddy. I did. I can recall a conversation with my girlfriend who lived next door. We were sitting on the front porch and she said, 'Who's that over at your house?' I said, 'Oh yeah. That's my daddy and his wife.' She said, 'Well, you don't call him Daddy.' And I said, 'Well, I don't.'

" 'Why don't you?'

" 'I don't know.' That was all I said. 'I don't know' worked real well at that age."

Jones would see her father just once more, and briefly, when she was twelve, about the time she learned she had an older sister who'd been given up for adoption. This was the same year she first became friends with Theresa Keaney, and invited Keaney over to a slumber party she had at her Nanny's house.

"I also knew by then that my father was a bad person," Jones continues. "I imagined him as something like a safecracker. My mother said he did worse things but wouldn't talk about it. I asked my grandmother, but she'd just say, 'Why do you need to know that? That's not necessary right now.' "

Bethene, says her mother, "always was to be protected. She's very naive. And it wasn't that I was not honest with her. I told her he was a bad person. I told her he was a criminal. I did not know he was a murderer until he was arrested in 1983."

Charlotte and Mike's daughter spent the balance of her unhappy youth romanticizing her absent father. Her innermost dream was that Daddy might suddenly reappear to rescue his sad Bethene from her melancholy.

The fantasy was brutally shattered in late May of 1984. Jones was living at the time with her Nanny. Saturday night, May 26, she came home from helping to host a friend's birthday party. Her grandmother called to her from her bedroom. "Bethene," said Nanny somberly. "Please sit down. Have you had any contact with your father?"

Jones exulted. "I was so excited!" she remembers. "I thought, 'He's called me and I wasn't here! But Nanny knows where he is! And he's alive!' Then I got mad at myself because I hadn't been home. 'Why did I have to have this function today? It didn't have to be today! I've *missed* him!' "

Her Nanny gave Bethene a nervous look.

"Well," she said, "he was on the television news tonight. He's been charged with counterfeiting and evidence shows that he's a suspect in rape and murder."

The next morning's editions of the *Fort Worth Star-Telegram* carried the story on the front page: EX-FORT WORTH MAN CHARGED IN KILLING SPREE.

The revelations devastated Jones. "All my prayers and my hopes and my dreams, my anticipation of him coming as my white knight to save me, it just all ended. Devastation just totally set in. A big knife came down on me and it hit me real hard."

The horror of what she learned turned Bethene even more resolutely inward. "I remember," she says, "that I was curious about my adopted sister, but not enough to go looking for her. I didn't want to tell her, 'Oh, your father's in prison.' I mean, I didn't have anything to offer a sister. Her life was bound to have been a lot better than mine. I just felt that."

Once Dr. Keaney initiated contact, however, Bethene proved an eager, persistent correspondent. In February of 1991, she penned her first letter to "Suzie." "You wrote that you were adopted by a wonderful family," said Bethene to her mystery sister.

> In some respects, I envy you. My mother remarried several times. Therefore I had to experience a step-father situation. As you can probably surmise, my home was a bit unstable. I think stability is what I wanted, what I envy most about you....
>
> In high school, I was an outsider. I was not in the 'In-Crowd.' I didn't want to be. My main activity I enjoyed most was choir. I like to sing and play the piano. I graduated in the top 25%.

Terry Keaney smiled as she read this first letter from her sister. "The funny part," says the doctor, "is that I was thinking, 'Yeah, I know. I was there.' "

Gradually, Bethene acquainted "Suzie" with their father. "She told me he was in prison for counterfeiting," Keaney recalls, "and that's kinda where we left it. Bethene later said he did a lot of other bad things. She said he wasn't eligible for parole, so I figured it must have been something pretty bad.

"At the same time, she kept pressing me to tell her

who I was. She really wanted to know. 'Can I at least have a picture of you? Could I at least know your real name?' "

Finally, in May 1991, Theresa sent Bethene her telephone number. "You already know me," she wrote with deliberate ambiguity. "As soon as you get this letter, call me if you want to know who I am."

Bethene came home from work, found the letter and telephoned her Nanny.

"What do I do?" she asked anxiously.

"Call her," said Nanny.

Bethene rang her mother. *"Call her!!"* ordered Charlotte.

With the enigmatic "You already know me," running through her mind, Bethene grabbed all her high school and college annuals, then sat down to telephone her sister.

"Can you guess who I am?" Terry teased on the other end of the line. "Do you have any idea?"

"No! Do we know each other from college or high school?"

"High school."

"I can't think!" Jones cried. "Did we have any classes together?"

"Not in our last few years."

Keaney tossed out a few more clues. Jones was helpless to interpret them. "She still couldn't guess," reports the doctor, "so I said, 'Does the name Terry Keaney mean anything to you?' "

"Your kidding!!" Jones exclaimed.

Both women started crying.

"She just couldn't believe it," Keaney remembers. "She was very sweet. She said, 'If I could have picked a sister, I could not have picked one better than you. I couldn't pick anyone nicer than you.' "

Two weeks later, Bethene visited Terry. "We just talked and talked and talked," says Keaney. "It wasn't exactly like we didn't know each other. Not only had we been friends in high school, but we'd written each other just about everything in letters. But we did talk about things you just can't write in letters. I told her how I wanted our relationship to continue progressing, and she did, too. I think we both kinda agreed that we're not going to live like we've been sisters all our lives. Yet we'll be good friends, with a closer bond."

Bethene and Terry discovered each other was a strong fundamentalist Christian. "Bethene went to church with me," says Keaney. "I told her I hoped that she wouldn't be offended if I didn't introduce her as my sister. I said, 'The people who know the story will know who you are. I don't want to get into it with the people who don't know. They've all met my adoptive sister, my *other* sister, and I don't want to confuse things.' "

"That was an interesting experience," adds Jones. "A good experience. I could tell who knew about me and who didn't. Some would come up and shake my hand and say, 'Oh, it's nice to meet you.' Then you'd have ones who'd come up and say, '*Oh!* Bethene! How *are* you?' "

At Thanksgiving time, Dr. Keaney, who was then pregnant with her second boy, came with her son to Nanny's to meet her mother, Charlotte. "Nanny's house," she explains, "is kind of small with a lot of little knickknacks all over the place. Bethene's baby was fussing and crying and the two boys were running around, hitting each other. You could tell that Charlotte was afraid to touch me. Nanny just came right over and hugged me and sat next to me, patting me on the knee.

"I could tell that Charlotte was kinda afraid. Always this nervous laughter. That's sort of what we did the whole time, exchange nervous little laughs back and forth. It was kind of an uncomfortable meeting.

"When we got up and left, Charlotte did hug me. We took pictures of everyone standing together. She put her arms around both Bethene and me. And then after the pictures we got in the car. I could see she was crying when we left."

Given time to reflect on what she's learned, Keaney cautiously concludes that her journey of self-discovery has been a success, with "a happy ending, to this point," she says. "I did envision my biological mother being a *little* different than Charlotte. As far as my father is concerned, it's something kinda in the back of my mind. I worry a little bit about it. I think, 'Oh, maybe I've got some of these genetic traits. I'm going to turn out to be some sort of criminal.' I've kidded with my brother-in-law that it probably skips a generation. So it's probably going to happen to my oldest son. I'm going to have to watch him like a hawk. He's already taking other kids' toys.

"I don't know what else to say. The truth did not upset me. Of course, reading some of the information Bethene has about him was horrible. To think that this person is my biological father is sickening. It's certainly not something I'm proud of. But on the other hand, if someone asked me about it I wouldn't lie to them. I'd tell them my father's a horrible person. He's in prison. There's even a book about him."

Several months later, Bethene Jones was jarred anew by a telephone call from Charlotte, who had word of yet another missing family member, 22-year-old Lindsey DeBardeleben, Faye's daughter. Lindsey had contacted the Secret Service, asking questions about her father and his wives and their children, if any. Now, Charlotte told Bethene, Lindsey was impatient to meet her older half-sisters.

Extroverted and talkative Lindsey DeBardeleben, who is fair with a high flush and an abundance of light brown hair, resembles both her parents. One moment she is the image of her lovely mother. Then she turns her head and there's Mike DeBardeleben, especially around her green eyes. The effect can be unsettling.

"My mom told me that I resembled my grandfather DeBardeleben," Lindsey recalls. "And I also can remember when I was younger and *quite* sassy my mom just looking at me, sort of frightened, saying, 'God! You remind me of Mike DeBardeleben.'

"She would tell me how manipulative I was, and I *can* be manipulative. It scares me sometimes how calculated and manipulative I can be. She told me Mike was just like that. Sometimes when she was mad at me she'd say, 'Okay, Mike. Go ahead, Mike.' "

Lindsey has no girlhood recollection of her father, whose name rarely was mentioned in her presence. "Mom was one of the most fearless people I've ever known," she says. "But when it came to him I could tell she was uncomfortable. She *really* stressed that she didn't want me to have anything to do with him. She let me know that he did things I didn't need to know about at that time. It was almost like, 'Look into my eyes. Understand this. Don't get hold of him. Don't contact him. He's no good.' "

By 1972, Faye and her daughter had settled near Tazewell, Virginia, the country community that Faye Davis just years before had so insistently yearned to escape. Her mother worked as a secretary, says Lindsay, and, like Charlotte Weber, was not always an ideal parent.

"Mom and I had a real odd kind of relationship," she says. "We would fight like cats and dogs. She'd say things to hurt my feelings. She'd drag me out to bars and leave me there at all hours while she had fun with her friends. Everybody loved her. I'd be in a booth asleep until three o'clock in the morning, until the bar closed, then go home. I didn't like that kind of lifestyle. I hated it as a matter of fact.

"Mom was pretty much a redneck. She was very intelligent, very articulate, but she just was a redneck. That was her upbringing. She liked going to country-western bars. She liked drinking. She like going four-wheelin'."

Yet Lindsey never felt a breach with her mother as Bethene did with Charlotte. She loved Faye very much, and it hurt the young girl to see all the pain her mother endured. "Mom just did not have it all together at all," she explains. "She had no luck with men, and she was always down on herself so much."

In 1978, according to Lindsey, her mother married an abusive, alcoholic truck driver who put Faye into the hospital several times. Twice, Faye tried to take her own life. Both attempts resulted in lengthy hospitalizations.

Faye pulled herself free of her second husband—they never did divorce—in 1984. Lindsey remembers her mother then taking up private duty nursing. She became a Licensed Practical Nurse. In the fall of 1987, Faye decided to try to become a Registered Nurse.

"She was enrolled in a nursing program at the local community college," Lindsey recalls, "and was studying quite fervently for exams. She'd really gotten run down. Mom smoked for years and she'd gained quite a bit of weight and she had a thyroid problem, so she wasn't the healthiest person in the world. Then she had a hysterectomy in October of 1987, and just never completely recovered from that. Around December 14, she started getting flulike symptoms; diarrhea, vomiting and fever.

"She refused to go to a doctor, so I took her to the emergency room and they gave her a shot. They wanted to keep her overnight, but she wouldn't stay because she had an exam and she wanted to study for it.

"So I took her home that night, and the next day she was one hundred percent better. I mean, she was still sick but she was sitting up and eating. Her fever and broken and she wasn't vomiting anymore. Had a lot more energy. So I thought, 'This is great! She's fine!'

And I didn't think anything more of it. Mom was 42 years old.

"That night I went to a friend's house to study. When I came back she helped me study, too. When I went to bed, she was up studying at the kitchen table.

"Next morning, I woke up, took a shower and then went into her room to rummage through her closet, as I did quite often, to find something to wear to school. Mom was lying on the bed. Her light was on at her bedside. She had an IV that the doctor let an RN friend of hers put in and monitor. I saw it was still in. She was lying on the bed on her back with her legs hanging off, like she'd been sitting on the side of the bed and fell back. Her eyes were open.

"It startled me to see her. I said, 'Mom, wake up. You're going to get a crick in your neck sleeping that way.' Then I realized what it was. But it didn't click. So I started yelling at her. 'Mom! Wake up! Wake up!' I thought I could wake her up if I yelled loud enough. I hit the wall. I thought that making noise would wake her up.

"I watched her chest and she wasn't breathing. Her eyes were open and glassy. So I knew she was dead. I guess I just didn't want to accept it. So I called an ambulance and they came and took her away. I went to my grandmother's."

Lindsey says her mother was autopsied, and that "acute viral infection" was listed as Faye's cause of death. "Her lungs had water in them, so I assume it must have turned into pneumonia."

Her mother's death overwhelmed Lindsey. "It's been the most unexplainable pain," she says, "and it never gets better. I still miss her more than anything in the world. And I still feel very alone in the world."

At first, Lindsey handled Faye's loss by trying to run away from it. "I just went on a rampage. Drank all the time and smoked pot quite a lot. I didn't do anything else, really. I was stoned every day because I was so miserable."

The binge lasted through Lindsey's senior year in high school, as well as her abortive freshman year of college. Then the teenager found Jesus. In 1989, she joined a Wesleyan sect she describes as "quite conservative and very evangelical. The church is now the biggest part of my life. If it wasn't for the Lord, I wouldn't have made it through the things I've made it through."

That summer, at a church function, Lindsey met a quiet young man from Canada. In the autumn they were married and moved north for a year before returning to the states in 1990. That's when Lindsey began corresponding with her father.

In 1984, as she explains, Mike had written Faye a note pleading for her help in his various legal troubles. He had included with it a note for Lindsey. "Mom sat me down and said, 'He wrote you this, but don't believe a word of it.' It was just a little half-page thing saying he loved me and that I was his daughter and he wondered how I was. He told me he'd written my mom my whole life and that she'd never written him back."

When Faye wasn't looking, Lindsey copied the return address from the letter's envelope and tucked it under her mattress. Six years later, while going through her personal papers, she ran across the address.

"I thought, 'What the heck?' So I called up his sister Linda and told her who I was. Then she gave me his address at Lewisburg and I wrote him and I got a reply within days.

"I got it on a Friday, and the whole weekend I just sat rocking back and forth, reading the letter, totally a basket case. *All* these emotions I'd had all my life about who my father was, and what he was, came together in one letter, it seemed.

"It was quite brief. It just said he was ecstatic I'd gotten hold of him and reestablished contact. He also wanted to know if I wanted to build on the relationship.

"My mother had told me he never wanted me. She said, 'He doesn't want you. He never wanted you. He doesn't want anything to do with you.' So I felt very unloved and unwanted. Then this letter contradicted what she'd told me. It was very confusing."

Mail traffic between father and daughter soon was steady. On her side, says Lindsey, "It was mostly questions: 'Why this? Why that? Why didn't you try to contact me? Why are you in prison?' " She remembers being aware that Mike was a counterfeiter and that he'd been tried for rape with Faye's cousin. At that time, she knew nothing more of his criminal career.

DeBardeleben's letters to Lindsey were of two sorts. In some, he bragged of his criminal genius and organized-crime connections. "*Nobody* can touch me," he boasted. "If I got out of here today I could call fifteen different people and have ten thousand dollars in my hand and a brand-new car within a day."

Alternately, DeBardeleben complained about prison conditions and the injustices he'd suffered. "He sent me all kinds of court documents and testimony from his trials and an article about a girl identifying a particular person. He wrote, 'As you can plainly see, I am not the type. My hair is not curly.' Also, he apparently had pneumonia at the time of one rape he is supposed to have committed."

The letters inflamed Lindsey's sense of justice. "I was upset," she says. "I was on the verge of trying to get hold of organizations and agencies that help people who are falsely accused. I really was. I remember him telling me the conditions he lived under, and getting *really* upset, saying, 'I can't *believe* they're doing this to you. How can they do this?' "

Her father assured Lindsey that despite all he still expected to be released soon. "He's determined," she says, "that he's getting out in two or three years. Almost every letter he wrote was, 'I have to go. I have an appeal deadline I need to get on right now. Sorry I haven't written lately, but I've been real busy on appeals.' "

DeBardeleben's only off-putting behavior surfaced during their weekly telephone calls. "I didn't like his laugh," says Lindsey. "It was weird and kind of sadistic. The first time we talked on the telephone he laughed and it was *really eerie!*"

After months of writing and talking to her father over the telephone, Lindsey resolved to visit DeBardeleben in person. Through the auspices of former Nixon aide Chuck Colson's Prison Fellowship Ministry, she found a Mennonite family with whom she could stay while in Lewisburg. When she could arrange transportation, she notified her father and set off.

The first day at the Lewisburg Penitentiary gate, prison authorities confiscated Lindsey's Bible. "I had no comprehension of a prison," she says, "so I didn't know what to expect. I was absolutely petrified. The place was hard, cold, desolate. I was amazed at the security precautions they took. And every guard I saw was my enemy, because I knew how badly they treated my father."

She was escorted through a series of clanging prison gates, down corridors and up some steps to a big visiting room furnished with rows of molded plastic chairs, bolted to the floor. Vending machines stood along the walls. Music was playing. Inmates and visitors chatted.

Lindsey handed a piece of paper with her father's name on it to a guard, who directed her to take a seat. Fifteen minutes later, as she recollects, she caught her first glimpse of DeBardeleben, handcuffed, dressed in blue prison overalls, being escorted in the same door she'd entered. After he was walked to the other end of the room and strip-searched, he came down the row of seats, sat down next to his daughter, and hugged her.

"This was an emotional moment," she says. "I didn't know what to expect. All those years of curiosity and wonder! It all came together in this person sitting next to me, who didn't look anything like what I expected. He just looked bad, unhealthy. He didn't talk at all the way I expected. His countenance was not what I expected. His *eyes* were like nothing I'd ever seen. I felt as if I was looking at the devil. The only word that comes to mind is disgust. I don't know why. Something inside me wanted to puke, for lack of a better word."

She describes DeBardeleben's gaze as cold and furtive, predatory. And when he looked at his daughter, the expression was anything but fatherly. "After we talked for ten minutes, I wanted to get up and leave. I was absolutely freezing. I know that had something to do with my nerves, but I have never felt so surrounded by evil as I did when I met my father. It took everything within me just to sit there. I went to the bathroom probably three or four times. And I didn't do anything! I just stood there and prayed, 'God, why am I here?' "

The answer, which came to Lindsey at once, was because her father needed her faith. "You've got to understand," she says. "Being a Christian I felt an obligation to share with him about my faith. Our whole purpose, we feel, is to spread the Word. And so I felt a very big commitment, and burden, for him and wanted to share with him about my faith, hoping that I'd convert him."

Lindsey remembers that between leers—"I felt really dirty around him"—she was able to keep the first day's conversation mostly focused on religion. Not that she made any progress toward rescuing Mike DeBardeleben's soul. "I realized that my efforts basically were lost," she says. "I found out that he didn't feel that he'd done anything wrong, and that *amazed* me. He of course also said he was totally innocent of everything he was in prison for."

She nearly fled home to her husband that first night. "I called him, crying. 'I want to come home! I can't go back in there! I'm scared!' " In the end, however, Lindsey found the strength to return to the visiting room for two more of the longest days of her life.

"I've never felt so helpless as I did at that point. Honestly, until then I'd thought, 'I'm his daughter. Even if he got out of prison he'd never hurt me.' But after I met him I really felt I was nobody to him. I just *felt* that way. I can't describe it. But I know I've never felt that way before, and I never want to feel that way again."

Lindsey went home and completely severed all contact with her father, as well as her aunt, Linda. Yet she still hasn't put aside the emotional turmoil caused by her confrontation with evil. Even after introducing herself by telephone to Bethene, exchanging letters and photos with her half-sister, making plans to visit one another, talking about Charlotte and Terry and discussing Courtney, the eight-pound, thirteen-ounce baby girl Lindsey bore January 27, 1993, Mike DeBardeleben is never far from her mind.

Nor Bethene's.

"This has been a big roller-coaster ride," says Charlotte's eldest daughter. "Terry has been good. Lindsey has been good. I'm real happy to find Lindsey, and I will try my best to be her friend. I'm not really sure you can be a sister on such short notice. She knows I'm very curious about our father and I think her main goal right now is to make sure that I don't try to visit him myself. 'Don't go,' she tells me. 'You don't want to see him.'

"As for our father, I already knew he was bad before I talked to Lindsey. I just learned from her that he was worse than I knew. Now with this book other people will start to learn about him and I'm sure he'll keep creeping up on my life.

"I know Terry will be there as much as she can. She

loves me and tells me, 'It's not your fault, Bethene, that everything is like this.' I don't think I'll lean on Lindsey so much, because I think she wants to lean on me. I'm the oldest. I have to be strong.

"And I have to work my way through it. I have a family, two children. I'm a mommy. I'm a wife. I'm a member of the church. I'm a sister, now, too."

Bethene considers for a moment. "All three of us have to work through it," she says finally. "There's no other way out."

There's an epidemic with 27 million victims. And no visible symptoms.

It's an epidemic of people who can't read.

Believe it or not, 27 million Americans are functionally illiterate, about one adult in five.

The solution to this problem is you... when you join the fight against illiteracy. So call the Coalition for Literacy at toll-free 1-800-228-8813 and volunteer.

Volunteer Against Illiteracy. The only degree you need is a degree of caring.